Surviving Diversity

Surviving Diversity

RELIGION AND DEMOCRATIC CITIZENSHIP

Jeff Spinner-Halev

THE JOHNS HOPKINS UNIVERSITY PRESS

BALTIMORE AND LONDON

© 2000 The Johns Hopkins University Press
All rights reserved. Published 2000
Printed in the United States of America on acid-free paper
9 8 7 6 5 4 3 2 1

The Johns Hopkins University Press
2715 North Charles Street
Baltimore, Maryland 21218-4363
www.press.jhu.edu

Library of Congress Cataloging-in-Publication Data will
be found at the end of this book.
A catalog record for this book is available from the
British Library.

ISBN 0-8018-6346-5

To Elyza, Avishai, and Davida

Contents

Acknowledgments

I FIRST TRIED to say something sensible about liberalism and religion at a panel at the 1994 American Political Science Association meeting. Luckily for me, Alan Houston was the discussant, and he quickly convinced me that most of what I had to say was actually rather indefensible. Alan's comments forced me to rethink my approach to religion and liberalism. I thank him for his wise advice and for his comments on other parts of the book. Alan was one of many people who commented on the book as it was developing. Eamonn Callan, Suzi Dovi, Tamar Szabó Gendler, John Hibbing, Andy Koppelman, Geoffrey Brahm Levey, Jim Rogers, Kevin Smith, and Beth Theiss-Morse all gave me insightful comments about my arguments. Margaret Moore's careful comments on the manuscript and our discussions over e-mail about various aspects of liberal theory were extraordinarily helpful. As I revised this book, I was also lucky enough to be able to read Monique Deveaux's book on cultural pluralism before it was published (*Cultural Pluralism in Liberal and Democratic Thought* [Ithaca, N.Y.: Cornell University Press, forthcoming]). While I mostly disagree with Monique, figuring out why wasn't always easy and helped improve my arguments here. My biggest thanks, however, must go to Gary Shiffman. Gary's comments on each chapter, some of which he read twice, proved invaluable. Gary was often able to understand what I wanted to say better than I did.

The bulk of the research for the book was done during the 1995-96 academic year while I was a Laurence S. Rockefeller Visiting Fellow at the University Center for Human Values at Princeton University. The Center is a terrific place to work, and I had the good fortune of being surrounded by five talented Visiting Fellows. During our many lunches together, in our conversations in the hall, and during our Fellows' seminars, Arthur Applebaum, Chris Korsgaard, Avishai Margalit, Arthur Ripstein, and Michael Thompson all discussed with me many issues that arise in the following pages. Amy Gutmann and George Kateb also participated in the seminars, where they gave me expert advice. Many thanks to Amy for inviting me to spend the year at the Center, and to George for his superb stewardship of the Center.

I also presented two chapters at the Young Scholars Weekend at Cornell University. Each chapter was the subject of a three-hour seminar, where the twenty or so participants had read the chapter and came armed with questions and comments. The experience was both grueling and illuminating. It made not only the two chapters I presented but the entire book much better. A special thanks to Kathy Abrams and Henry Shue for inviting me to participate in the program. Kathy and Henry convinced Sandy Levinson and Will Kymlicka to each be lead commentator for a chapter I presented. The comments of each proved to be particularly valuable. Will later commented on yet another chapter. Kathy and Henry worked hard at making the weekend a success. Their hard work turned into my good fortune.

Various parts of this book were also presented at the 1996 APSA convention, at Syracuse University, at the Political Philosophy Colloquium at Princeton University, at the European University Institute's Conference on Multiculturalism, Minorities, and Citizenship, and at the Canadian Center for Philosophy and Public Policy's conference on Citizenship and Diversity. Thanks to Stephen Macedo, George Kateb, Steven Lukes, and Will Kymlicka for their invitations to present my work. Many in these audiences offered thoughtful comments and asked important questions. I want to also thank Beverly Busch, Matt Johnson, and Andy Stock for excellent research help.

I am grateful to the Department of Political Science at the University of Nebraska for providing financial support in the summers of 1996 and 1997. I am also indebted to the National Endowment for the Humanities for providing financial support for this project when it first began in the summer of 1994.

This book is dedicated to my wife, Elyza, and my children, Avishai and Davida. They often patiently allowed me to work on this book, but they were also good enough to take me away from it on many occasions.

Earlier versions of some of the arguments in this book have appeared in the following articles: "Difference and Diversity in an Egalitarian Democracy," *Journal of Political Philosophy* 3, no. 3 (September 1995): 259-79; "Cultural Pluralism and Partial Citizenship," in *Multicultural Questions,* ed. Christian Joppke and Steve Lukes (Oxford: Oxford University Press, 1999), 65-86; and "Extending Diversity: Religion in Public and Private Education," in *Citizenship in Diverse Societies: Theory and Practice,* ed. Will Kymlicka and Wayne Norman (Oxford: Oxford University Press, 2000).

Surviving Diversity

Introduction 1

THE RELIGIOUS DIFFERENCES between Barbara Zeitler and Jeff Kendall didn't prevent them from getting married. Barbara was a mildly observant Reform Jew, and Jeff a not very devout Catholic. They agreed to raise their children Jewish, which meant they would be raised as Reformed Jews. This arrangement didn't strike them as odd or problematic since both were part of a broadly liberal religious framework. They both accepted the idea that there were different paths to heaven and that being a member of one particular religion was not a prerequisite to being good, trustworthy, or righteous.

Over time, however, Jeff became attracted to a fundamentalist Christian church and Barbara turned to Orthodox Judaism. The liberal religious alliance within their household began to crack — and eventually Jeff and Barbara divorced. As they became part of conservative religions, they became part of exclusive groups. That their marriage failed is hardly a surprise. A liberal Christian and Jew can marry and raise a family with a few obstacles that can be overcome, but a conservative Christian and Orthodox Jew will typically have fundamentally opposing beliefs that even the best marriage cannot withstand. The problems with Barbara and Jeff didn't end with their divorce, since they had three young children. When the children were with Barbara they lived in a Jewish household; when they were with Jeff they lived in a Christian household. While this is no longer an unusual arrangement in the United States, the arrangement breaks down quickly when the parents are members of conservative religions with antagonistic beliefs. Following his church's doctrine, Jeff taught his children that everyone who didn't accept Christ as savior would end up in hell, where there would be much weeping and gnashing of teeth. Jeff also cut off nine-year-old Ari's sideburns (*payes*), which many religious male Jews wear, and opposed teaching his children about the Holocaust.

Barbara took Jeff to court, demanding that he no longer teach his Christian beliefs to their children. The court found that Ari was experiencing considerable distress and conflict because of the religious dispute between his parents. Ari worried that both he and his mother would go to hell, and was upset when his father made him do things on the Jewish Sabbath that his mother taught him were forbidden. Further, the court found that Moriah, their six-year-old daughter, began to experience emotional distress because of the parental conflict and expected that their four-year-old-daughter would as well when she got older. The court declared that the father had to refrain from teaching his children about his religious beliefs. The court said that the "best interests of the children" meant they should not have to worry about their mother going to hell or that their identity as Jews damned them forever.

I am less interested in whether the court was right in its decision (though I think it was) than I am in what this case highlights: the exclusive nature of conservative religions and the tensions that arise between conservative religions and liberal democracy.[1] Exclusive religions are what Avishai Margalit calls "encompassing groups," or "a competing group in the sense that anyone belonging to it cannot in principle belong to another encompassing group of the same type." One cannot, for example, be both an Orthodox Jew and a fundamentalist Christian — nor can one raise children in both religions. Living both a rural and urban life, Margalit contends, is a technical impossibility because the ways of life are incompatible. But being an Orthodox Jew and a fundamentalist Christian is a principled impossibility because the rules of membership in one community prohibit belonging to the other. "Forms of life are incompatible if it is technically impossible to live them both simultaneously. Forms of life are competing if they contradict one another, in the sense that the beliefs and values of each one contradict those of the others."[2]

Members of different encompassing groups cannot marry one another, but the exclusion runs deeper than that. They restrict the access that outsiders have to their institutions. Some religions do not want to welcome everyone into their church, synagogue, or mosque: only members may congregate there. Some religious people want to exclude certain people from their place of business or from their associations. Encompassing groups also want to restrict the lives of their members. Depending on the group and doctrine, they may want to restrict what their members eat and wear, who they marry, and how they raise their children. They sometimes want to set up exclusive schools for their children. They object when public schools teach everyone to respect one another's beliefs, when some people's beliefs are (they maintain) obviously mistaken.

This exclusiveness clashes with liberal democracy in at least three important ways. First, liberals today often stress the importance of autonomy — autonomous people do not inherit their lives, but actively choose them. The contemporary liberal account of autonomy is often inspired by John Stuart Mill. Choice was not quite enough for Mill: he wanted people to cultivate their individuality. A person is said to have character, Mill declared, if his desires and impulses are his own. The person who does things because it is customary to do so is someone who does not make a choice; this person does not have character.[3] Autonomous people should be able to evaluate critically their own life to decide if that is how they want to live. This means more than following the lives of their parents; for people to have a meaningful choice about their lives they must confront and learn about the lives of other people. Encounters with others aid autonomy since dialogue between different kinds of people provokes them to think about their own values and practices as they try to defend them. This process may enable people to become more committed to their ideas, but it also may lead them to revise their ideas.[4]

Second, liberal democrats often stress the inclusive nature of citizenship. Liberal democratic citizens need to meet, learn about each other, and talk with one another, since it is important that in a democracy people learn to cooperate and compromise. Some liberals take this to mean that common schools and a common secular language are needed to ensure that citizens learn how to engage in the kind of dialogue that is needed in a democracy. Citizens who speak in languages based on their faith might not really be able to communicate enough with one another to make democracy work. Third, some liberal democrats suggest that the importance of citizenship means that most kinds of discrimination are illegitimate. Equal citizens meet on equal grounds in many different arenas. When citizens are excluded from important institutions, their opportunities are often restricted and their dignity damaged. Some liberals maintain that this can easily undermine the idea of equal citizenship.

Many religious conservatives, however, do not want to encourage their members to express and foster their individuality. They want their members to follow their customs, as informed by God and their leaders. They do not want their members to examine their lives critically; they want their members to obey the dictates of their religion. Religious conservatives want to insulate their members from others, to some degree at least, so they will not be tempted to leave the religion. They frequently want their children to attend school with other believers; and they typically want to speak the language of faith among fellow believers, not a secular language accessible to all their fellow citizens. They rarely believe in equality. Rather, they often believe that men should be in charge, with women taking on subservient roles in their communities. Religious conservatives want to shield their members from the influence of nonbelievers. By doing so, the community protects itself and the souls of its members.

While many liberals have recently argued that liberalism needs to better account for the role that culture plays in people's lives, these arguments do nothing to ease the tensions between liberalism and conservative religions. These recent arguments argue that culture is a means to an end — to be autonomous, people must live within a secure cultural structure or context.[5] Liberals who advocate this argument do not argue that culture should be valued as a good for its own sake. They claim instead that culture is important since it undergirds autonomy in crucial ways. People make their choices and discover their opportunities within their culture. The culture has social, political and educational institutions; people within the same culture share a vocabulary and an understanding of certain social practices. Since culture is an aid to autonomy, according to some liberals, it is best if the culture is diverse so members can encounter different kinds of people and be accorded a variety of opportunities. But if a culture is not diverse, and if its social practices and institutions do not support autonomy, as many religious conservative ones do not, then liberal support for the culture fades away rather rapidly.

The Kendalls' case highlights the tensions between some religions and liberalism. It can be hard for members of encompassing groups to cooperate and compromise. The Kendalls certainly had a hard time cooperating with one another. It is sometimes hard for believers to trust nonbelievers; the Kendalls surely didn't trust one another very much. Members of encompassing groups are rarely interested in living an autonomous life, or in teaching their children to be autonomous. Neither parent wanted to raise the children to choose their own lives. They each wanted to raise their children to believe in a certain faith. They both wanted to shield their children from the influence of others. The idea of the autonomous citizen, someone who is willing to listen sincerely and discuss with others, understands the importance of cooperation and compromise in a liberal democratic state, is able to evaluate different ideas and to construct one's own life plan, will sometimes stand in tension with the life of faith.

This account of the tension between liberalism and religion has some truth to it, yet it is too easy to dismiss many religious people as illiberal. Viewed from another Millian perspective, the religious conservative deserves a place in the liberal polity. A religious conservative may reject the life of individuality, but this does not mean that he or she is not autonomous in any way. More than many people in liberal societies, the religious conservative is aware of the life he has chosen. It is certainly an exaggeration to say that he is the Millian hero in today's society, but it is the religious conservative who stands out as different in liberal society today. Mill celebrated people who were different; he wanted people to depart from public opinion and from mainstream practices and norms. He wanted people to engage in "experiments in living." This describes the religious conservative, who departs from many cultural norms and practices today.

I do not think this departure is easy. We live in a permissive and consumerist society, yet many religious conservatives live a life full of often intimate and constant restrictions. The lure of mainstream society is relentless. Living a restricted life takes a depth of commitment, is a matter of constant choice, and, at least sometimes, takes character. The lives that Barbara and Jeff Kendall chose are not easy ones to choose today.

Still, the religious conservative is not the model Millian character: he may choose his life, but he has little individuality. This person is autonomous, but only in a limited way. He has chosen a life, but it is a life of little choice, at least in many important spheres. This has some disturbing implications for liberal theory, particularly for liberal citizenship, which must be considered, but liberalism is about autonomy, not individuality. A person should be able to choose to live a life where he does not cultivate his talents in his own individualistic way. The difficulty is that few arguments for cultural diversity recognize such a choice.

I do not want to suggest that living a devout religious life always means having no or little individuality. Some religious people combine a life of restrictions with autonomy. I want to defend the choice that people make to live an illiberal life. I also defend the idea, however, that living a devout life, one full of religious restrictions, is sometimes fully compatible with and perhaps even supportive of liberalism. Few arguments for cultural recognition, however, have a place for the religious moderate who wants to live a life of some, not complete, restrictions; for one who wants to protect his or her identity by reducing, though not eliminating, the contacts one and one's children have with others. Few arguments for cultural recognition have much room for the religious life of faith, except for liberal ones. These arguments instead emphasize the individual and his choices; they rarely make room for groups of obedience. Recognizing the authenticity of choosing a religious life, which means living by restrictive rules, means developing an argument that allows for both individual diversity and group difference. I try to develop such an argument here.

The Religious Silence

What is surprising is that while discussions of diversity and difference have permeated the academy and the larger culture for much of the last two decades, religion is rarely discussed in these multicultural debates. Political theorists, in their edited volumes and book-length treatments on difference and diversity, include little or nothing about religion.[6] Some of these works refer to certain religious groups, like the Amish, Jews, or Pueblo Indians, but treat them as ethnic groups. Few theorists take seriously these groups' belief in God and ask what that means for difference and diversity. I do not think that it is a problem that any specific volume ignores religion. Few treatments of difference and diversity can be so comprehensive that every possible group is discussed, and so I do not blame any single author or editor for omitting any lengthy discussion of religion. But it is a problem when *none* of the major works on the subject discuss religion in any detail. Writings by educational theorists fare no better. Robert Fullinwider explains: "Although religion almost always appears on the list of 'differences' that multiculturalists address, it seldom received any substantial discussion. . . . Indeed, the multiculturalist understanding of ethnicity itself must remain pretty shallow if it doesn't take account of the distinct religious observances and beliefs [of different groups]."[7]

Motivating the discussion of difference and diversity is the idea that many groups have been wrongly excluded from mainstream life in the United States. Textbooks have been rewritten to emphasize women, blacks, and other excluded groups. Universities and corporations talk about their commitment to hiring members of excluded groups. These public celebrations of inclusion, however, often exclude religious groups. Not surprisingly, some religions are unhappy with the liberal public culture because it excludes them. Even if this exclusion is acceptable or morally right, and sometimes it is, it has to be defended; ignoring religious groups is not the right way to defend their exclusion.

Not everyone passes over religion. Since the 1940s religion has often been at the heart of constitutional questions in the United States, leading legal scholars to discuss religion to a large degree. They are mostly interested, however, in how religious liberty and the establishment and free exercise clauses can coexist. These are important questions, but the legal scholars do not discuss the issue of the place of exclusive groups in an inclusive polity. Some political theorists also discuss religion, typically in the context of education. These discussions, too, are important, and I address them in chapter 5, but the issue of religion is more than an educational one. Political theorists need to broaden their discussion of religion.

Multiculturalism is supposed to be a doctrine that alerts us to often-ignored sources of diversity, yet it neglects religion. Even more striking, religious groups tend to last longer than other groups. One reason for religions' longevity in the United States, and in some other liberal democracies as well, is simple: religion has constitutional protections. The First Amendment of the U.S. Constitution declares that Congress cannot prohibit the free exercise of religion. While this declaration is balanced by the establishment clause — Congress cannot establish a religion — no analogous protection is given to other groups. There is an extensive history of court cases on religious matters in the United States, at least since World War II, that is not matched by the history of ethnic groups. The First Amendment helps explain why.

Another important reason why religious groups tend to last a long time is their use of rules and boundaries. The best way to retain your group's identity is to establish clear boundaries around your group. Establishing who is a member and who is not, and making rules that make it clear who is and isn't a member, is an important way to retain group identity. Few groups are able to do this well. In the United States white ethnic groups, for example, have lost much of their distinct identity. If the policy of liberal diversity succeeds — this is by no means certain — then the distinct identities of people of color and of gays and lesbians will almost surely fade as well. This can be seen as a victory for liberal individuality. Although arguments and policies of recent years have increasingly rejected the assimilationist model that has governed many liberal states, these arguments tend to be based on strong notions of equality and autonomy which don't recognize group differences as much as they support individuality.

Encompassing groups, however, often reject individuality. They are able to maintain a strong sense of community among their members because they are governed by exclusive rules. Moreover, these groups tend to have internal norms and rules that are hierarchical and patriarchal. While a group *can* be exclusive without being patriarchal and hierarchical, and this is sometimes the case, it is much easier to keep a group together when the rules are enforced through a hierarchical structure.

When people follow a set of rules that affects their lives in significant ways they are bound together in a community. Handing down these rules maintains the community over time. By firmly establishing the rules of membership, religious communities can guard the boundaries of their communities more closely than can other communities. Clearly established boundaries, which presume there are guardians of the boundaries at the top of a hierarchy, help maintain a community by preventing its erosion.

Rules also restrict what members can and cannot do. Jews who keep kosher cannot eat either in the homes of people who do not keep kosher or in nonkosher restaurants. If you will not eat at most other people's homes, you don't share an intimate experience with those outside your religious community. What keeps Catholics distinct from other Christians is their church hierarchy and their specific rituals. If Catholics decided that the Pope had no special status, and that they could decide on church doctrine for themselves, the distinctive nature of Catholicism would fade. If Catholics could make their own rules, eventually a person could do anything he or she wanted and remain Catholic. People could then say they were Catholic if they felt in the mood to say so. What keeps a community distinct over time is adherence to a set of rules that sets them apart from others. Believing in their church hierarchy is one of the things that keeps Catholics distinct from others.

Religions bring people into a community mentally and physically. People come together to pray, perform rituals, and listen to their religious leader speak. It matters in Judaism that you need at least ten men together to pray; praying with others is better than praying alone (and praying alone is better than not praying at all). Religious communities have rituals that mark life-cycle events. Circumcising infant boys, bar mitzvahs, first communions, confirmations, funerals, and weddings are all ways in which religious communities mark the entrance (and exit) of members in their community. These rituals bring parts of the community together, so they can celebrate the event; they celebrate the continuity and strength of their community with these rituals. These rules and rituals also help the community last. Passed down from one generation to the next, marked in different life-cycle events, rules and rituals give the community continuity and provide the past with a connection to the future. Few nonreligious communities can match the exclusiveness and the rules of religion, which is why few of them match the perseverance of religious communities.

Some may object to my statement that groups in a liberal society have a hard time staying together. After all, it is *possible* for some groups to remain together in a liberal society. It is possible that an Italian immigrant community will retain its Italian identity generation after generation. It is possible that few of its members will marry people from other groups, that each generation will teach Italian to the next one, that each generation will learn little from the mainstream culture, but will mostly maintain the traditions of their parents. This is all highly unlikely, however, without a large measure of insularity. When people attend common schools, they learn about others and become influenced by them. Indeed, if the liberal state does not fund private schools, as some do not, then it works to undermine particular communities, since it encourages people from different backgrounds to encounter one another in public schools. This process continues when people attend college, where they may even find a spouse with a different heritage. It happens at diverse work settings and in mixed neighborhoods. It is hard to maintain one's language if most of the people one and one's children encounter speak a different language. Moreover, many cultures have few hard and fast rules. What rules do you follow to be an Italian-American? Italian-Americans define for themselves what it means to be Italian-American. It is not surprising that the meaning of being an Italian-American has become vague over time, since there is nothing that one must do to belong to the community.

Many religions also have an institutional framework that helps them remain together more than ethnic groups. Many religions run or are affiliated with hospitals, nursing homes, schools, universities, child-care services, funeral homes, social services, and charities. These institutions provide religions with a way to communicate their values to their members. It also provides their members with a set of institutions to inhabit, contribute to, and to give one's loyalty. These institutions are centered around something powerful that few ethnic groups can match: a certain belief in God. People's beliefs change, of course, but beliefs in God and religion change more slowly than those of ethnicity.

Not all religions remain together very well; not all are the same. I mostly discuss here *moderate* and *conservative* religions. Tensions arise between these religions and liberalism much more frequently than between liberalism and the liberal religions. While religious divisions in the United States have historically been between religions—Protestantism versus Catholicism versus Judaism—now the debates often run through the religions. Orthodox Protestants have more in common with their Orthodox Jewish, Mormon, and Catholic counterparts; they are aligned against their more liberal coreligionists. They are what James Davison Hunter calls "conservative religions."[8] These conservative or orthodox religions believe in an external transcendental authority. Typically they believe in the literal truth of the Torah, Bible, or Koran and have a culturally conservative outlook. Members of these religions believe that their religions are true, and that people who deviate from or ignore them risk God's wrath, perhaps his everlasting wrath. Since religious conservatives think that only their way is the route to salvation or to please God, the distinction between insiders and outsiders is quite important. If outsiders influence their members too much, then they may stray from the true path. This is why following the rules of the religion is so important: the rules ensure that people remain true to God's way.

Conversely, the worldview of Reformed Jews is more similar to liberal Episcopalians than it is to Orthodox Jews. Liberal religions tend to try to understand their sacred texts more metaphorically than do conservative religions. Liberal religions also suggest that there are many ways to please God. What is important is the deeds one does and the spirit in which one lives. Liberal religions often emphasize living a spiritual life instead of a life according to rules, stress equality and inclusion, and seek alliances with others. These liberal religions are quite compatible with liberal democratic theory, and so I say little about the relationship between the two here. It is with religions that reject liberalism, or at least some parts of it, that the interesting questions arise.

Like many analytical distinctions, distinguishing between conservative and liberal religions is both useful and misleading. In a world of many religious groups, dividing them into two camps would collapse important differences among many of them. Yet dividing them into groups is convenient, since many have similar tendencies (which some of them recognize when they make coalitions). Moreover, to talk about religions generally means generalizing about them.

Still, I qualify the conservative-liberal dichotomy in one way. I will discuss religious moderates in the following pages. Like religious conservatives, religious moderates believe that their religion is true, but are more willing to work and live among others than conservatives. Still, religious moderates seek to retreat to some exclusive social space on a regular basis, where outsiders are not welcome. They worry about their members straying from their particular path, but they also find that they can learn from others and that they want to be part of mainstream society in at least some ways.

Conservative and many Orthodox Jews, evangelical and some fundamentalist Protestants, many practicing Mormons and orthodox Catholics inhabit some exclusive institutions, but they also tend to work, live, and sometimes learn among others.[9] These are religious moderates. I want to be clear that many religious moderates believe that their sacred texts are true, and that others who do not share their views are creating an eternal problem for themselves. Religious conservatives include some fundamentalist Protestants, some Ultraorthodox Jews and Hasidic Jews (together called the Haredim), and some Catholics and Mormons. The Amish, the Hutterites, some Haredi Jews, and perhaps some fundamentalist Protestants separate themselves from the world to a much larger degree. They form a variant of the conservative religious group, the conservative insular group. It may be possible for a liberal or moderate group to be insular, but since these groups tend to have only some rules and relatively porous boundaries, it is harder for them to remain insular than their more conservative counterparts.

Religion and Classical Liberalism

Though my argument is set in the context of contemporary debates about diversity and difference, classical liberalism has much to say about religion. My argument in this book is not a historical one, but it is worth briefly explaining the liberal tradition's view toward religion to see what this view is, and why this view is only of limited value to liberals today. Though many classical liberals have written about religion, I will examine John Locke, John Stuart Mill, and John Dewey, since they all take religion seriously, and their writings capture much of the classical liberal attitude toward religion.[10]

What Locke, Mill, and Dewey did in their writings about religion was to argue with their fellow citizens. Their hope was to convince their fellow citizens to change their religious views; they hoped to make their religions more open, more based on reason than on revelation, and more of a glue to bind different people together, rather than a repellent that keeps them apart. In all, they wanted to make religion more liberal. These liberals hoped that their arguments would be convincing, that people would turn toward more liberal religions.

JOHN LOCKE

Locke argued for toleration of those with different religious beliefs, but he also argued against toleration of atheists and Catholics.[11] Belief in God will restrain people's appetites and become the foundation of morality. People who cannot be trusted to act morally, Locke said, have no place in the commonwealth. People need a good incentive to act morally: the promise of heaven and the threat of hell are proper inducement to good behavior. Without a belief in the afterlife, without a fear of God, people will act solely in their self-interest. This is why atheists are not to be tolerated. They cannot be trusted to fulfill their obligations in society. "Promises, covenants and oaths, which are the bonds of human society, can have no hold upon an Atheist."[12] That trust is important in a society based on a social contract is not surprising. We need to know that people will keep their word and their contracts. People who do not fear the afterlife, Locke thought, cannot be trusted to keep their word.

While Locke did not tolerate nonbelievers, he thought that toleration should be far-reaching. "Toleration" is the "chief characteristical mark of the true church." The true church does not argue about minor doctrinal matters. "Why am I beaten and ill used by others, because, perhaps, I wear not Buskins; because my hair is not of the right cut; because perhaps I have not dip't in the right fashion; because I eat flesh upon the road, or some other food which agrees with my stomach?" What a person eats and when, how feet are washed, when a child is baptized—these matters are not of major importance, although at the time Locke wrote people were killing each other over them. Locke wanted churches to stop arguing about different forms of worship. He argued that what really mattered is teaching and practicing Jesus' moral message, a message of love and peace. Toleration does not mean merely begrudging those with different beliefs to live nearby in peace: "We must not content ourselves with the narrow measures of bare justice," he proclaimed, "charity, bounty and liberality must be added to it."[13]

It is not just individuals who should treat each other well, important as this is. Churches, too, should look upon other churches in friendship, with their ministers teaching this friendship from the pulpit. Churches should be messengers of love, not hate. "Peace, equity and friendship are always mutually to be observed by particular churches, in the same manner as private persons." Ministers, Locke contended, are obliged to preach goodwill toward all men, the erroneous and the orthodox alike. Ministers who do otherwise do not understand their calling and will one day have to answer for their behavior before God.[14]

Getting in the way of Locke's religious message of peace and goodwill are religious fanatics. Their problem is that they do not see that reason and revelation should support one another. Reason, Locke declared, is natural revelation. Revelation is "natural reason enlarged by a new set of discoveries communicated by God," which reason "vouches the truth of, by the testimony and proofs it gives that they come from God." The problem with "enthusiasts" is that "reason is lost upon them" because a light has supposedly "infused into their understandings." This light, however, blinds the enthusiasts from judging what propositions are from God. Their beliefs are grounded in a tautology, not in something that can judge them true or false: "It is a revelation, because they firmly believe it; and they believe it because it is a revelation." In fact, however, God leaves humanity's faculties in their natural state. People are able to judge God's inspirations: "Reason must be our last judge and guide in everything."[15]

With reason as the basis for his Christianity, it is perhaps not surprising that Locke's Christianity was unorthodox for his times. He may have been turning toward Unitarianism in his writings about Christianity, since he was uncertain about the doctrine of original sin and the divinity of Christ.[16] Locke thought reason led to a belief in God, but Christianity itself was based more on belief.[17] This led him to argue that toleration should be extended to non-Christians, as long as they believed in God, since belief in Christianity is ultimately a matter of faith. "To you and me the Christian religion is true," Locke said in a reply to a criticism of his doctrine of toleration, but "how do you and I know this?" He answered that no one can know that Christianity is true: "For faith still it is, and not knowledge." Locke did add that the toleration of non-Christians does afford Christians an opportunity to convert them, since persuasion and not force is the best way to get true converts.[18] Still, those who believe in God can be tolerated (unless they are loyal to "another prince"). What is crucial for Locke is their belief in some higher power that will punish them for acting immorally.

JOHN STUART MILL

Locke's reasonable Christianity, with goodwill, friendship, and liberality at its center, is clearly leaning in a liberal direction. While God played a important role in Locke's political theory, God dropped out in the religion of later liberals. John Stuart Mill did not merely want churches to treat nonmembers with goodwill; he questioned the idea that a belief in God and the afterlife must underpin morality. Mill argued that the afterlife is too remote to affect people's conduct in any concrete way, and that few people think that whatever ills they have done deserve to be punished with everlasting hellfire.

Mill thought Christianity would undermine the morality of liberalism. Since its maxims of morality are thought to have a supernatural origin and therefore are static, Christianity stands in the way of discussion and progress.

Society changes, and a moral doctrine of two thousand years ago may not be appropriate for today's society.[19] Mill thought that people are progressive beings, meaning that moral truths must be discussed and sometimes change as people progress.

By telling people the most important thing is getting into heaven, Christianity casts human morality as essentially selfish, giving them little reason to care for others. It teaches people to submit to the "Supreme Will" but doesn't do anything to try to create a better world.[20] The passive character of Christianity conflicts with Mill's view of people as autonomous and progressive beings. People who are resigned to the way the world is because they attribute it to God's will or because they hope to get into heaven will not be motivated to improve the world.

Finally, Mill complained that Christianity contains a negative morality and not a positive one, due to Christian morality being in great part a reaction against paganism.[21] Christian morality tells people what not to do but is not as good at telling people what to do. Christianity is good at telling people to deny their lusts. This does not do enough, however, to encourage people to act cooperatively and autonomously, as Mill wanted them to do. Mill wanted people to debate and discuss how to move society forward. He wanted people to try out different ideas, both in discussion and in practice. He wanted people both to cooperate with one another and to feel comfortable dissenting from the views of others. Christianity inhibits people from acting autonomously and from pursuing the common good. Liberal society, in Mill's view, needs to move past Christianity.

This does not mean that every doctrine of Christianity had to be discarded. Mill thought that Christian morality contained some useful parts. Jesus was a man of great morality and had much to teach people. Christianity chose well to hold up such a person "as a standard of excellence and a model of imitation." Even unbelievers can admire Christ, who was "probably the greatest moral reformer . . . who ever existed upon earth," and who tried to lead humankind to virtue and truth. Believing that Jesus was a great man need not entail a belief in the divine. The people who gathered around Christ, "far from believing the doctrines to be excellent because they came from God, believed them to come from God because they felt them to be excellent." An excellent person with such good ideas was ascribed to God, as were most unusual things back then. Events and people that were extraordinary did not send people scurrying to their labs to figure out a scientific explanation for the phenomenon; rather, it was assumed that God was behind them. We can admire remarkable things as our ancestors did, but we are not bound to their divine explanations. Doing so can have dangerous consequences. Jesus's teachings may be good, but other teachings in the Bible or the Koran may need to be revised. If they are thought to come from God, however, revision will be difficult. Since Jesus is not divine but only an excellent man, we can discard the fiction that he is the son of God and still retain his teachings.[22] This will allow us to develop a morality that moves beyond Christianity.

Mill did not want to dismiss the idea of religion. He warned that there is little reason to think it will disappear, with philosophy taking its place, as some intellectuals might hope: "whatever some philosophers may think, there is little prospect at present that philosophy will take the place of religion." The fact that religion has been believed for so long means that it cannot simply be dismissed. Its long duration means that even if it is not true, then it probably fills some requirement of human nature.[23] The solution is to create a religion that has the necessary spirituality without Christian servility or negativity. A morality that is grounded on "large and wise views of the good of the whole," that neither sacrifices the individual to the whole or the whole to the individual, would derive its power in the best people from benevolence and the passion for excellence. People would act on benevolent motives not because of a promise for a heavenly reward, but because of the approval of the people we respect and admire, whether they are dead or alive. This kind of morality, Mill claimed, constitutes a real religion: the Religion of Humanity. "The essence of religion is the strong and earnest direction of the emotions and desires towards an ideal object, recognized as of the highest excellence, and as rightfully paramount over all selfish objects of desire."[24]

To people who might question whether the Religion of Humanity is a real religion, Mill replied that it has the essential qualities of religion. Indeed, Mill even said that "it is not only entitled to be called a religion: it is a better religion that any of those which are ordinarily called by that title." This is because the Religion of Humanity is disinterested and does not ask people to believe the unbelievable. It asks people to act out of their best motives, not out of self-interest for a heavenly reward. The Religion of Humanity challenges people to act well because the deed is good. Furthermore, it also does not ask people to suspend belief by believing in a perfect God while the world is so "clumsily made and capriciously governed." It is not so easy to combine the worship of a perfect God with the belief that this world, with all of its flaws, was made by such a Being. Many believers do not even try, saying only that we cannot understand the justness and goodness of Providence. Moreover, the

Religion of Humanity would not insist, as does Christianity, that people believe in a Being that would condemn millions to everlasting torture for not having heard of Christ.

JOHN DEWEY

In the early twentieth century, John Dewey's ideas of religion paralleled Mill's in several ways. Like Mill, Dewey called for a religion that had little to do with traditional religion. He called instead for a religious humanism. A religious humanism would encourage a religious quality to life, a quality that he thought was anesthetized in the hands of institutionalized religion. Religion, Dewey maintained, prevents "the religious quality of experience from coming to consciousness and finding the expression that is appropriate to present conditions." The problem with most religions is that they are caught up in an old world, a world with fixed ends created by a supernatural being. Religions are committed to immutable beliefs. Furthermore, throughout history religion has prevented people from fully using their powers to work for a better world because religion has taught them to wait for an external power to improve things. The Christian belief in the power of prayer to change things is also too passive in the face of the problems faced by people: "It leaves matters in general just about as they were before."[25]

Dewey called for faith in intelligence, a collective faith that can become religious in quality. He wanted people to have faith in their ability to act in concert to solve the problems of the day. The future of religion, he declared, "is connected with the possibility of developing a faith in the possibilities of human experience and human relationships that will create a vital sense of the solidarity of human interests and inspire action to make that sense of reality."[26] Collective devotion to great ethical and social ideals can have a religious quality to it. While Mill thought that Christianity encouraged people to be selfish, Dewey contended that the problem with both atheism and supernaturalism is that they leave humans isolated. A religious attitude like the one Dewey called for, however, "needs the sense of a connection of man, in the way of both dependence and support, with the enveloping world that the imagination feels is a universe."[27]

What Dewey wanted is a religious faith in the intelligence of the community's members to face and solve the problem of the day through an experimental empiricism. He wanted people to have faith in their ability to experiment cooperatively to solve problems as they arise. This translates into believing that people can change and, more important for Dewey, to grow intellectually as they respond to problems with the social experiments that will help them find a solution. Dewey was concerned that religion and philosophy are caught up in the quest for certainty. He maintained that both religion and philosophy were involved in the misguided attempt to find certain moral truths in a dynamic and changing world. But we need to become comfortable with the uncertainty of our world.[28] The world is always changing, and people must change in order to respond to it. Having dropped faith in the supernatural or in philosophy's quest for fixed ends, Dewey wanted people to have faith in their ability to solve the problems of society. Since society's problems are never fully solved, since change will inevitably occur and bring new challenges with it, the cycles of change and growth continue endlessly. Ultimately, this translates into a belief in the democratic community: "Democracy as the way of freedom and growth is Dewey's American secular form of spiritual practice."[29]

THE END OF PROGRESS?

I want to put aside for now the question of whether Locke, Mill, and Dewey's views on the relationship between religion and morality are correct. What I want to emphasize in this very short survey of liberalism's views toward religion is that liberals thought that over time people would lose their attachments to revealed religion and would embrace a religion that centered around humanity, not God.[30] Locke did not share this view, but his liberal Christianity was aimed at mostly bringing people together instead of keeping them apart. Mill and Dewey knew this would not happen overnight, but as humanity progressed they thought there would be less need for God. Mill said that the one disadvantage the Religion of Humanity has compared to revealed religions is that it can hold out no prospect of the afterlife. But in time, Mill suggested, this disadvantage would fade. As "the condition of mankind becomes improved" and people become happier, the hope of heaven will become less important. "They who have had their happiness can bear to part with existence: but it is hard to die without ever having lived." This is true for the unselfish anyway. Those who are "wrapped up in self . . . require the notion of another selfish life beyond the grave."[31] In a society, however, where autonomy was encouraged and the common good pursued, and where the Religion of Humanity held sway, there would be few selfish people.

To a certain degree, Mill and Dewey's—and Locke's—hopes have become true. Many Christians downplay doctrinal differences in the name of friendship and goodwill to others. While a Religion of Humanity hasn't caught on, many people today are not religious or are only barely so, unwilling to live by maxims announced centuries ago. For a variety of reasons, people no longer adhere to the rules of religion as they did in the past. Religious conservatives do not dominate the liberal polity, and the violence that often accompanied religion in Locke's day is now largely gone in the West. Religions do not keep people apart in the West as they used to do. But not all people are irreligious or belong to a liberal religion. Locke, Mill, and Dewey's success has been limited. Conservative religions are alive and well today, and there is no reason to think they will soon disappear from the Western liberal democracies. This is not to say that they will not get smaller in the future, but it is just as possible that they will get bigger. The liberal project to turn people toward more liberal religions will not be completely — or even close to completely — successful any time soon. Liberals should still argue with conservatives about religion. But liberals must also stop assuming that progress means that religious conservatives will eventually fade away or disappear. We cannot assume with Locke, Mill, and Dewey that the future will be a world without conservative religions. Locke, Mill, and Dewey could try to construct a liberalism without religious conservatives. We liberals cannot do the same, however.

Nor can liberals simply say that religion is a private affair and leave it at that. This is partly because religious people want to bring their religious views into public settings, like public schools and public debates. It's too simple to tell these people they need to leave their religious views at home. This is not just because many religious people will not follow such an injunction, but because there are important considerations of liberty at stake, and because the consequences of the view that religion should never appear in public may harm the liberal state more than necessary. Further, it is inevitable that there will be points of contact between religion and the liberal state. What should be taught about religion in schools? Should religious organizations be allowed to discriminate because of the dictates of their religion? Can religious communities shield their children from a secular education? These questions and more cannot be answered by assuming religion to be a private affair.

Recognizing Religion

That religious conservatives are no longer in the center of the liberal polity is not a reason to ignore them. A main idea behind the multicultural movement is to better recognize those sources of diversity that are usually ignored. Moreover, while religious conservatives may not stand at center stage in the West, they are a relatively large minority in some countries, including the United States, certainly too large to dismiss. Though few arguments on difference and diversity discuss religion in much detail, part of what I plan to show in the following chapters is how many of these arguments implicitly leave little room for the conservative and moderate religious life. I place my argument within the context of the contemporary diversity debate since its lack of attention on religion is conspicuous and so obviously needs to be remedied. Some liberals do, of course, discuss religion in their arguments, usually in the context of specific issues. When discussing education particularly, but also deliberation in the public square, and antidiscrimination law, liberals sometimes discuss religion.

The leading liberal accounts of cultural recognition place autonomy at their center. My main dispute with these arguments is not that they emphasize autonomy too much, but that they too relentlessly place choice and opportunities in their conceptions of cultural recognition and autonomy. The cultural recognition argument maintains that every cultural community within a liberal state needs to support autonomy. By arguing that each community should support autonomy, these theorists restrict the opportunity of people to choose to live a life of obedience. Group difference is then sacrificed in the face of individual diversity. I do not think this tradeoff must be made. Not every community within a liberal democracy must support autonomy to ensure that all citizens have meaningful choices about their lives. The argument that every community should promote choice actually gives people less of an opportunity to choose to live a religious life and thereby undermines autonomy.

When liberals turn to the specific instances of education, religion, and public debate, their arguments have different, but still illiberal, consequences. In the name of mutual respect and inclusion, liberals typically argue that public schools should not accommodate religious conservatives in a class or two. This argument often has the unfortunate consequence of driving religious conservatives out of public schools altogether, and into religious schools. Despite a class exemption or two, religious children will still learn many liberal values by attending the other classes in public schools. In their religious schools, however, they will learn little of these values. Some liberals have recently argued that no religious argument has any place in the public square. This premise further isolates religious conservatives, making them more hostile to liberalism and more illiberal. It is usually better to engage religious conservatives in public debate; doing so will force them to make public arguments, to turn from private sources of evidence to more public ones. This will often have the salutary effect of making them more liberal.

Some liberals have taken the idea of inclusion to mean that religions themselves should be inclusive. While a religion may choose this route, doing so will often lessen the distinction between that religion and others. It will give people fewer religious choices. Liberalism, however, should allow a plurality of religions to flourish; it should allow these religions to make their own rules of membership. If diversity will succeed in liberal democracies, then people should be able to belong to their own groups that establish their own rules.

My defense of choosing the religious life is qualified in important ways. One problem with people who choose to live the nonautonomous life is that their way of life often undermines liberal democratic citizenship. While liberal arguments about the need for a common citizenship can also become too relentless, and crowd out much possibility for a religious life, some institutional support for citizenship is necessary, even if doing so sometimes makes it harder to lead a religious conservative life. An argument like the one I present here, which aims to recognize the legitimacy of choosing the religious conservative life, cannot escape the tensions between liberalism and conservative religions. Many liberal institutions work to encourage liberal attitudes and beliefs, which will often undermine conservative religions. This is not a problem as long as there is space in the liberal polity for the religious conservative to choose and live his life. The liberal state may aim to produce liberal citizens, but it also must allow for dissenters.

Allowing people to choose the religious conservative life within the confines of citizenship leads me to develop three principles. The first is *noninterference*. A cultural community that meets certain minimal conditions can exist without interference from the liberal state. The second is *inclusion*. I argue that the liberal state should try to include religious conservatives in its institutions and in public debate when religious conservatives want to do so, and when doing so does not undercut citizenship. The third principle is *exclusion:* people should be able to exclude others from their institutions, as long as doing so does not harm citizenship.

Just as there are many religions, there is no one view of liberalism. I take liberalism to be a doctrine of individual rights and of limited government; the government should be divided so the power of any one branch is circumscribed; liberalism is characterized by the rule of law rather than of men and women. Liberal citizens are equal to one another; they have the same political rights and, one hopes, something close to equality of opportunity. They also have equal liberty, more or less: each is able to pursue his or her plans and projects. This places autonomy at the center of liberalism. Autonomy means that we are to choose our way of life. This means we should be able to choose to live a life in a community of fellow believers who stress obedience and faith over individuality.

Some liberals object to the idea that autonomy is at the center of liberalism. I cannot canvass all possible liberalisms here, but I do discuss two alternative views of liberalism in the following chapters. I look at Chandran Kukathas's argument that tolerance is the central virtue of liberalism, and what we must do is tolerate the practices of different communities. Kukathas's view of liberalism has a remarkably weak sense of citizenship that is based on an inapt description of liberal society. More important, I argue that it is not as tolerant as it first appears. If some liberals sacrifice group difference at the expense of individual diversity, Kukathas does the opposite: he wrongly sacrifices individual diversity at the expense of group difference. While I think many liberals wrongly restrain group difference to enhance individual diversity, some restraints on group difference are needed in order to support the ability of people to live autonomous lives in a diverse setting.

I also examine Rawls's argument that liberalism is a neutral doctrine, and that an autonomy-based liberalism wrongly imposes a version of the "good life" on liberal citizens. I doubt that this is the case. An autonomy-based liberalism does place certain limits on the kinds of life that people can live, but it also gives them considerable options. That autonomy has an important place in liberalism is seen in Rawls's own work. In chapter 4 I explain my agreement with many of Rawls's critics who maintain that his version of liberal citizenship places autonomy at its center. Since Rawls admits that his doctrine may work to undermine traditional religious communities, he is in some agreement with his critics.

Autonomy is at the core of my argument, but citizenship also matters. I understand liberal government to be democratic. While liberalism and democracy are conceptually different, liberal governments today are also democratic. Liberal citizens have some power over the government, and they must be able to cooperate and compromise with one another. This means that liberalism is also a moral doctrine. A variety of moral virtues undergird liberal citizenship. While these virtues are limiting, they are also limited: liberalism gives people considerable space to decide how they want to live their lives. The main virtues of citizenship often coincide with robust versions of autonomy. Autonomy admits of degree, and people can meet the conditions of autonomy in a minimal way and not be very good citizens. People should be able to choose to be neglectful citizens. The virtues of liberal citizenship should be encouraged, with the realization that the liberal state can easily survive if some citizens do not live up to these virtues.

Outline of the Argument

I hope it is clear by now that I write as a political theorist, not as a theologian. How religions should react toward liberalism, how they can remain vibrant and vital in our world, what exactly are the doctrines of the various religions, how to reconcile church doctrine with people schooled in democracy are all important questions that I mostly do not discuss here. My focus is on political matters. I discuss autonomy and citizenship in the next three chapters. While arguments about these matters can remain abstract, arguments about culture and religion are best made in a specific context. It is hard to discuss the role of religious communities in liberalism without discussing specific religious communities. It is hard to know exactly the tensions that may arise between liberalism and religion without examining tensions that have in fact already arisen. The context of my argument is self-consciously American. Most of my examples—though not all—come from the United States. Further, hovering in the background of my argument is the U.S. Constitution. Some states have constitutional provisions for aid to private schools, for example, while the United States does not. This is an important difference that affects how one argues about education and religion. This does not mean my argument is not applicable to other countries. It does mean that care is needed when applying them elsewhere.

I tend to use examples from three American groups, though these groups exist elsewhere: Protestant fundamentalists, Orthodox Catholics, and Orthodox and Hasidic Jews. I say little, in particular, about non-Western religions. I suspect that much of what I have to say applies to Islam, but I am considerably less certain about Buddhism and Hinduism. I also use the word *church* rather expansively here, as a convenient metaphor for religions and their houses of worship in general.

Chapters 2, 3, and 4 outline the theoretical framework of the book. This part of the book is the most general and perhaps the most applicable elsewhere. In chapter 2 I contend that most recent arguments about cultural recognition do not allow for as much cultural difference as they first appear to do. I am mostly interested in the arguments of Joseph Raz and Will Kymlicka because they place autonomy at the base for their arguments for cultural recognition. The way they misapply autonomy to cultural matters is instructive. I also look at the arguments of Nancy Fraser and Iris Young, to show that arguments based on identity or group difference place considerable limits on cultural difference.

In chapter 3 I argue that while Raz and Kymlicka both contend that cultures give their members opportunities and choices, they ignore the converse: the role that communities or culture restricts people's lives. I argue that, contrary to most liberal arguments, living with restrictions need not be incompatible with choice. Some of these restrictions can enhance the autonomy of people by giving them a meaningful way of life that they can reject, modify, or accept. I suggest here that religious people — here I am thinking of religious moderates — can lead an autonomous life with the restrictions dictated to them by their community. I also explain the principle of noninterference here.

In chapter 4 I enter the area of citizenship, where I contend that a common citizenship is important. I examine the view that religion supplies a morality that supports liberal citizenship, a view I find might be true for some religious moderates but is rarely the case for religious conservatives. This is because the encompassing character of conservative religions clashes with the inclusive nature of liberal citizenship. I outline here my two principles of inclusion and exclusion. I apply these two principles in chapters 5 through 7, to education, to matters of public debate and discourse, and to matters of association and discrimination. In the concluding chapter I examine the issue of the special character of religion. I also speculate on the weaknesses of liberal religions and the sometimes apparent strength of more conservative ones.

I also point to the irony that many recent arguments favor diversity but do little to ease the tensions between liberalism and conservative religions and may even increase them. Liberalism and religion have clashed since the days of Locke; and it's true and even fortunate that many religions have changed to accommodate liberal theory. But some religions remain stubbornly illiberal. Contemporary liberalism, which strives to be attentive to diversity, should make room for minorities like religious conservatives by recognizing that minorities in liberal societies almost always choose their life. A liberal theory like the one I present here better recognizes the different sources of diversity than other liberal theories. It will nonetheless be difficult for conservative religions to coexist with liberalism, though they are in a better position to survive liberal diversity than most other minorities.

2 | The Limits of Cultural Recognition

THE RELIGIOUS CONSERVATIVE haunts liberalism today. This person has not faded into the background as liberals since the Enlightenment have supposed would happen. Instead, the number of religious conservatives is growing as I write this book. Religious conservatives are especially troublesome because they do not have a place in the new, increasingly influential arguments for recognizing cultural diversity and difference. Instead, the presence of religious conservatives reveals the limits of such a position. Arguments for cultural diversity can rarely account for religious conservatives because these arguments are often based on autonomy and individuality, or equality, ideals that religious conservatives often reject.

I argue here and in the next chapter that arguments for cultural diversity overreach their bounds and narrow cultural differences too much. In this chapter I show how these arguments curtail the chosen life of the religious conservative. While few discussions about diversity directly address religious people, I show the implications that several leading arguments have for conservative religions. I am mostly interested in the liberal viewpoint, and so I discuss two leading liberal arguments for cultural recognition, by Joseph Raz and Will Kymlicka, and follow their work into the next chapter. Their beliefs about autonomy and culture are important, and my disagreements with them should not mask the extent to which we agree on the importance of autonomy in liberal theory. The way Raz misapplies his influential view of autonomy to cultural groups is illuminating; examining his argument allows me to make a few minor changes to his idea of autonomy and to show how it should be applied to cultural groups. While I am mostly interested in liberalism, I am aware that not only liberals have limited arguments about retaining group differences, and so I also show how the arguments of two "identity theorists," Iris Young and Nancy Fraser, also narrow group differences.

The main problem with these arguments is that they do not present a conception of society that is pluralistic enough. By assuming that all communities within a larger society must adhere to the standards of autonomy (or equality), they refuse to give people the option to live in a community of obedience. Such a choice, I believe, should surely be respected in a liberal state. I begin by defending the idea that living a deeply and conservative religious life is indeed made by choice.

Choosing the Restricted Life

It is common enough, and sometimes true, to contend that some religious people have not chosen their life, but merely live the life of obedience they were born into. In today's liberal societies, people who are committed to living a deeply religious life are often regarded with suspicion by others who wonder about their values and their way of life. This very suspicion, however, is reason to think that many religious people do think about their commitments. When you live the strange life, when you are the one who is different, it is hard *not* to think deeply about your life. In today's Western liberal democracies it is not the feminist or the punk rocker who is different. Rather, it is deeply religious people who are different. The religious person stands out in our culture — in the cultures of the West — as someone who does not conform to many of mainstream society's norms and practices.

Resisting the mainstream society is often hard to do, especially since religious conservatives live a life full of restrictions that people in the mainstream society do not have. Living a life with restrictions, restrictions that can be ignored (although that may mean leaving the community), is usually harder to do than living a life without restrictions. We live in a materialist and consumerist culture that encourages people to discover and fulfill their desires. Religious conservatives spend much of their lives trying to deny their desires. It is not easy to live the restrictive life when coworkers and neighbors eat whatever they want and spend the Sabbath at the beach, while you pray in a sweltering church or synagogue and pass up the shish-kabob for your kosher bologna sandwich. It is harder to wear a black suit and a black hat or a long-sleeved dress in the hot summer than it is to wear shorts. It is hard to avoid television, radio, and the movies. People who are different are constantly reminded of their differences. When these differences can be so easily spurned — the fundamentalist Christian can always turn on his television set — then they are surely chosen. Living the restrictive life takes a depth of commitment and character that many people lack.

How can one possibly think that the Hasidic Jew who lives in Brooklyn and works in Manhattan is not aware that there are ways of life that are in many ways clearly easier than the life he lives? The fundamentalist Christian who watches little television or movies will be reminded of her differences every time the talk at her office turns to popular culture. Living the restrictive life takes a commitment that is not always easy to maintain and certainly requires some thought. Few members of minority communities can ignore the majority culture. It constantly surrounds them. Even religious people in rural areas will often see others who are different. When they go into town, or talk to their neighbors, they become aware of their differences from others.

It is not only those who join conservative religions, as the Kendalls did, who consciously choose their faith. These people certainly exist, and they are not just poor or uneducated people looking for an opiate to deal with their misery of life. Many people who join conservative religions are well-educated and wealthy.[1] Most people born into conservative religious communities understand they have a choice about their life as well. Except for the most insular groups, religious conservatives easily see and confront a mainstream society that celebrates choice. Its advertisements and media are ubiquitous. Walking down the street one can see its members living in different ways. How can a city dweller avoid a confrontation with mainstream society? Its existence and perhaps its lure will be constantly present.

In contrast, people who live in the mainstream society can live lives without any deep commitments and can live unchallenged or, at the least, rarely challenged as intensely as are religious people. They may be taught about other cultures or ways of life, but only occasionally confront others who live lives that are different in any meaningful way. Those who live in the mainstream of liberal societies can breeze through life without consciously choosing their way of life. This is because they are not living a different kind of life. It is religious conservatives who are often different.

While religious conservatives will often routinely face secular society, few members of the mainstream society will confront a religious community in any meaningful way unless they seek one out. Religious conservatives can rightly ask how many liberals allow their children to experience a conservative religious life. To do so means more than attending church one day. It means spending time living a life according to the rules of the church. A child raised within the church will eventually see that there are other ways of life out there. These children will see that their neighbors or schoolmates live differently than they do.

To say that religious conservatives choose their lives may strike some as odd, and not only because they seem to live a life of obedience. Michael Sandel argues that many religious people do not choose their beliefs. Rather, they follow their beliefs because that is what their conscience dictates.[2] Yet describing the religious person's convictions as a matter of choice is appropriate from the perspective of liberal institutions. Religious people may object to the idea that they choose their life — they may say that following God is not something they have a choice about. Whether people feel their beliefs and way of life are chosen or dictated by their conscience, however, is immaterial from a liberal perspective. It only matters that people are able to live a different life if they so wish. This means the liberal state needs to make sure that people are aware that they have options in their lives, that they are not coerced by others to live a certain kind of life, and that they have enough of an education to survive in another life if they desire. If this is accomplished, then from the perspective of the liberal state, people have a choice about their lives, even if some of their commitments don't necessarily feel like a choice.

The Decline of Religion

Religious conservatives are not the only ones who live different lives in liberal society, but they are an important example of group difference. American culture is not relentlessly secular, but the religion accepted in the mainstream society is mostly a privatized one. There is little religion in public schools or public institutions. The fights that occur about religion in public show how its public role has been accepted by most as minimal. I believe it is wrong to have a teacher-led prayer for a few seconds in schools, but this sort of prayer is hardly inserting religion into the public schools. I'm against crèches on public property, but this too doesn't mean the Christianization of government. These are symbolic gestures, and if they succeed they will only mask how secular our public life has become.

This wasn't always the case. Not all that long ago, liberalism and religion, or at least Protestantism, were intertwined in the United States (and surely elsewhere). Nineteenth-century American liberalism rested on the idea of the church-going patriarchal family in a capitalist economy. It assumed that liberty was not license, the ability to do whatever one wants. Rather, many people in the nineteenth century assumed that liberty depended on virtue, and any account of virtue had self-restraint high on the list. If people were not virtuous, liberty would devolve into license and chaos.

Virtue, not surprisingly, depended on religion. Religion was nurtured in the family, at church, and in the schools. Tocqueville observed that religion often fails to restrain men directly, but "it reigns supreme in the souls of the women, and it is women who shape mores."[3] He was only partly right. Women were often influenced by the church, and then tried to impart the church's morality on their husbands, but sometimes, however, the church's influence on men was direct when the men attended church themselves.[4]

While there may not have been any constitutional ties between church and state, the influence of Protestantism on education was pervasive. The King James Bible was routinely used in public schools. Most private universities and colleges were associated with a church. In the 1840s most presidents of public and private institutions of higher learning were members of the clergy. Attendance at the campus chapel was often mandatory and noncontroversial.

Protestantism's influence on society was clear in other ways. Most business closed on Sundays, the day of rest, often because of laws that mandated their closing. Some employers took it upon themselves to teach their employees about the evils of drinking alcohol.[5] The monogamous patriarchal family was upheld when the government decided to stamp out Mormon polygamy. Until the late nineteenth century, many Americans considered themselves evangelical Protestants, though many people, often working class, were not very religious at all. Educated people often were, however, and they simply assumed that there was no conflict between Protestantism and liberalism. Where Protestantism prevailed, so did liberty and the flourishing of the human intellect. Since religion was so important to liberty, it is hardly surprising that in the first half of the nineteenth century almost every state in the Union had blasphemy statues that were routinely enforced.[6]

Religion's influence was never as great as its adherents wanted: if it was, there would have been no need for the antidrinking crusades of the nineteenth and early twentieth centuries. Nonetheless, much of society considered itself to be Protestant and to prize liberty. Theological and social changes by the end of the nineteenth century, however, weakened evangelical Protestantism's dominance in the United States. While many intellectuals questioned the veracity of Christianity since the Enlightenment, it wasn't until the end of the century that this thinking had a widespread impact in America. The publication of Darwin's *Origins of Species* shook the belief that many had in the literal interpretation of the account of Creation in the Book of Genesis. For many, the Bible could no longer be considered literally true. Furthermore, immigration brought large numbers of Jews and Catholics to the United States, undermining the notion that America was a Protestant country. Catholics fought the use of the King James Bible in public schools, while Jews were often suspicious of the use of any Bible in public schools. Universities slowly accepted religious pluralism and atheism by relaxing their chapel requirements and by choosing nonclergy as presidents and chancellors. With the onset of the plurality of religions, and with atheism becoming more respectable, American liberalism could no longer quietly accept the role of Protestantism at the center of society.[7]

All of these manifestations of public religious life are nearly unimaginable today. I don't want to pretend that everyone — or even most people — in nineteenth-century America were devout, but the culture of public life was based on a thick Protestant model. This is no longer the case. Public schools no longer teach Protestantism, all public and many private colleges and universities are thoroughly secular, and the idea of blasphemy statutes is inconceivable. To be sure, the Protestant influence on public life still persists, but its influence is thin and mostly symbolic. American debate about a short teacher-led prayer in school is a sign of that. To be publicly religious, to believe in the errant truth of a sacred text today, is to be different.

Autonomy and Cultural Recognition

While religious conservatives may choose their life, they clearly clash with some versions of liberal autonomy. Although Mill did not use the word *autonomy*, he clearly thought of autonomy in terms of individuality. Mill wanted people to think about their lives and the choices they made within them. He wanted them to express their individuality. He didn't think this meant ignoring one's tradition: "It would be absurd to pretend that people ought to live as if nothing whatever had been known in the world before they came into it; as if experience had as yet done nothing towards showing that one model of existence, or of conduct, is preferable to another." Mill, however, clearly hoped that people would redefine tradition in their own individualistic ways: "It is the privilege and proper condition of a human being, arrived at the maturity of his faculties, to use and interpret experience in his own way." Mill wanted people to make their own choices, choices that come from the inside, not the outside. People should be inner-directed, not outer-directed. "A person whose desires and impulses are his own — are the expression of his own nature, as it has been developed and modified by his own culture — is said to have character. One whose desires and impulses are not his own, has no character, no more than a steam-engine has character."[8]

The person who chooses a life of obedience fails Mill's conception of individuality. A more Kantian formulation would be to say that people should lead a life directed by reason. People do not become Hasidic Jews or Protestant fundamentalists to express their inner nature in their own way, nor do they want to interpret their experience in their own way. They don't lead a life of reason, but of faith. (Some lead a life of reason *and* faith.) To say they lack individuality, or that they do not live by reason, however, is not to say that they haven't made or are incapable of making a choice. (The lack of individuality will often be a matter of degree: the more conservative the religion, the less individuality it will allow. Some religions may be a little less conservative than others, and so allow for a certain amount of individuality.) Religious conservatives choose their way of life, a choice that many of them are reminded of almost every day in liberal societies.

There is a difference between choosing a life of obedience and living the Millian life of interpreting one's tradition and experience in one's own way. There is a difference between living a life of faith and living a life of reason. It is wrong, though, to rob the person who chooses the life of obedience of all autonomy. If someone chooses a way of life that many liberals find odd or incomprehensible, that is no reason to deny them their choice. As long as they are not hurting others and still allow others to make their own choices (important caveats that I explain in chapter 3), liberals need to respect their choices. Autonomy, as Raz says, is a matter of degree: some people will have more of it and some less of it.[9] People who choose the life of faith and obedience have enough autonomy. Those who live the Millian life of individuality, or the Kantian life of reason, may be autonomous in a robust manner. But there is no reason to think that everyone in a liberal society should or will choose such a life. The problem is that most accounts of cultural recognition assume that every community must vigorously support the autonomous life.

JOSEPH RAZ

Joseph Raz follows Mill in his *Morality of Freedom,* where he argues against the idea that liberalism can be neutral toward the good life, a view perhaps most famously advocated by John Rawls. The neutral view of liberalism argues that the state's job is to allow people to live their lives as they see fit. The state should not impose any view of the good life — the kinds of activities and practices it deems valuable — on its citizens, though it should ensure that citizens allow one another to live their lives as they wish. The neutrality view, though, has been criticized by many other liberals for a variety of reasons. Perhaps the most incisive is that the idea of a neutral state is impossible. Raz argues that every culture favors and encourages certain kinds of lives over others, a view that even Rawls agrees with.[10] Cultures provide their members with certain opportunities and not others. They can't be neutral about what sorts of opportunities they supply. Raz, for example, argues that certain cultures support autonomy. These cultures offer their members opportunities that cannot be had in a nonautonomous environment.[11] It is hard (though perhaps not impossible) to be autonomous in a culture that doesn't support autonomy; conversely, it is hard to be nonautonomous in an autonomous culture.

Raz, however, goes further than simply noting that particular cultures promote certain values. He contends that the liberal state should embrace perfectionism. That is, it should promote the well-being of its citizens. This means the state should promote what is valuable in life to choose. It could, for example, discourage television watching and encourage book reading through taxes and subsidies. Raz does not think there is only one valuable thing in life; he is a pluralist and thinks that there are many valuable goods. Just the same, there are goods that are not worthwhile and the state should not encourage its citizens to choose those goods. Raz, however, does not want the state to choose for its citizens, for the very act of choosing is part of a valuable life. "We value autonomy to the extent that it adds to the well-being of the autonomous person. We regard the fact that a life was autonomous as adding value to it."[12] Autonomy is an essential ingredient of living a good life. A state that wants to support the well-being of its citizens (as it should) would then support autonomy.

Still, autonomy and well-being are conceptually distinct in Raz's account, and someone may choose badly. The good life is not only the autonomous life; it is the autonomous life where good choices are made. What happens when bad choices are made, like when someone watches television for hours each day? Should the state force the person to choose well? Raz argues that it should not, that doing so can too easily violate that person's autonomy in a general way. His worry is that the state will not merely prevent the person from making a bad choice in the one instance, but will more broadly interfere with the person's life, decreasing that person's autonomy in many ways. Autonomy is not the only ingredient in a good life, but it is a crucial one. Any broad interference with it will probably harm the person more than one bad choice. Raz's perfectionism is not designed to justify the states' scrutiny of citizens' individual choices. Rather, it is designed for general state policies that can encourage good choices and discourage bad ones. Raz unfortunately has few examples to show how this may be done. He says that the state can promote monogamous marriage through legal recognition of it. This doesn't force anyone to marry, but through the state's recognition it may encourage people to do so.[13] We can imagine other ways, however, for the state to promote well-being and discourage bad choices. The state can promote well-being by encouraging people to live a good life by, say, supporting and promoting the arts and museums. This does not force anyone to attend the museum, but it enables people to do so. The state can also discourage bad choices by refusing to subsidize religious schools (if this discourages well-being on Raz's account), or forcing communities to expose their members to a variety of choices.

While there may be a variety of ways in which the state can promote well-being, encouraging autonomy is obviously central to Raz's argument. Raz says that there are three conditions for autonomy: appropriate mental abilities, an adequate range of options, and independence. If a person is to be autonomous, he must be able to make complex plans for himself and figure out how to realize them. He must have minimum rationality, the ability to understand the means needed to realize his goals, and so on. Presumably, he also needs to be educated adequately to realize his mental abilities. He must have a variety of adequate options from which to choose. Simply giving someone a choice about one thing or another is not sufficient. Nor is simply giving someone many choices of a similar nature enough. Variety, not merely numbers, matters. Further, a person should be able to have a range of options that have "long term pervasive consequences as well as short term options of little consequence, and a fair spread in between."[14]

Finally, his choices in life, if he is to be independent, must be free from coercion and manipulation from others. Coercion and manipulation subject the will of one person to another, taking away his autonomy. Coercion means one person has interfered with another person's choices. Manipulation means one person perverts the way another person reaches decisions, forms preferences, or adopts goals.[15] Though I will contend in the next chapter that the manipulation condition should be relaxed, Raz's conditions generally establish the background conditions that enable a person to choose the life he or she wants to lead.

The conditions for autonomy do not take place within a vacuum, but within a particular culture. This is where the liberalism of neutrality fails. It does not recognize the role that culture plays in the autonomous life. By leaving culture alone, neutrality liberalism takes the risk that the conditions to support autonomy may atrophy. Raz contends that the claim of cultures to "respect and to prosperity rests entirely on their vital importance to the prosperity of individual human beings." Culture is important as "a precondition for, and a factor which gives shape and content to, individual freedom." Raz contends that "only through being socialized in a culture can one tap the options which give life a meaning."[16] By and large, one's cultural membership determines the horizon of one's opportunities, of what one may become. Culture is important because it is only through a specific cultural context that we can become autonomous.

Because culture is so important to how we live our lives and the opportunities we have in it, Raz argues that it is in the interest of everyone to be fully integrated into a cultural group. Raz also argues that culture is an important part of one's identity, and so "slighting one's culture, persecuting it, holding it up for ridicule, slighting its value, etc., affect members of that group. Such conduct hurts them and offends their dignity."[17] We should respect and support people's cultures in order to respect and support the people who are part of these cultures. We identify with our culture, since it is our culture that gives us our identity; our culture also structures our choices and opportunities.

Since Raz argues that culture is important because it is through a culture that we become autonomous, it is not surprising that not all cultures are valuable. He contends that cultures that do not encourage their members to make their own choices do not merit much support. If culture should support individual autonomy, it is hard to support illiberal cultures that do not give their members much freedom. The way cultures — and governments — support autonomy is by supporting Raz's three conditions for autonomy. Perhaps most important, cultures should provide their members with a variety of options. Raz says that governments "can help people flourish, but only by creating the conditions for autonomous life, primarily by guaranteeing that an adequate range of diverse and valuable options shall be available to all."[18] But this is not true only for the society at large. It holds true for the cultural groups within it. Raz argues that each cultural community should provide an "adequate range of options" for its members.[19] Each cultural group should offer its members meaningful choices about their lives. Each constituent cultural group within a society should provide an adequate education to its members so they can construct and pursue their own life plans. He maintains that political societies are required "to discourage repressive practices in their constituent cultural groups." Further, Raz contends that cultures should not repress their own members or refuse them the right of exit.[20]

Moreover, Raz argues that peaceful coexistence in a multicultural society means that the members of the society's different cultures should become acquainted "with the customs of all the people and ethnic groups in one's country." Each culture within a society cannot be intolerant of other cultures. The young should learn about their own culture, and learn about other groups and to respect them. Learning about other cultures will sometimes create the temptation to drift out of one's cultural group and into another. Indeed, it may be that in a liberal society some cultures will disappear over time.[21] That some people may leave one culture and enter another is a choice that should be respected in a liberal society. This support fits in with Raz's autonomy-based account of culture. He supports cultural groups that support individual freedom, and he thinks culture is important since it is within a culture that people find their opportunities and choices.

Though Raz makes his argument in the name of cultural recognition, he certainly reduces many culture differences. He argues that the conditions of autonomy should apply not only to the society at large, but also to every cultural group within it. Raz wants each culture to educate its young so they can choose their own lives. No culture should try to coerce or manipulate its members' choices. And each culture must furnish its members with an adequate range of options. Raz does not suggest that cultures that fail these tests should be stamped out. He recommends tolerance of illiberal communities, with the view that perhaps they will gradually disappear.[22]

Raz's insistence that each culture within a society support autonomy weakens group differences, since historically and currently many cultures do not support autonomy. While Raz's argument undermines many group differences, I want to point out how it particularly affects religious conservatives. Because Raz wants each culture to teach its members to think for themselves, and because he wants each culture to supply an adequate range of options for each member, he places a version of autonomy that is very much like Millian individuality as a value that each cultural community should support. Communities and cultures that do not prize individuality are a problem for Raz, and so his argument calls into question the life of the religious conservative (and others). Yet the religious conservative almost always chooses his life, even if his choice of life is one that does not prize individuality. The only way he can choose this life is to live in a community that does not teach people to think in certain respects for themselves and that does not provide much of a range of options.

Raz wants to close out this option, but by doing so he would prevent people from choosing to live a life that many consider to be valuable. This would unnecessarily restrict people's choices and reduce cultural diversity. People should be able to choose the life of obedience in a liberal society. What Raz does not explain well is why each community must provide a range of options for its members. He seems to think this is necessary to ensure that people make their own choices, but religious conservatives today surely understand there is a range of options from which they can choose. Raz's account undervalues the choice that people make to live in a community of obedience.

WILL KYMLICKA

A similar dynamic appears in Will Kymlicka's writings. He has argued that people have a right to their "cultural structure."[23] The idea is that it is through a "rich and secure cultural structure that people can become aware, in a vivid way, of the options available to them, and intelligently examine their value." Cultural structure is important because it is the context in which people make their choices. Our cultural structure gives us options: "We decide how to lead our lives by situating ourselves in these cultural narratives, by adopting roles that have struck us as worthwhile ones."[24] If the cultural structure is weak, then it will be hard for us to make good choices because we won't have good options available to us. Having a strong cultural structure is an important ingredient in choosing the life we want to lead.

For Kymlicka, cultures are important because it is within a cultural context that people discover worthwhile options to make. We find our opportunities through our culture. Furthermore, since our identity is tied up with our culture, a weak culture ridiculed by others will harm our self-respect, making it harder for us to construct and pursue our life plans. Minority cultures may have a hard time surviving for a variety of reasons, and they may need state support to help them along. Majority cultures rarely need special support, since these larger cultures typically dominate a state and so are supported by society's main institutions and by the majority of the population.

Kymlicka initially stated that a liberal political community might have several cultural communities that deserve to have their cultural structure protected. His argument could possibly be applied to many groups, including immigrant and religious groups. Partly because of this expansiveness, Kymlicka has more recently narrowed his statement, saying that his argument applies only to societal cultures, which are relatively large and provide their members "with the meaningful ways of life across the full range of human activities, including social, educational, religious, recreational and economic life, encompassing both public and private spheres."[25] Societal cultures also have a distinct language or culture, territorial concentration, and no desire to integrate into the mainstream culture or society's main institutions.[26] These cultures are able to maintain themselves with a few protections from the outside. Kymlicka maintains that only societal cultures deserve special protection, and that the liberal political community is an example of such a societal culture.

Kymlicka is now willing to give only a few cultural communities—the societal cultures—considerable power over their members. Most ethnic and religious groups in the United States and Canada do not meet his requirements since most are not territorially concentrated, and only a few have a distinct language or culture, at least a generation or so after immigration. This narrows considerably the application of Kymlicka's theory of cultural rights. In North America, at most only indigenous peoples count as a national minority. In Great Britain perhaps only the Scots and the Welsh count.[27]

Within liberal societies, Kymlicka allows for cultural diversity, but each religious and ethnic community must adhere to the standards of liberalism. The cultural rights Kymlicka gives to national minorities are not given to other cultural communities. Immigrant, ethnic, and religious groups—groups he calls "polyethnic groups," groups that generally aspire to integrate into the mainstream society—must adhere to the norms of a liberal society. Kymlicka does discuss polyethnic rights, but these are rights that support integration into the larger political community.

Like Raz, Kymlicka sees culture as an important ingredient in protecting people's autonomy and so prefers that cultures be liberal. Since his support of cultural structure is predicated on the importance of individual autonomy, he says, "any form of group-differentiated rights that restricts the civil rights of group members is therefore inconsistent with liberal principles of freedom and equality."[28] Kymlicka is suspicious of granting communities the right to restrict the kind of education provided for children.[29] An autonomy-based culture for Kymlicka means it provides its members with opportunities, choices, and roles; a cultural community that does not provide its members with choices and opportunities is not one that deserves much respect. Kymlicka's account of culture and autonomy is similar to Raz's, and its application to religious groups will have a similar effect. Not surprisingly, Kymlicka is explicit about the influence of J. S. Mill on his account of autonomy.[30]

Like Raz's arguments, Kymlicka also narrows the range of group differences. Polyethnic groups, which include immigrant groups, their progeny, and religious communities, cannot exempt themselves from providing a cultural context that supports choice.[31] Communities should not be allowed to restrict the lives of their members in any way. Once again, every community (with the exception of national minorities) needs to support choice and opportunity for its members. Kymlicka does not grant communities the opportunity to live a life that doesn't support the choices of its members. Moreover, on Kymlicka's account, polyethnic groups should be encouraged to be included in mainstream society. The rights that they do receive are often designed to encourage this inclusion, though this sort of inclusion allows them to hold onto some symbols of their ethnic identity. This inclusion will further narrow group differences. As people study, learn, work, and play together, the differences between them narrow. (I further explain this argument below.)

While Kymlicka rightly suggests that many polyethnic groups want to be included in the mainstream society, it is telling that many religious conservatives want some sort of separation. They want to separate partly so they can live in a community that doesn't celebrate choice. They do not live in cultural communities that provide much in the way of choice or encourage people to express their individuality. They want to live within communities that restrict people's choices, sometimes in large ways. But this does not mean that their members do not choose to live in these communities. Like Raz, Kymlicka leaves little room for people to choose to live in a community of obedience.

Identity Politics

The standard account of liberal diversity has been criticized by identity theorists, who contend that one problem with liberalism is its failure to acknowledge explicitly the role that groups play in society. This failure results in the oppression and inequality of these neglected groups. This is because it is white men, or perhaps wealthy white men, who establish the standards of our political and social institutions. Nonwhite men, excluded from participating in establishing these standards, are either excluded from these institutions or inhabit them at a great comparative disadvantage to white men. The first step toward rectifying this problem, according to identity theorists, is to recognize the exclusion of particular groups and take steps toward including them.

While theorists like Kymlicka and Raz do recognize cultural groups, it is still the idea of individual autonomy that drives their arguments. The group is still not primary in their arguments, as identity theorists argue should occur to rectify their oppression.

Despite their claims to the contrary, groups are not nearly as primary in the account of identity theorists as they claim. What drives the account of identity theorists is not the celebration of groups, but the desire for equality. Replacing a version of autonomy with equality, however, does little to protect cultural differences. The problem with the account of identity theorists isn't their historical analysis. Many of Western society's institutions were created by white men and excluded other groups. There may be times when the political recognition of groups is necessary to end subordination. The problem with the account of identity theorists is their belief that group difference will remain intact with the onset of equality and the decline of subordination. Identity theorists fail to see that the end of subordination introduces the decline of many group differences and advances the primacy of equality and individual autonomy.

INCLUSION AND THE DECLINE OF DIFFERENCE

Many group differences arise from subordination. Groups that aspire to be part of society's mainstream institutions, but face obstacles that others do not in their attempts to do so, are subordinate. Members of subordinate groups routinely face more obstacles in their attempts to achieve their life plans and projects than others; they have more barriers to living their lives in fulfilling ways. They often face more barriers when they try to enter the political process and economic institutions. In an egalitarian society, careers are open to talents. For members of subordinate groups, talent is not enough. They are judged, and judged badly, based on ascriptive characteristics (like gender or race) that have nothing to do with the qualifications for the political office or job they are seeking; or they may be ignored because they lack the money to get the education necessary to qualify for certain positions. These economic and political barriers can often, but not always, be overcome. This is the case because while subordination is sometimes overwhelming, it is not always all encompassing; in some ways, members of subordinate groups can have advantages over others. They may be wealthy, or educated; they may have connections to people who can help them succeed in society. Yet at some point, sometimes at an important point, members of these groups will have to try to overcome discrimination to achieve their goals.

That subordination leads to group difference can be seen by looking at certain oppressed groups. Many homosexuals, for example, have created their own institutions because of their exclusion from mainstream life. The gay ghettos that exist in large cities, Mark Blasius writes, are largely a creation of subordination:

> To be sure, the ghetto exists because lesbians and gay men, to the extent that they come out, have been forced by societal rejection to find other means of livelihood, other sources of emotional sustenance, and other institutional frameworks within which to pursue their life objectives; the gay ghetto is significantly a manifestation of forced ghettoization.[32]

Many lesbians and gays have developed social institutions apart from mainstream society, places where they can meet and socialize and pray and work together without fear of harassment. That's why, in part, gay bars exist. The sprouting of gay churches and synagogues is due mostly to the inhospitable atmosphere of many mainstream churches and synagogues for homosexuals. If mainstream institutions welcomed lesbians and gays, the number of alternative institutions would be fewer. If places of worship were more welcoming to all and were willing to treat all their members equally, fewer gay churches and synagogues would have been built.

As the subordination of a group decreases, the practices that arose out of the subordination may fade. Not all practices will decline, but doctrines of equality and inclusion, liberal or otherwise, will lead to the fading of some differences. More lesbians and gays would probably marry, enabling homosexual couples to get the same insurance and tax benefits as others; gay couples would adopt more children; they would show affection in public, just as straight couples do. Gay bars would not be in obscure locations in nondescript buildings, as they often now are, particularly in smaller cities, but would stand alongside other bars downtown. This does not mean that people will no longer identify themselves as gay, or that being gay will become meaningless. It does mean, though, that identifying oneself as gay will no longer be as central to the lives as many gay people as it is today. Some separate institutions will fade away, though not all will. It does mean that being gay is something that no one will have to hide, and that it will not lead to the sorts of social, economic, and political exclusions it now does. Gay people will no longer be forced into a certain kind of identity, but will have more options in fashioning and refashioning themselves.

The usual vehicle for ending subordination and oppression is inclusion. Those who are oppressed want to be included in democratic discussions as full and equal citizens; they want to be heard, and they want to be treated fairly in social and political life and in the schools. When members of excluded groups, who are forced out of mainstream society, argue that their history is wrongly neglected from history textbooks, they are not attempting to maintain a distinct cultural identity. Rather, they want their history to be included in the country's historical narrative. They want to make their history part of the country's history. When Black history and Jewish history and Italian-American history are taught in schools as part of American history, as they should be, these histories can be claimed by all Americans. Those who advocate this kind of inclusion are promoting liberal diversity.

Some forms of inclusion do defend cultural boundaries, but usually in a rather soft way. When Jews want to wear their yarmulkes while in the military, or Sikhs want to wear turbans while serving as Canadian Mounties or in school, these people want to retain something of a distinct identity. I say "something" here because these differences are not enough to sustain a robustly distinct identity. Jews that want to be radically different from non-Jews don't join the American army; they stay in the yeshiva. Nonetheless, serving in the army with a yarmulke or a turban is showing a form of cultural identity that distinguishes the wearer from (some of his) fellow citizens. Diversity does not entail the eradication of all cultural differences, but the differences that might be preserved are often less robust than the similarities that coexist with it. Indeed, this pluralism is often quite like cosmopolitanism. When a devout Sikh serves as a Canadian Mountie, eats hamburgers at home, and attends Toronto Blue Jay baseball games, and his children attend the University of Toronto, then he and his family are living the cosmopolitan life, one that draws on several cultural traditions.

NANCY FRASER

In some ways, Nancy Fraser agrees with this account of group difference. She argues that "subaltern counterpublics," made up of subordinate groups, have arisen in response to their exclusion from the mainstream public square. These smaller publics are often "involuntarily enclaved," yet they want to talk to members of the larger public in order to get their ideas and arguments out to a wider audience. Fraser asks what happens to these subaltern counter-publics if they succeed in reaching the larger public, and if the inequality that forced the establishment of these smaller publics disappears. To her credit, Fraser understands that "subaltern counterpublics formed under conditions of dominance and subordination."[33] She notes that ending oppression will change the oppressed groups. The differences between women and men may very well narrow, while African-Americans will change from a "subordinate racialized caste into an ethnic group."[34] Her account of group difference is nuanced and subtle.

Yet Fraser still wants to retain the idea of a widely culturally diverse society *and* of social and political equality. She worries, however, that public spheres cannot be culturally neutral, but are culturally specific. The institutions of all public spheres have "culturally specific rhetorical lenses that filter and alter the utterances they frame; they can accommodate some expressive modes and not others." This means a society with only one public sphere will necessarily be less diverse than a society with several public spheres.[35] Still, Fraser says she sees "no reason to rule out in principle the possibility of a society in which social equality and cultural diversity coexist with participatory democracy." She contends that for the continuation of different cultural traditions there needs to be several publics in a society, with one overarching public where everyone can participate. This wider public is necessary since there will be many debates over issues that affect everyone. The need for a common and equal citizenship means that members of the different publics will have to speak to one another. People will have to gain "multicultural literacy," which they can do through practice.[36]

Quickly, however, the group boundaries that Fraser wants to maintain begin to slip. She contends that "under conditions of social equality," and because "intercultural communication" is important, different publics will be characterized by "porousness, outerdirectedness, and open-endedness." Moreover, people will often participate in more than one public, with many having overlapping memberships.[37] The reason for the establishment of these groups —subordination—has now ended. Now people will move between porous groups. Under these conditions, it is hard to see group boundaries remaining very robust.

Behind Fraser's hope of intact group boundaries appears to be the idea that the traditions of a group can continue unvarnished alongside equal interaction with others. But history isn't enough to carry a tradition forward, especially when that history was based on a subordination that Fraser now assumes (for her argument) has ended. Traditions and practices partly depend on specific institutions. Many smaller publics were created, as Fraser understands, precisely because the members of these groups could not enter the larger public. Part of what these smaller publics do is fight for acceptance and equality. When they succeed in reaching equality, their specific traditions and practices will alter and often become fused with other publics and the larger public. If alternative publics were created because of oppression, many will fade away when this oppression ends. We should expect this to happen, since this is frequently the outcome of an equal common citizenship, overlapping memberships and porous boundaries.

Fraser wants people to be equal and to communicate with one another. What she does not want to admit, but where the direction of her argument points, is that equal interaction often leads to a decline in cultural differences. In some ways, Fraser understands this. She argues, for example, that differences besides culture, like differences of class and perhaps of gender, will fade when oppression ends.[38]

Furthering this decline of cultural difference is Fraser's belief in social equality. Fraser does not think that political equality is enough for a fair society; political equality can mask wide social inequalities that often serve to perpetuate patterns of dominance and oppression. To end oppression and dominance people must be socially equal. This does not mean that people have the same amount of income or wealth, but it does mean that power is distributed roughly (not exactly) equally. The basic framework in society should not generate "unequal social groups in structural relations of dominance and subordination." An egalitarian society has no classes or gendered or racial divisions of labor.[39] People should be socially equal to others, regardless of their group membership. Fraser does not suggest that some cultural groups can continue their patterns of social inequality or patriarchy (though she understands that some groups have these patterns). Rather, she wants to get rid of all dominance and subordination. If all cultural groups, however, adhere to the idea of social equality, if all citizens are members of the larger public square and communicate with one another, then group differences begin to narrow and fade, just as they did for Raz and Kymlicka, though individual diversity will still continue.

IRIS YOUNG

Like Fraser, Iris Marion Young wants to preserve group differences in an egalitarian society; and like Fraser, Young's egalitarianism, and her commitment to individual autonomy, undermines her arguments for group differences. Unlike Fraser, Young does not understand that oppression is often the cause of group differences, and that ending oppression changes the nature of these groups.[40] While Fraser's argument for group differences in an egalitarian society is something of a hope, Young declares it an inevitable fact. She says that "group differentiation is both an inevitable and a desirable aspect of modern social processes." Young declares the good society "does not eliminate or transcend group difference. Rather, there is equality among socially and culturally differentiated groups, who mutually respect one another and affirm one another in their differences." Perhaps it is this vision that allows Young to rather tellingly refer to "Arabs" or "Asians" in the United States, instead of using the more accurate "Arab Americans" or "Asian Americans."[41] Young's terms imply that Arabs and Asians live in the United States as members of an Arab or Asian culture that is not much integrated with mainstream U.S. culture. Beyond the obvious objection that it is a misnomer to imply that there is one Arab or Asian culture, Arab- and Asian-Americans are often well integrated into American society. To be sure, this integration takes some time. Like most immigrant groups, the integration of Arab- and Asian-Americans may take two or three generations, but this is hardly surprising or unique.

Young claims that people do not give up their social group identifications "even when they are oppressed."[42] This idea, however, contains a backward misunderstanding of how group identity is often created and preserved. Social groups typically do not keep their identity even when they are oppressed, but *because* they are oppressed. Once the oppression is over, then group boundaries begin to fade and merge with other groups.

Though Young declares group differences to be an inevitable part of the good society, her vision of an egalitarian society undermines these group differences. She wants groups to be equal, but she also wants equality among individuals, and she imagines a society where people have a multiplicity of identities. Indeed, Young says that group memberships are "multiple, cross-cutting, fluid and shifting." She suggests that in "complex, highly-differentiated societies like our own, all persons have multiple group identifications." In an argument that strives for both autonomy and equality, Young contends that in a just society there will be "full participation and inclusion of everyone in a society's major institutions, and the socially supported substantive opportunity for all to develop and exercise their capacities and realize their choices."[43]

Moreover, though Young does not discuss groups that contain internal patterns of subordination and dominance, she clearly wants to get rid of subordination wherever it is found. While too often her book reads as if it is only the mainstream culture that contains oppressive elements, it is hard to imagine that she would want patterns of subordination and domination preserved, even in marginalized groups, given her firm commitment to equality. Indeed, she argues that culture should be politicized, so we can ask "what practices, habits, attitudes, comportments, images, symbols, and so on contribute to social domination and group oppression and to call for collective transformation of such practices."[44] If an egalitarian society is to be reached, then groups that may be both oppressed and oppressive will have to change.

The society that both Fraser and Young envision is an inclusive society of equality and diversity, full of multiple, cross-cutting, and fluid identities. What Young and, to a lesser extent, Fraser don't realize, however, is that even if we recognize groups in order to end oppression, group differences will fade in a society where equality reigns. When group boundaries are opaque and shifting, when people are members of different groups, when equality is realized and society's main institutions are inclusive, the individual becomes primary and the group secondary. This sort of society, one where Young hopes that people can "exercise their capacities and realize their choices," is a society of diverse individuals who construct themselves from a variety of cultural sources.[45] The goal of identity theorists like Young and Fraser is a society where people can lead the lives they choose to lead, where people fashion and refashion themselves as they like.

This is clearly an attractive vision of society in many ways. But it would cause many group boundaries to fade, including those of conservative religions. It would make it hard for religious people to choose to live a life they consider to be valuable. Conservative religions understand that the way to retain their differences is to reject equality, have boundaries that are neither porous or open-ended, and ensure that their members have few fluid, multiple, and cross-cutting memberships. Members of these communities do not "exercise their capacities and realize their choices." Rather, they realize one important choice, one that they are often reminded of: the choice to live a life that is different from most of their fellow citizens.

Difference and Diversity

I want to be clear that individuality and equality will not end all group differences. The movement to recognize different cultural practices is in part a reaction to the idea that all immigrants and outsiders must assimilate to the mainstream culture in order to be fully accepted. Kymlicka, Raz, Fraser, and Young all argue that many cultural practices that may have been formerly frowned upon should be accepted and sometimes incorporated in the mainstream society, as long as these ideals are compatible with liberalism. These arguments are important and generally right.[46] Mainstream society and its institutions should learn, for example, to accept different modes of dress and of worship. Educators should try to be more sensitive to different cultural methods of learning. While there are limits to the acceptance of cultural differences, Western liberal democracies can do much more to accept cultural differences that are compatible with liberalism.[47]

There is no doubt that the recognition of cultural practices compatible with liberalism is an important improvement over the assimilationist model. This idea of assimilation had some unbelievably unjust consequences, like the forcible taking away of indigenous children from their families and their placement with white families. Other times, however, the assimilationist ideal had considerable less effect. The many immigrants who have come to countries like the United States, Canada, and Australia often lived in ethnic enclaves, with a vibrant ethnic life. Over time, however, as the children of immigrants made their way into the mainstream society and embraced many liberal ideals, these enclaves lost their vigor.

Insisting upon individuality and equality in the context of cultural recognition will not end all differences, but it will end some group differences, while other group distinctions will become quite opaque. The dulling of group differences does not always mean the end of individual diversity. Individuals will choose to lead their lives in a variety of ways, drawing on a multitude of cultural strands and traditions. Indeed, the diminishing of group differences may allow for more individual diversity, as more individuals are able to create their lives in their own way, compared to the times when groups had considerable authority over their members. When individuals interpret their traditions in their own way, however, as Mill and his followers want, then groups have a hard time maintaining their boundaries. If groups cannot command the obedience of their followers to a particular way of life, then they cannot stay together for very long.

While subordination is one route to maintain group differences, voluntary separation from others is another way. Some religious groups follow this latter route. I suggested in chapter 1 the reason why religious groups are more apt than most groups to retain their difference: they live according to a set of rules, rules that help set religious conservatives apart in a community of their own, rules that are based in a certain belief in God. These rules of religion are exclusive: they establish who is a member and who is not. They are almost always hierarchical. A hierarchy is needed to establish the rules, and to discipline or expel people who break them. It's hard to be expelled from the Italian-American community, but a church or synagogue can expel a member. While liberal churches are hesitant to do so, conservative churches are less reluctant to enforce their rules. The hierarchy of conservative religions is often patriarchal as well, but this hardly means that only women are under the dominance of men. Both male and female members of a conservative religious community are supposed to follow the rules, rules that often limit their freedom. There are often more rules that apply to women, and women are often supposed to obey their husbands. To say that women are often shackled in conservative religions does not mean that men in these communities are free to do what they want. Equality is not prized in many conservative religions; obedience and hierarchy are.

To be sure, many people disdain the rules of their religious community. Religious liberals reduce the rituals and rules that set them apart from others. Religious liberals attend church or synagogue only sometimes, depending on their mood. If they wish, they ignore their religious leaders. They treasure their autonomy over obedience to the rules of religion. Having fewer differences with others, they are more apt to go to school, work, live, and marry people outside their faith. And then their ties to their religious community usually weaken.

Religious communities, even insular ones, are not complete cocoons, away from the influence of others. But this influence is limited and carefully watched. Conservative religious change over time, but members who change too much can and often are expelled. Certain core beliefs and practices are resistant to much change, while the more peripheral beliefs and practices change more. Hasidic Jews wear the garb of their Polish ancestors, but they happily use telephones and cars. However they change and however they resist transformation, though, conservative religions maintain a set of rules that sets them apart from others. These rules are often exclusive: they make certain kinds of interaction with others, particularly intimate kinds of interaction, off limits. It may mean that working, eating or socializing with others is taboo; it certainly means that marrying others is prohibited. Religious conservatives can survive liberal diversity because they live by a set of rules that rejects the kind of inclusion that is fostered by diversity. Their differences are not only rooted in history or culture, in a set of different beliefs, but in also a set of rules that distinguishes insiders from outsiders.

The Choices of Pluralism

What is right about arguments for cultural diversity is their support for individual diversity. Individuals in a liberal society should be allowed to choose from different cultural traditions as they fashion their lives. Yet liberalism is not only about the celebration of individuality. A liberal society should allow for communities that do not prize individual diversity and that treasure obedience instead. The mistake Raz makes (which is paralleled by Kymlicka, Young, and Fraser) is to suggest that each condition for autonomy — appropriate mental abilities, an adequate range of options, and independence — must apply to every community within a society. Raz's argument is paralleled by Kymlicka, who says that all polyethnic groups aim to integrate into liberal society and must support liberal autonomy. Fraser wants social equality and inclusion to spread to each cultural community. Young wants all members of all groups to be fully included in society's main institutions.

These arguments too relentlessly apply to all groups in society. These unyielding arguments crowd out the choice to belong to a group that does not want full inclusion in society's mainstream institutions, that doesn't aspire to give its members many options, and does not think much of social equality.

I agree with Raz that each community should educate its members so they have appropriate mental abilities and not coerce them. It is mistaken to argue, as Raz does, however, that *each* community within a society must give its members an adequate range of options in its support for autonomy. Raz's argument rests on his assumption that a society consists of different, fairly self-contained communities. Raz assumes that a multicultural society is one of distinct groups, though these groups are not geographically separated. He speaks of members of cultural groups that may wish to leave one group for another. He says we "should learn to think of our societies as consisting not of a majority and minorities, but of a plurality of cultural groups."[48] Raz speaks of enclaves, of particular cultural communities. His vision of society is of a Muslim community, a West Indian community, a Hindi community, and so on. He says that "multiculturalism insists that members of the different groups in society should be aware of the different cultures in their society." He assumes that we think of the state as a community of communities, with the state not being the same as these other communities.

Raz's assumption that we live in a society of different cultures is mistaken. Raz insists that members of each culture be taught about "all the cultures in the country," and be taught to respect them.[49] He argues that each culture should have few restrictions on their members and their members should be taught to be autonomous in a vigorous manner. Moreover, Raz contends that members of these different cultures will "inhabit the same economy." They will "tap the same job market, the same market for services and for goods." Members of these different cultural groups will also belong to the same political society. "They will all be educated and placed to enjoy roughly equal access to political power and to decision-making positions." Raz says that members of all cultural groups will have to "acquire a common political language, and common conventions of conduct." Finally, a multicultural society should have a common political culture.[50]

Given the strong notion of common institutions that Raz has, which even stretches to "common conventions of conduct," the amount of learning about and respect for members of different cultures should have for one another, and the importance he places on autonomy, it is hard to see how society will be made up of different and separate cultural groups. Rather, Raz's vision here leads to one of considerable cultural sharing and of intermarriage. It is one where a mainstream society that has fused elements of different cultures is surrounded by communities that are to some degree separate, though since they all must be internally liberal and lack restrictions, the separation here isn't very large. Raz's understanding of common institutions undercuts his own vision of a society of separate cultures.

Kymlicka has a much softer recognition of different communities within a larger society. More than Raz, Kymlicka recognizes that many communities want partly or sometimes completely to integrate into the mainstream society. He does argues that "polyethnic" groups often deserve certain rights, but these rights are typically rights of recognition and inclusion. Polyethnic groups want to be included into the polity, but they want to do so without shedding all marks of their heritage, so they ask that the terms of inclusion be modified to accept their cultural markers.[51] These terms are also compatible with liberal autonomy.

Kymlicka is explicitly suspicious of communities that want to be recognized so they can withdraw from the larger society (unless the community is itself a "societal culture," something that religious groups are not). Kymlicka worries in part that giving groups certain rights of withdrawal allows them to deny their members liberal rights or a liberal education.[52] Unlike Raz, Kymlicka does not see a society of self-contained groups. Rather, he sees many polyethnic groups, most of who want to retain some symbols and practices of their cultural identity but who are also integrated into the larger society. These groups are all part of the societal culture of the liberal society and should support autonomy and lack internal restrictions.

Similarly, neither Fraser nor Young gives an account of how groups in a liberal society can restrict the lives of their members. Rather, they aspire to have groups with open boundaries and citizens with multiple memberships. Despite their arguments for difference, neither one presents an argument for the maintenance of group difference in face of the equality and open-endedness of groups that they desire.

Instead of thinking of the state as merely a plurality of groups, as Raz does, I assume that communities are surrounded by a mainstream society and other communities, some of which are more enmeshed with the mainstream society than others. Given this assumption, I see no reason why *each* community within a larger society must provide its members with an adequate range of options from which to choose. This is only true if one assumes that each community is fairly well contained, with minimal contact between them or that a group's desire for withdrawal can be largely successful. If the state is more than a plurality of groups, however, and contains a mainstream society with few restriction and provides its members with a range of options, then a particular community within it need not. Raz and Kymlicka, of course, recognize that some people in a liberal society will not be very autonomous or will choose to be autonomous in only a limited way. But they want every community within a liberal society to support the conditions of autonomy.

Public institutions that serve all citizens, and civil society institutions that serve the public, make up mainstream society. Public schools and public colleges and universities are part of the mainstream, as are private schools that do not serve a particular population, like some religious schools do. Newspapers and other forms of media that strive to reach the widest possible audience, and to give news that affects the society as a whole, are part of the mainstream. Popular culture, like movies and television shows that hope to be viewed by most members of society, is also part of mainstream society.

More peripheral are those institutions that aim only to serve a particular

community. Asian-American newspapers try to give their audience information of particular importance to the Asian-American community. Many
churches and synagogues see only a specific community as their constituency.
Some parochial schools want to provide a particular kind of education to
members of their community.

Some people live completely in the mainstream, some live mostly in their
smaller communities, and many people live in between. The mainstream society should support the conditions of autonomy. It is within the mainstream
society that individual diversity should flourish. It is there where people will
take from different cultural traditions and incorporate them into their lives as
they wish. Here I agree with Raz and Kymlicka. I disagree with their argument that all the communities that surround the mainstream must support the
conditions of autonomy.

Most Hutterites, the Amish, and Hasidic Jews all know that they are sur-
rounded by a society with different ways of life. Protestant fundamentalists,
Orthodox Jews, and conservative Catholics know this as well. Many Hasidic
Jews live and work in New York City. How can one possibly argue that they
do not see a wide range of options of how they might want to live their lives?
The Hasidic children in Alaska may be given a narrow education, but they
certainly are aware that there are different ways to live. Even Hasidic Jews in
Jerusalem are aware that there are other ways of life. How could it be otherwise? Protestant fundamentalists live throughout the United States and surely
are aware of the way others live around them. The same is true for conservative Catholics. Modern, pluralistic societies give their members many options.
There is no reason to think that every community within these societies must
provide their members with a similar wide range of options, as long as the
larger society does.

I agree with Raz that a society that supports autonomy gives its members a
range of options when they consider the kind of life they want to lead. We
disagree on what counts as a society. Raz's (and Kymlicka's) argument that
every community within a society needs to provide its members with a range
of options is not necessary to support autonomy. Young and Fraser's assumption that every community support social equality and be open-ended suffers
from the same flaw. These arguments flatten out too many communities: it
makes diversity run through communities in a way that will make them more
similar. If we think that members of restrictive communities need not have a
range of options as long as the options are present in the larger society, then
liberals need not think they have to open up these communities. The result

will be a more pluralistic society. It will support individual diversity within the mainstream society (and perhaps within some of the smaller communities as well) and it will support group differences. Supporting diversity and difference does not mean giving up on autonomy.

Many religious conservatives do not value autonomy. They do not want to give their members choices about many fundamental issues. Yet this does not mean their members do not have this choice. As long as the community does not coerce its members or deny them a basic education, these members have a choice about their lives. This would be different if the community was self-contained, if it had little or no contact with outsiders. But this is rarely the case in a liberal society. As long as the community's members can see the ways of life of others, then the conditions of autonomy are met, though sometimes in a minimal way. Similarly, a community cannot undermine its members' political equality.[53]

Autonomy is a matter of degree, with some people being more autonomous than others. People who glimpse other possible ways of life from afar for their whole childhood and adolescence will be less autonomous than those whose glimpses turn into sustained examinations as they become teenagers. There is a wide range of autonomy. Some people will understand they have a choice in their lives. Others will examine their choices thoroughly and thoughtfully. Many will fall in between. Those who merely understand they have a choice about their lives meet the standard of autonomy minimally, but that is still meeting the standard. Undoubtedly, many religious conservatives will fall in the bottom range of this scale, but so too will many others. Yet some religious conservatives and a good many religious moderates will be at the top end of this scale.

Still, Raz might object to my argument. Having a choice is one thing; being autonomous is quite another. Autonomy does not mean that one decides when "young what life to have and spends the rest of it living it out according to plan." Raz quotes J. L. Mackie to suggest that the choices an autonomous person makes are ongoing throughout one's life: "there is not one goal but indefinitely many diverse goals, and . . . they are the objects of progressive (not once-for-all or conclusive) choices."[54] It might be said that religious conservative choose their way of life early on, and from there live a life of obedience. Further, Raz's account of liberalism is a perfectionist one. He argues that the liberal state should not only promote autonomy but also promote the good. Autonomy is valuable, Raz contends, only in the pursuit of the good. Since religious conservatives do not live an actively autonomous life,

Raz might say that their way of life is not a good one. Unsurprisingly, Raz suggests that some communities do not promote good lives because they do not value autonomy. He mentions immigrant communities, indigenous peoples, and religious sects in this context.

To apply this argument to religious conservatives, however, assumes too much. It assumes that they only make one choice at one moment on how to live. It may be, though, that they review their choices at different times throughout their lives. They may be plagued with doubts, or they may be tempted to leave the fold at times. My argument throughout this chapter suggests that both possibilities may occur.

Still, I have granted here that some religious conservatives may not be very autonomous. But their choice of what kind of life to live is surely defensible on liberal grounds, and it's possible to tease out a defense of their choice from Raz's own arguments. While Raz argues that autonomy is part of well-being, and that the state should promote well-being, Raz also admits that autonomy is "inconsistent with various forms of alternative forms of *valuable lives*." He suggests that autonomy is valuable for us because we in the Western liberal democracies value autonomy. "Since we live in a society whose social forms are to a considerable extent based on individual choice . . . we can prosper in it only if we can be successfully autonomous." Only those who are autonomous will do well in our culture: "those who live in an autonomy-enhancing culture can prosper only by being autonomous."[55]

The argument that those who live in an autonomous-enhancing society can only thrive by being autonomous begs for more argument than Raz supplies. This contention appears to be a simple descriptive claim, that those who live nonautonomous lives and think they are prospering are simply mistaken. Raz suggests that perhaps in another culture they could prosper, but not in ours. Why can't they, however, prosper in our culture?[56] The sociological accounts of religious conservatives reveal a mixture of well-being: some people feel stifled in their communities, some revel in them, and others bounce in between.[57] This is hardly surprising or unique. Undoubtedly, the range of feelings that people have about conservative religious communities is paralleled in more liberal communities.

As an empirical claim that only those who live autonomous lives can prosper in our culture Raz's argument looks incorrect. If this is the case, and the primary concern of the state is well-being, then there is no reason to be much concerned with religious conservatives. I don't know why liberals or the liberal state should presume that only fully autonomous lives are worthy of being chosen. Moreover, if we live in our different and separate groups, as Raz sometimes suggests, why can't some of them have autonomy as a value? Why can't some promote valuable lives that are nonautonomous? If nonautonomous lives can be valuable in cultures that do not value autonomy, as Raz admits, and the state should promote well-being, there seems to be no reason to transform these communities.

An important flaw with Raz's account is the way he shifts his assumptions on how liberal societies are constituted. Sometimes he assumes that each community within the larger liberal society is mostly separate from others; other times he does not. When he assumes that cultural communities are fairly separate, it is hard to figure out why each community must support autonomy. Raz says that nonautonomous lives can be valuable within nonautonomous cultures, and so a society of separate cultures may very well be able to have some autonomous and some nonautonomous cultures, each supporting different kinds of valuable lives.

If these communities are not really so separate, like I believe and like Raz sometimes suggests, then there is no reason to insist that every community provide a range of options to each member. If these different communities are part of the same job market, economy, and political society, then the different communities collectively provide options, along with the options that the mainstream society offers people. People need not have their own community provide them with many different options, since peering into other communities and the mainstream society to see what they have to offer will not be hard to do.

By casting well-being prior to autonomy, Raz confuses his account. It begs the further question of what counts as well-being. There is no reason to think that only autonomous lives full of choices are good. By arguing that the state should promote well-being and autonomy, Raz invites questions about what happens when the two diverge. His argument that in our world this is not possible is unconvincing.

Kymlicka is less ambiguous than Raz about autonomy's place within liberalism. For Kymlicka the prior value is autonomy: the liberal state should promote autonomy, which presumably leads to well-being. To be sure, some people will make bad choices, but an autonomy-promoting state will lead to more well-being rather than less. Having autonomy as the main liberal value allows Kymlicka to avoid the confusion that seeps in Raz's account when he adds well-being. Such a liberal state is not a neutral one; a government that promotes autonomy will encourage certain kinds of lives and institutions and not others. Further, since liberalism is now tied to democracy, the government may have a interest in advancing good citizenship, taking the state further from neutrality.

There are, of course, different ways to be autonomous. While Raz and Kymlicka leave little room for the religious conservative in their arguments, it is certainly odd for a liberal to argue against chosen lives that do not (physically) harm others, particularly in the name of cultural pluralism. Making autonomy central to liberalism means that the liberal state's proper concern is to ensure that people are to make a choice about their lives. Having a choice about one's life is much different than insisting that the life chosen be a life of Millian individuality. Liberalism demands that the conditions are in place so people can choose or reject a life of individuality if they wish. Even Mill understood this.

Mill doesn't hope or pretend that everyone will lead a life of individuality. His concern is that a stagnant culture will prevent those who to lead such a life from doing so. One way to read *On Liberty* is as a plea to the masses to stop putting pressure on the eccentrics to conform to the lifestyle of the "ascendant class." Mill complained that "originality is the one thing which unoriginal minds cannot feel the use of." He certainly hoped that the number of people who would exercise their individuality would rise. He hoped that increased discussion, more political involvement, and giving workers more power at work would help people use their minds more. He didn't pretend, however, that everyone would exercise their individuality. He assumed that many would not. He knew, for example, that most debates would not be listened to impassionately by most people: "I acknowledge that the tendency of all opinions to become sectarian is not cured by the freest discussion. . . . But it is not on the impassioned partisan, it is on the calmer and more disinterested bystander, that this collision of opinion works its salutary effect."[58]

Liberalism aims to enable the life of individuality, but it does not insist that people choose this life. The religious conservative may lead a life of minimal autonomy, a life guided by one main choice. But this life is safely within the confines of liberalism, as long as this life is chosen, people are given a decent education, and are not coerced. Liberalism demands that people choose the sort of life they want to lead, not that they live lives couched in constant choices. When he wrote *On Liberty,* Mill was quite worried that a stagnant culture stifled all attempts at encouraging individuality. He maintained that liberal democracies should protect and promote those who act differently from the mainstream. Mill celebrated people who were different; he wanted people to depart from public opinion and from mainstream practices and norms. When the mainstream is liberal, however, it is the nonliberals, such as religious conservatives, who depart from many cultural norms and practices today. A liberal theory that fails to recognize the right to be different and live a life of faith and obedience is not consistent enough with the liberal ideas of liberty and pluralism.

The dominant arguments for cultural pluralism wrongly undermine pluralism. A society that has some communities where autonomy is not prized and its conditions met only minimally offers its members *more* choices than a society where every or most community meets the conditions of autonomy more robustly. This society will allow its members to choose a life where autonomy is not particularly prized. While few people who are not born into the community join the Hutterites or the Amish, a number of people do join the Hasidim. The ranks of Protestant fundamentalism has grown over the last few years, as has Orthodox and Ultra-orthodox Jewry. The Church of Jesus Christ of Latter-day Saints (Mormons) is one of the fastest-growing churches in the world. And, of course, people have been leaving and joining the Roman Catholic Church since before Martin Luther. It is certainly true that some people have a hard time leaving their religious community, but people have been doing precisely that throughout history. A liberal society, one that is also pluralistic, will allow these choices to continue. Liberal theories that condemn the choice to be part of partly closed communities in the name of autonomy mistakenly restrict people's choices, and reduce the pluralism of society.

This suggests another difference between my account and that of Raz and Kymlicka's. They both argue that cultural communities or societal cultures need to be protected since it is through cultures that people make their choices and find their opportunities. The difficulty with this argument is that many cultures do not support choice and opportunity, which leads Raz and Kymlicka to want to revise the practices of many cultures. This account of culture and autonomy is backwards, however. Instead of supporting cultural communities or cultural structure because they support autonomy — something that is only sometimes true — liberals should support people's autonomy, which may mean, as Geoff Levey explains, "respecting the cultural commitments and attachments of individuals and even groups."[59] It means respecting people's attachments and commitments, even if they are illiberal. Supporting people's choices of cultural practices is more pluralistic and better honors the value of autonomy than only valuing those cultures or cultural practices that support autonomy. I am supporting the right of a person to choose to live a restricted life, but such a life is often guided too much by the idea of obedience to be admired by liberals. Still, not all chosen restrictions are the mark of the compliant and submissive person. Sometimes restrictions can aid autonomy. I explain how in the next chapter, where I turn away from religious conservatives and to religious moderates.

Autonomy and the Religious Life 3

THOUGH I HAVE JUST ARGUED that liberalism must allow people to choose to live in communities that do not support autonomy, liberals may still be nervous about this choice. Living within a community that sets restrictions upon its members often appears to be antithetical to liberal values, but that is not the case. Raz and Kymlicka both argue that culture is important because it is within a cultural context that we make our choices and find our opportunities. Unfortunately, neither explicitly discusses enough how cultures *restrict* our opportunities in many ways. This must be the other side of the opportunities cultures give us.

In the previous chapter I stated that not all restrictive communities need to support all the conditions of autonomy in a liberal society. Here I go further and argue that restrictions can sometimes aid autonomy. Of course, as with many principles, restrictions can be used in both good and bad ways. Liberty is an important liberal principle, and it can be used positively and negatively. While I want to defend community restrictions here, I also want to say that not all restrictions will support autonomy. Even restrictions that do not aid autonomy, however, must be allowed in a liberal society. The key to making this argument work is to insist that members of groups where autonomy is not prized have the right to exit, and that they can exit to a society that encourages autonomy. Yet the conditions needed to ensure the right to exit are typically more minimal than many liberals think. I end this chapter with a discussion of Chandran Kukathas, who presents a powerful theory of group difference, but whose argument does nothing to ensure individual diversity or autonomy.

Cultural Restrictions and Opportunities

Raz argues that cultures give us choices within a context, which means that autonomy will always be constrained in some way. Indeed, autonomy is only possible within some constraints. Autonomy, he rightly insists, is only possible within "a framework of constraints. The completely autonomous person is an impossibility."[1] Raz doesn't say much more about this in a direct way. The most we are left with is the idea that since every culture or every society must constrain in certain ways, it is best if these constraints work to support autonomy instead of inhibit it.

Kymlicka criticizes cultural restrictions more than Raz does, and he distinguishes between internal and external restrictions that particular communities have. External restrictions are restrictions a certain community has against outsiders, to prevent them from coming into a cultural community and changing its key norms and practices. Internal restrictions are those that a community—or those in charge—wants imposed against members of the community. These restrict the basic civil and political liberties of a group's members. An external restriction might be implemented to prevent non-members from having voting rights in a particular indigenous tribe. An internal restriction might be one that restricts the kind of education members of the community receive or one that limits the role of women in a cultural community.[2]

There is a difference between restricting insiders and barring outsiders from one's community, yet this distinction masks the fact that many external and internal restrictions have the same motive: to protect a particular culture's practices. Avishai Margalit and Moshe Halbertal have argued, with some justification, that many cultural communities want external restrictions so they can impose internal restrictions. Some communities want outsiders to have no influence so they can control the education and gender relations within their community.[3] An indigenous community may want to prevent the sale of its land to outsiders in order to maintain its way of life.[4] Keeping outsiders away is an important way for the cultural community to maintain its practices.

Another problem with the idea of internal restrictions is that Kymlicka doesn't define it very precisely. He does contend that internal restrictions are suspect because they restrict the basic civil and political liberties of a group's members. One of his main examples of an internal restriction, though, is the educational exemptions that some religious groups receive. Kymlicka notes that some of these groups can withdraw their children from school before the legal age of 16, and are not required to teach the usual school curriculum. Children, though, don't have the same civil and political liberties as adults so it is not clear that changing their way of education is a violation of their liberties. Moreover, there is no "usual school curriculum" in the United States (although there is in other countries). The curriculum is typically constructed at the local or state level, and as I'll show in chapter 5, all states in the United States allow parents to send their children to private schools and most have minimal requirements on home-schooling. In the United States everyone can be exempted from the curriculum established by their local public school. Since private schools are legal in most Western democracies, this is true in most liberal societies. What seems to bother Kymlicka is that some people restrict their children from a liberal education, from an education that will expose children to others. A liberal theory, he maintains, "will view interaction with and learning from other cultures as a good."[5]

THE NEED FOR RESTRICTIONS

While the distinction between internal and external restrictions isn't always clear, it is sometimes useful, and I will use it here. Since all cultures restrict their members in some ways, however, general admonishments against internal restrictions are too vague to be helpful. Some restrictions surely are worrisome, but this means that arguments against them need to be precise.

Looking at how communities restrict their members' lives and their interaction with others allows us to see that communities restrict their members in all kinds of ways, ways that also give people choices. This is actually implicit in Kymlicka's example of indigenous peoples. He argues that their culture needs to be strengthened so they have a strong cultural context from which to make choices about their lives. If the culture of indigenous peoples is fortified, and more indigenous people stay within their culture, then some opportunities will be closed to them. If an indigenous community decides to have communal property ownership, then one could not be a member of the community and own property in the community. (By contrast, one could live in a society with individual property rights and choose with others to buy and live on land communally.) This choice is unavailable to people who live in indigenous communities. Furthermore, they cannot become major league baseball players or astronauts, work for large corporations, or become a concert pianist.

Raz, too, suggests that cultures both restrict and enable us to take on roles.

Options exist for us not because they are naturally part of the world, but because they are created by our culture: "One cannot have an option to be a barrister, a surgeon, or a psychiatrist in a society where those professions, and the institutions their existence presupposes, do not exist."[6] Both Raz and Kymlicka agree that models and roles are typically culturally specific. While this argument implicitly suggests that cultures will restrict us, they don't work out the important implications of this suggestion.

It would be wrong to think of cultural restrictions simply as internal restrictions that confine people's choices. Living in an indigenous community also opens up certain opportunities for its members. An indigenous person can become a chief or a shaman or a traditional healer, or take on some other role in an indigenous community, but nonmembers cannot. This is true for other cultural communities as well. A Jewish person can become a rabbi or a cantor, but would find it difficult to become a priest. Further, Jewish people can become members of synagogues, active in Jewish organizations, and so on. Others cannot, or can do so only with great difficulty. Catholics can receive communion (if they are in good standing), but others cannot.

All cultures and communities close off some options as they open up others. No culture provides limitless options. Rather, cultures provide people with certain kind of options; they tell us what are worthwhile options, what is valuable and what is not. As Kymlicka says, activities have significance because they are "culturally recognized as a way of leading one's life." We learn about these activities through stories. "They become potential models, and define potential roles, that we can adopt as our own." Particular physical movements have meaning for us because they are culturally significant, "because they fit into some pattern of activities which is culturally recognized as a way of leading one's life."[7]

Kymlicka doesn't suggest that we can only take on roles that have been defined by our culture, but that certainly is where we begin in leading our lives. Some practices of a culture—like the way it organizes property—establish certain possible roles (property owner, perhaps) and makes other roles impossible. Other cultural practices establish certain roles (rabbi, minister, healer, altar girl, Hebrew school teacher, palace guard, and so on) and give them meaning. Raz notices this when he notes that barristers and psychiatrists exist only within a society that have the necessary institutions to endow these roles with meaning, but he never pushes this insight into particular communities within a larger society. Rather, Raz's constraints remain, at best, as background conditions within the wider society.

Community or culture can be thought of as an "enabling constraint": it enables us to have choices just as it restricts the choices we have. Enabling constraints are fairly common in our lives. Think of the rules of chess. The rules enable us to play the game, as Raz notes, just as they restrict the way we can move the pieces. "One cannot play chess by doing what one wants, say, by moving the rook diagonally. One can only play chess by following the rules."[8] The rules of grammar work similarly. They restrict what we say and how we say it, but without some rules we would be unintelligible to others.

Cultures and communities restrict people's choices in all kinds of ways, but they also enable other people to pick certain roles. They take away and give us options at the same time. No culture can give us limitless options and opportunities; no culture can teach us to become anything. Communities give their members choices by giving meaning to certain roles. These communities restrict members' choices, since some roles are not possible or have no meaning within a certain community. Since cultures and communities restrict their members as they enable them, we need to be careful of blanket condemnations of internal restrictions. It is impossible to imagine a culture or community that doesn't restrict its members in some way. Some restrictions will surely be educational. Much of culture is passed through education, and so it is hardly surprising that many communities will try to restrict the education of their young in some way.

Cultures and communities also restrict the choices of outsiders. They are often excluded from both formal and informal roles and opportunities offered in a particular community. As a general matter, these exclusions should not automatically be condemned. It would be wrong to say that Judaism restricts people's autonomy by insisting that one be Jewish to become a rabbi. Rather, Judaism enables some people to take on certain roles, while other communities enable their members in different ways. If Judaism (in, say, the United States) could not restrict membership in the rabbinate, then being Jewish might very well lose its meaning; and this could lead to the end of Judaism. Many roles are infused with meaning by a culture or a community, and in order to keep their meaning must only be held by the members of these communities. These certainly restrict the choices of nonmembers but does not harm their autonomy. To be autonomous does not mean that one can become or do anything. Without some restrictions and limitations, it would be impossible to have many meaningful choices.[9]

THE RESTRICTIONS OF COMMUNITY

Since all cultures and communities restrict their members in some ways, it is not enough for liberals to simply be against restrictions, either internal or external. Still, one might say that fewer restrictions are always better than more restrictions, all else being equal. People may be able to choose to live in a community with restrictions, but liberals may be disdainful of such a choice. Cultures, or communities (terms I've been using interchangeably so far), can be enabling constraints. Living within a culture or a community can both restrict our options and give us opportunities.

The large Western democracies, however, have within them many communities. With the context of the American culture, there are Protestant fundamentalist, Vietnamese-American, Hasidic, Mormon and other kinds of communities. Whether Hasidic Jews, the Amish, or Protestant fundamentalists make up their own cultures or are part of the American culture is an issue I want to sidestep here. Rather, I want to recall my argument in chapter 2 and say that these are communities within a larger society. These communities are not national minorities, like indigenous peoples, who should be thought of as sovereign nations in some way. The communities I am discussing are part of the larger society, but have some distinct norms and practices that set them apart. Some of these communities are far apart from the mainstream society, so far apart that perhaps calling them a distinct culture may be accurate; others are closer to the mainstream, but have certain distinct communal practices that set them apart and make them into a definable community.

People living within the mainstream society are restricted by the roles and opportunities their culture provides them, but they are free to try to develop new roles for themselves. To be sure, they may fail but the only restriction that prevents them from trying is what the law forbids. In the mainstream society people often establish new roles, drawing upon different cultural traditions. In the smaller communities I am discussing here, though, members' lives are restricted in various ways; they cannot fashion themselves as readily as members of the mainstream society. These communities self-consciously try to perpetuate their specific cultural traditions, and they often have people in charge of making of new rules when needed and enforcing the old ones. By contrast, there are few cultural guardians in the mainstream society.

These smaller communities may restrict how their members can dress, what they can eat, what kinds of jobs they can take, how much money they should contribute to the church, how their children are educated, who they can marry and under what conditions they can get divorced, what holidays they should celebrate and how they should be celebrated, and so on. These restrictions can run deep into people's lives, though this is by choice, at least for adults. If they do not like the restrictions, they can leave the community. Members of the larger mainstream society have none of these restrictions. They can dress, eat, and work however they wish.

If these restrictions can be thrown off by adults simply by leaving the community, what force do they then have? First, they certainly have force for children. How people raise their children is significant, since it affects how they act and think as adults. There are so many philosophical and political disputes over education and child-rearing practices because they influence so much of our lives. This leads to the point about voluntary restrictions. People can leave a community, but it is often hard to leave the community one is raised in. One has made psychological attachments to the community and its members. Of course, adults can leave any community within a liberal society, but some may find it hard to do so. They may accept restrictions they dislike in order to remain in the community. Other people may dislike the restrictions, but think that the path to Heaven lies through obedience to their church. Leaving may be possible but not easy.

The mainstream society has only legal restrictions and is welcoming to all citizens. It cannot kick someone out the same way a church can expel a member. All citizens are welcome in the mainstream society, as are all cultural practices that are compatible with liberalism. Smaller exclusive communities, however, need not be as welcoming. They can guard their rules and their cultural practices much more vigorously. This does not mean that the mainstream society has no culture—I'm not sure what it would mean to have a society with no culture. It does mean that the culture of the mainstream society is considerably more pluralistic and fluid than that of exclusive communities. As different kinds of people enter the mainstream society, its culture changes, though it always is (or should be) compatible with liberalism.

One could argue that the Western cultures are enough of an enabling constraint, and what we need to do is try to ensure that their various communities do not constrain its members any further. One might contend that a society need not have any smaller communities that restrict its members. I have argued here that the idea that we gain our opportunities through our culture implies that these cultures restrict our choices in some ways. To say that societal or national cultures restrict our choices, however, does not mean we must endorse the further restrictions of smaller communities within these cultures.

Kymlicka and Raz might say that the formal restrictions of the national culture are enough, and that any further community restrictions are oppressive, even if they are voluntary for adults.

This argument, though, is too restrictive. A large, dynamic society will typically contain many choices for people. People who are raised without any community or strong set of values, who are told they can choose any life they wish, may very well not know how to choose anything. We can't choose our way of life like we choose clothes; it's not something we try on for a few minutes and decide whether it fits after a quick look in the mirror. Western societies offer their members many choices, but not all these choices are particularly meaningful. The choice of which cereal to buy, or at what mall to shop, are not the choices that a liberal society should display as proof of the advantages it gives its members.

We should worry when children are raised with seemingly limitless choices. Liberal society celebrates choices and offers some of its members a wide range of options.[10] When children have lots of choices, how will they be able to choose? How will they know how to value certain things and disdain others? When people are raised with a sea of choices, they may not be raised with any deep values. When a person is taught to value many possibilities, none of these values can be felt in any deep way. It is not clear that a person raised to live a superficial life with many choices considers anything deeply enough to have made a real, considered choice.

No person can consider taking on every possible role or option. Too many choices can even be paralyzing. A short story can illustrate this point. My wife and I recently had to pick out a new kitchen floor. We went to the store to look at our options. Much to my surprise and distress, there were hundreds and hundreds of choices, perhaps more. My immediate response was panic, since I had no clue how to begin to narrow the options. My immediate response quickly gave way to a second, more considered response, which was a very strong desire to flee the store. I wanted choices, but only ten or twelve, not seven or eight hundred.

Though this story may tell us something about gender in our society (guided by my wife's sure hand, we managed to pick out a new floor), it also tells us why having more options isn't always better. A culture can tell us what sorts of roles it considers to be valuable. It may consider some roles to be less valuable and it may not even consider still other roles. By limiting opportunities and roles for their members, cultures can provide their members with meaningful opportunities.

It may be an advantage in a large society to be raised within a particular community. People raised in a community are given values and a way of life that they can reject or revise when they are older. The community can provide structure in a society that may seem like it offers many choices to its members. That children are raised in a community with a tradition, and not exposed to all the alternatives, does not mean that they are not autonomous or that community is a bad idea. Growing up within a secure tradition gives people the background to examine their choices and the choices of others. It gives them something to reject, if nothing else. For children "to learn what it is have a way of life, they must first be given a way of life."[11]

Children who grow up within a community will have a deep understanding of a way of life, but that does not mean they will have an inability to see or examine other ways of life. It may mean that the child has an idea of what it means to live a life guided by deep-seated values. A child who grows up with a particular way of life can reflect on this life and decide what parts to retain, what to reject, and what to alter. As a teenager and adult the person can look at other ways of life and compare them to his or her own. A child who is given many different options about how to live and often chooses differently, however, will not experience any way of life deeply enough to have a basis for comparison.

This argument is not a communitarian one. I'm not suggesting that people can only discover who they are, and not change their identity. People can certainly change their attachments, goals, and identity over time. In a pluralistic society, people will sometimes interpret and mesh cultural practices in their own way. It's important that a deep way of life given to a child changes over time, and that the child is given the chance to confront and learn about other ways of life. This person still has a choice about life if not given the chance to learn about others. That a person raised in a restrictive community may be autonomous, however, does not apply to a person who never steps outside such a community, but lives within it, from cradle to grave.[12] Nonetheless any defense of community restrictions must allow for this possibility.

It is wrong to assume that any community restrictions are automatically suspect. Some restrictions are woven into a particular way of life, a life that need not be repressive. While liberals may be suspicious of restrictions, it is not automatically the case that a life without restrictions, a life with seemingly limitless choices, is a life of autonomy in any way. It may be a shallow life. To be sure, some people who live within restrictive communities do so without much deep thinking. But people who do not think deeply can be found in many places and in many communities.

One could say that a society only needs to have parents who are willing to restrict their children's lives in some way. The restrictions of a religious community may be overbearing, burdensome, or undermine autonomy. While parents can restrict their children's lives on their own, it is often easier to do so within a particular community. A community can help guide parents. Religious communities, particularly conservative and moderate ones, have long-standing traditions that can be relied on. They have established rules of authority for interpreting the rules when conditions change. They also have institutions that teach, practice, and support the rules of their community. They may have schools, camps, child-care services, nursing homes, counseling services, charities, and even ambulance services established for members. Often these institutions will negotiate with the state over various matters. The institutional support of conservative religions is an important way the community is tied together.

Religious communities can also police themselves. Not directly, not with police powers, but with social pressure and with the threat of excommunication. Many conservative churches and synagogues know when their members are absent; they may know whose children are attending the wrong sort of movies downtown. Members are prevented from entering their houses of worship if they are not dressed appropriately. Members are often expected to contribute financially to the church if they are capable. The Church of Jesus Christ of Latter-day Saints asks that all members who are able to give 10 percent of their income to the church, which means members show the church their tax returns. Members can refuse to abide by these rules and leave the community. Many parents, though, turn to these communities for help and guidance. Communities with long-standing traditions, which will often mean religious communities, have the institutions and resources to guide and influence parents in ways that many will find helpful.

Raz would probably find social pressure to stay within a religious community disturbing. Raz follows Mill in arguing that liberalism should try to prevent one person from harming another, but Raz's version of harm moves past offense and physical harm. Raz also maintains harming a person may mean to "diminish his prospects, to affect adversely his possibilities."[13] This broad definition of harm could easily be used against religious communities that pressure their members to say within the fold, or threaten members with economic retaliation or shunning if they deviate from the community's practices or leave. Certainly, these practices — which are common enough[14] — are meant to undercut people exploring their prospect and possibilities.

Yet without these threats and pressure, the community itself may be threatened. One important argument in Raz's *Morality of Freedom* is that the social conditions that support the options within a particular culture are collective goods. This means, for example, that autonomy will best flourish within a society that supports autonomy. Autonomy will only thrive if the "general character of one's environment and culture" support autonomy.[15] Surely this insight applies to smaller religious communities as well: their particular practices will only survive within a community that is supportive. Certain individual practices can best flourish within a community or society that supports these practices.

Raz might want to suggest that autonomy-centered cultures are simply better than other cultures, and so the state should support the former and discourage the latter. Furthermore, Raz is clear that autonomy is only worthwhile if it is used in pursuit of the good, and it is doubtful if Raz would think that religious conservatives pursue a worthwhile good. If my argument here is correct, however, secular mainstream society is not necessarily more supportive of autonomy than the religious communities that lie within it. Moreover, some ways to influence people to remain within smaller religious communities is necessary if these communities are to survive in a liberal society. One good worth preserving in a liberal society is pluralism; I argued in the previous chapter that pluralism, religious communities, and choice are all compatible. Now I want to argue that this pluralism will become thinner without some community restrictions.

MINORITY COMMUNITIES

The largest problem with liberal accounts of culture that emphasize choice and opportunity is that they provide no resources for a minority community to retain its identity. Minority communities rely on both internal and external restrictions to protect their character. Unless such a community can manage to gain status as a societal culture, there is little chance that most liberals will sanction their restrictions. Without these restrictions, however, it is hard to see how a minority community can survive.

Religious parents may want to raise their children within their church, but as the children get older they may be increasingly exposed to other ways of life. The children may eventually attend a secular high school or college and work and perhaps play with nonbelievers. The parents aren't trying to seclude their children from the outside world. What they want is a chance early in their children's lives to instill in them a certain set of values. If minority communities are going to be able to survive diversity, they need a chance to restrict their children's encounters with the outside world, at least for some time. This will often mean some restrictions on education, an issue I return to in chapter 5. Children who confront others in a significant and constant manner at an early age — children who confront diversity — will more readily be pried from the life of their parents and community before they even have a deep understanding of this life.

The mainstream community is large and alluring. It contains few restrictions, and so children may be particularly attracted to it, since children rarely rejoice when they live the restricted life. The unrestricted life will be hard for many children to reject until they have had some time to live according to the restrictions of their community, both to become habituated to these restrictions and to understand the rationale behind them. A community that is unable to impose its internal restrictions on its members, especially its children, will see its boundaries and eventually its identity fade. To enable communities to survive diversity, and to give their members the option to remain in their community, some amount of internal restrictions are often necessary.

As their children grow up they will have to figure out for themselves what they think of these values after they confront others. If this is right, then liberals should not always be suspicious of religious communities, even religious communities that aim to teach their children about their tradition in a fairly sheltered way. Liberals should also better recognize the constructive role that internal restrictions can play in a community. Internal restrictions can help children lead valuable and autonomous lives when they are older. It gives them a chance to live a particular way of life that calls for a deep commitment; it also allows them to reject it if they so choose, if they are exposed to other ways of life when they get older. If liberals insist upon teaching their children the value of choice from a very early age on, then experiencing a way of life deeply will be even harder to do in a liberal state than it already is. But a restricted life can be valuable and sometimes liberal.

My account of moderate minority communities depends on them living within a pluralistic culture. I argued in the previous chapter that religious conservatives cannot help but see and often be tempted by the larger mainstream society, and so their community need not support autonomy. Similarly, liberals need not worry so much about moderate communities sheltering their children, since over time they will be exposed to others. The community itself, however, need not present these other ways of life to its charges to support autonomy. It can expose its children to those in the mainstream society and in other communities. This exposure, which is deeper and more meaningful than the exposure that religious conservatives have, means that community members live an autonomous life. The community's partial openness to others, not its own internal structure, can ensure that its members see up close other ways of life. Some internal restrictions and some educational sheltering can be compatible with and even supportive of autonomy in the context of a pluralistic culture. Indeed, these communities themselves will add to the pluralism of society.

MANIPULATION

I can now say why I am skeptical of Raz's argument that being free from manipulation is part of the autonomous life. Raz says that manipulation perverts the way a person makes decisions, forms preferences, and adopts goals.[16] Unfortunately and rather surprisingly, he says very little about manipulation, which is clearly a complex notion. A community that restricts people's options is manipulative in some ways. But this is true for almost all parents—and it is true for good parents. It is hard to see how parents could give their children limitless options. I doubt this would be a good idea, even if it were possible. Doing so would mean that the child would never be able to grasp the meaning of any of the options before him in any substantial way. Parents try to steer away their children away from certain kinds of lives and into others. Eamonn Callan notes that "the desire to perpetuate their own deepest values in the lives of their children is fundamental to the project of parenthood as most people understand it."[17]

While Raz wants each cultural group to teach its members to be independent so they can choose their own life, few cultures are willing to teach their young to choose *any* reasonable life, even to the point of exit. Cultures usually try to sustain themselves over generations by teaching their members that their culture is important, that continuing in its ways is a crucial value. It would be mistaken to object to something that many parents and communities deem essential to their desire for continuity, something that is indeed inevitable and often good and important. Nor is it the case that the attempt to perpetuate one's community or way of life necessarily inhibits autonomy, though it may do so.

Still, I don't want to suggest that all forms of manipulation are good for the child. It is hardly admirable or good for a parent to tell his child that she will be disowned if she doesn't become a doctor. This is certainly different from the parent who takes his child to the Lutheran church every Sunday. Surely, this is often an attempt to convince the child to live a life that involves the Lutheran church. The parents are not wrongly manipulating their child because they do not attend a different church, synagogue, or mosque each week.

A parent who tells his son that if he doesn't attend church each week he will end up in Hell is also manipulating his child. I am uncomfortable with such manipulation, because I think the threat is false. Yet if I thought the premise was true I would certainly think differently about the threat. Manipulation appears to be inevitable and is not always wrong. Raz's sparse comments about manipulation give no hint as to what he thinks of everyday and perhaps inevitable manipulation that parents (and friends and children and siblings) engage in.[18] That people should be able to make their own decisions, despite being manipulated, is probably the best liberals can hope for. This means that this child should be exposed to other ways of life. Yet if this exposure takes place too early in life, minority communities will have a hard time surviving.

Nonintervention and the Right to Exit

Internal and external restrictions are necessary for a community to retain its identity, and these restrictions can sometimes be used to aid autonomy. Indeed, there is reason to believe that a life without restrictions is a superficial life, not an autonomous one. It is important for liberals to emphasize the need for people to have choices and opportunities, but in the process they often neglect the role that restrictions play in the autonomous life and in retaining group differences.

The problem is that restrictions can easily be misused. Restrictions can be used to reduce or even subvert autonomy altogether. Kymlicka's worry about internal restrictions is not wrong, it is just too vague. Restrictions can be used to create a tightly woven community, one that is all encompassing throughout life. I argued in the previous chapter that many religious conservatives must consciously choose their way of life since it means they have to live surrounded by a society that greets them with suspicion. But some religious communities remove themselves from the mainstream society to a large degree, so their members do not confront others on a daily basis. Sometimes a community is not an enabling constraint but a disabling constraint.

This is something that liberalism will have to accept. The rights that parents have (or should have) in raising their children can be used in an extreme way by some. But as long as the difference is in degree, and not in kind, liberals must accept the misuse of restrictions. Parents often restrict the lives of their children. Communities often try to restrict the lives of their members. What I try to show below is that the many routine ways parents use to restrict and manipulate the lives of their children can be abused, but not in a way that calls for intervention. When parents and communities have considerable leeway in how they raise their children, as they should, it will not surprising if they sometimes raise their children in ways that liberals will dislike.

This does not mean that any community or parental restriction is acceptable. Principles need to be established to know when a community restricts its members too much. What is needed is a principle of nonintervention, describing the conditions that a community must meet in order to avoid intervention by the liberal state into its practices. The conditions for the principle of nonintervention are suggested by Raz's conditions for autonomy. People must be given a minimal education so they are able to consider their options and function outside their community and in the larger society. This is Raz's condition of appropriate mental abilities. Members must not be completely—or mostly—shielded from the larger society (though some partial shielding is acceptable). This meets the condition of having an adequate range of options from which to choose. Restrictive communities cannot harm their members without permission (and children's consent to harm is always open to question) or force them to remain within their community. This meets the condition of independence, as it ensures that no one in the community is coerced. In sum, there must be a real right to exit. Communities can meet this right, though, and still shelter their members to a considerable, though far from absolute, degree.

THE DIFFICULTY OF EXIT

While both Raz and Kymlicka are suspicious of insular groups, the case against them has been best developed by Leslie Green, who worries that minorities within insular groups will be wrongly oppressed. His main example is Mill's argument about polygamy. Mill decried polygamy as an odious practice, but also maintained that it called for no state intervention since Mormon women could leave the fold if they wish. Green argues, however, that members of religious groups are not "like members of a tennis club who assessed the options and then freely joined and who remain free to resign." Rather, he points out that adult converts are a minority of most religions; most members are born into the religion. They find themselves "members of an institution whose character is largely beyond their control but that structure their lives."[19]

There is certainly some truth to Green's argument, but his example illustrates the other side of the story. When Mill wrote about Mormon polygamy in 1859, Mormonism was a relatively young religion, not yet 30 years old. Certainly then many — if not most — of its adult members were, in fact, converts. What Green inadvertently alerts us to is the fact that some people do voluntarily join religious groups. Others, of course, are born into them, as Green says. Green does not say what should be done to ensure a right to exit from insular communities, since "everything depends on the character and weight of the particular rights involved and on the social context."[20] More can be said than this, however, though circumstances will obviously matter a lot.

My deeper argument with Green is at our initial assumptions. He assumes that something should be done to increase the chances of exit for people living in insular (he calls them "organic") communities. It is "risky, wrenching, and disorienting to have to tear oneself from one's religion of culture."[21] I believe that risky, wrenching, and disorienting matters are not a matter of state concern except in exceptional circumstances. That people do risky things is not cause for state intervention (unless they put others at risk).

Liberals must allow people who raise their children in an insular community to do so since their children have formal choices about their lives — they *can* leave — even though this may be very hard to do. This is what liberal autonomy demands. Liberals cannot insist that every child experience all the different kinds of lives out there since this is impossible; and if it were possible it would still be a bad idea. Most religious conservatives, even those in insular groups, know they have a choice about their lives and so meet the minimal requirements of liberal autonomy. They see other people around them living different kinds of lives. Members of insular groups leave all the time. Members of these groups may have psychological difficulties in leaving their community, as Green suggests, but there is little that liberalism can do about that. What the liberal state should ensure is that members of insular communities have a right to exit and that they know they can exercise this right.

THE HUTTERITES

I can best illustrate the dilemmas of the right to exit with a stark case, which is exemplified by the Hutterites. Like the Amish, the Hutterites are an

Anabaptist group that fled Europe to avoid persecution. Most Hutterites live in western Canada, in small colonies of about a hundred people. When a colony gets too big, about 150 people, it splits into two, with the mother colony taking on half of the daughter colony's debt. Everyone works according to his or her abilities, and everyone's needs (which are defined minimally) are cared for. Everything in the colony is owned communally. There is absolutely no private or personal property, except what is kept by stealth. People get to keep a few things as their own, like clothes and some personal effects, but they are not owned by the users. The Hutterites are farmers and because they work hard and reinvest much of their earnings into farm equipment, their colonies are often quite wealthy. They don't use the wealth for luxury items, or even for items that most North Americans consider essential, because they live simple lives.[22] Saved money that is not used for new farming equipment or for kitchen appliances is used to help begin new colonies.

The difficulty here is one of having the economic means to exit, which a court case illustrates. In the early 1960s four members — all brothers — of a Hutterite colony began to stray from the faith, as they become converted to the beliefs of the Radio Church of God. When this became apparent, the Hutterites tried to show the Hofer brothers the error of their ways. The brothers, however, showed no remorse and, in fact, began to practice their new beliefs in the colony, flouting many of the colony's rules. The Hutterites expelled the brothers from the colony and the brothers retaliated by suing, saying they deserved their share of the colony's assets.[23]

The force of the Hofers' lawsuit against their former colony is clear: they worked hard in the colony, and it is unfair that because they changed their mind on a few religious matters they became penniless and homeless. The colony had a legal charter (as all Hutterite colonies do) stating that members who are expelled have no claim on the colony's property. A strictly legalistic approach, however, won't do.[24] A legal document that says in exchange for work a person will be given food, along with clothes and shelter, but no money, makes the coercion of members quite possible. Members may feel unable to leave the colony since they can't take any money or possessions with them. Without any assets, members' choices are quite restricted. A liberalism committed to giving people choices about their lives ought to be concerned when the choice to leave one's community is severely circumscribed. The liberal state ought to be wary of a contract that means a person will work hard for his adult life (and part of his adolescence) but receive no money. Not all contracts are legal in the liberal state. No one can agree to become a slave or an indentured servant. While the Hutterites are neither, they give up considerable rights as members of their community.

Yet the Hutterite community cannot remain true to its religious ideals if it must give every member a proportionate share every time someone leaves. If every person who left received a proportionate share of the colony, many colonies would collapse. Since colonies are small, it would take only a few members to leave at around the same time for the colony to disintegrate. If liberals sided with the Hofers in their case (which they lost), this would reveal the extent that religious toleration is predicated on an individualistic conception of property. Religious groups that had a communal view of property would find themselves out of luck in the liberal state. There is no reason, however, to think that liberalism precludes communal living. No one forced the Hofer brothers to work in the Hutterite colony after they became adults. They could have left when they were younger, and worked outside the colony.

Some people may wonder if the Hutterites really understand that they can leave the colony. They almost certainly do. Few members of insular groups are unaware of the outside world. The lure of modern culture is rather powerful, and it is hard to hide people from it. People who try to shield their children from outside influences rarely completely succeed. Furthermore, small groups must routinely deal with outsiders for many reasons. The Hutterites regularly make trips to town to sell their goods and buy equipment and other items they do not make, to meet other Hutterites, and sometimes go to the bar to drink. The Hutterites don't baptize children, but wait until adulthood to do so, which means the decision to remain part of the Hutterite community must be a deliberate one. A Hutterite knows the ramifications of accepting baptism into the community.

Many liberals point to education as the place to liberate children raised in sheltered environments. While they attend school with other Hutterites in the colonies, Hutterite children are taught about the world from a very worldly perspective. Since the Hutterites are taught by state teachers, as well as by Hutterite teachers, it is hard to argue that they fall below Raz's conditions of adequate mental abilities. The Hutterites have a basic education that is probably equal to many Canadians. What the Hutterites show is that a state education in an atmosphere that is permeated by a worldview hostile to many of the state's ideals will have only a limited effect. Some Hutterites leave their communities, and some undoubtedly do so because of the education they receive, but that many Hutterites stay shows that education alone is only of limited effect in influencing insular communities. Still, this education ensures that the Hutterites meet Raz's first condition for autonomy.

Despite these outside influences, it is difficult for someone raised in a colony to refuse to become a Hutterite, since doing so means leaving the colony, one's family, and the world one knows best. The psychological difficulties in leaving must be large, and I don't at all want to minimize them. This is what bothers Green when he says that leaving insular communities must be risky and wrenching. Yet the difficulty in leaving one's parents' way of life is a common one and not peculiar to Hutterite children. Many parents shield their children from the influence of others; many parents restrict their children's lives in a variety of ways. Many parents frown upon what they consider to be bad choices by their children. Many children have difficulty straying from the path their parents set out for them because doing so means rejecting that path. This can often be psychologically difficult. So what? There is nothing in liberalism that says the state should make children feel comfortable about rejecting the path of their parents.

Green does not say why departure from one's parents is a matter of state concern. If it were, the state would have to get involved in many parent-child relationships. Liberals want to make sure that children are able to depart from their parents' way of life, but are not concerned that they should feel good about it. Hutterite parents are not the only ones who try to influence their children to follow their path. Lots of parents do. It can't be the fact that the Hutterites (or Amish) heavily influence their children that bothers liberals. Since the Hutterites are educated by state teachers, it can't be their education either. Some may object to the lack of diversity in Hutterite schools, but their nearest neighbors are rarely close, so the only option is busing over long distances, which is not an attractive possibility.

One key difference between Hutterite parents and others is that the choice Hutterites give their children is a stark one. They say, in effect, "either you live like us, or you are severed from our community." Since the Hutterites prescribe the way one lives in a rather detailed fashion, if one chooses the Hutterite way, one is giving up a considerable part of one's individuality. Yet if one rejects the Hutterite way of life, one's ties to the community are usually completely severed. A stark choice indeed. Here we see that the difference between Hutterite and other parents is not a difference of kind, but of degree. Parents routinely try to influence their children and express disappointment when their children make what they consider to be a bad choice. Some parents even occasionally refuse to talk to their children or withhold money.

Few parents and communities are so resolute, however, in demanding their children live a particular life or be expelled from their community. Liberalism allows communities and families to be so uncompromising if they wish. In a liberal society you can talk and associate with whom you choose, and you can avoid certain people if you want to do so, even your children, even if this does not happen very often. Some Orthodox Jewish parents have said the prayer for the dead when a child of theirs has married a non-Jew. The threat of being considered dead by one's parents certainly makes the choice of marrying a non-Jew rather daunting. But this reaction to children who stray from one's chosen path is allowable in a liberal regime.

Other families who successfully influence their children rarely give their children such a harsh choice. They may influence their children, but when the children are grown they will probably choose their own clothes to wear, what they want to eat each day, and where they want to live. They can decide what movies or television shows to watch (unlike the Hutterites, they can choose to watch movies and television). They may choose their occupation and perhaps deviate from how their parents worship. Few families present their children with the sort of choice that the Hutterites do.

A stark choice, however, is still a choice: as uneasy as liberals may be with the choice the Hutterites give the children, there are no liberal grounds for insisting that the Hutterites give their children more options. There is nothing in liberalism that insists that parents sanction the choices of their children. Uncomfortable and difficult choices are still choices. All sorts of parents cut off their children or reduce contact with them for a variety of reasons. We should not single out the Hutterites because they have an explicit policy about doing so. Liberalism does not insist that parents refrain from inflicting psychological harm on their children — this sort of thing happens all the time, in all kinds of settings. As long as they do not physically harm their children and prevent people from leaving, the liberal response to the Hutterites has to remain a rather muted one.

Another reason why groups like the Hutterites make liberals uneasy is that while the Hutterites may understand that there is another world out there, they are always spectators of that world, seeing it from afar. The Hutterites surround themselves with fellow believers; they are not members of multiple groups. Their children have no meaningful interaction with non-Hutterite children. These reasons should make liberals squirm a bit, yet here too liberals cannot do very much. If parents want to raise their children in a sheltered environment, the liberal state cannot prevent them from doing so. It is one thing if parents refuse to let their children leave the house, do not teach them how to read and write, and raise them so they are incapable of understanding the world outside their home. But this does not describe the Hutterites. Even if they do raise their children in a sheltered way, that is also true for many parents in liberal states. It is not just education in schools that helps make people autonomous. The influence of one's parents and community, and who one interacts with on a daily basis, also affects autonomy. These are matters, however, over which the liberal state has limited direct influence.

EXIT AID: FUNDS AND ORGANIZATIONS

Still, the issue of the right to exist from insular communities dangles. Without any money or much knowledge of how the outside world works, it must be a rather daunting experience to leave the community.[25] Many members may feel unable to leave. An older member may realize that he made a mistake joining the Hutterites, but this should not mean that he is bound forever to a decision he made when he was 18. People ought to be able to change their minds. Without any money, however, the option to leave the community is severely restricted. The difficulties in finding their way in the outside world may lead some young adults to accept baptism in the community even though they prefer to leave. To enable people to leave by easing the transition to the outside world, the Hutterites should set aside a small fund for members who leave their community. The amount of money given to someone who leaves the Hutterites should not be an incentive to leave, because then the state would be nearly closing down the community. No one should become wealthy by leaving, but a few thousand dollars would help members leave the community if they wish. Some money will give members the choice to leave. This money is not meant to be compensation for work. Though by the time they are 18 many Hutterites have worked for several years on the colony, many children work for family businesses for little compensation beyond the food, shelter, and clothing that we expect parents to supply their children.

The exit fund will allow members to leave; it will mean that members who stay choose to do so. Older members are compensated for their work by the food, shelter, and clothing they are given and by the intangible goods they receive by living in an unusual community. The Hutterites won't set up this fund voluntarily but they should be forced to do so.

It is difficult to leave other insular communities as well. But apostates in the

Amish or Ultraorthodox Jewish communities can and do own property, so leaving their communities does not have such harmful consequences as leaving the Hutterites does. They can plan to leave beforehand, and save up money to move if they wish. The Hutterites cannot do this. Still, there are worries when it comes to exit. Young adults may own very little, know little about how to live in the outside world, and have few job skills. (This is more likely with Ultraorthodox Jews than with the Amish, who are usually raised on farms. Some Ultraorthodox Jewish boys know a great deal about Jewish texts, but little else.) The same is true for women of all ages. The psychological difficulty in leaving one's family and community, combined with the lack of funds, will make it very difficult for these members of insular communities to leave. Older couples or men, who when they leave the community may find themselves pressured to sell their house at a cheap price, or find that the clientele to their business suddenly evaporated, may also have a hard time leaving.

To ensure that there really is a right to exit, organizations are needed to help members of insular communities leave if they wish. These organizations (they can be run by the government, but need not be) can help apostates leave their communities without becoming destitute by giving them advice on legal matters or on how to reestablish their businesses. They can help train young adults for jobs or help them go to college. Here I am sympathetic to Green's argument that leaving insular groups can be disorienting; it is useful to help those that leave become oriented to the mainstream society. Again, these organizations should not help make people who leave wealthy but ensure that the right to exit really exists. Just as some countries assist immigrants adjust to their new home, refugees from insular communities need assistance as well. We should not, however, expect these organizations to become very busy, since leaving one's family behind is hardly an easy decision to make.

Though the Hutterites should be forced to create an exit fund, few other groups should be made to do the same.[26] I doubt that exit funds are needed for those religious conservatives who are not as insular as the Hutterites, Amish, or Hasidic Jews. My larger point here is not about the Hutterites, though, but about the right to exit. Barring those groups that completely shield their members from the outside world, there is little that liberals can do to ensure that all people have the psychological resources to make a fully autonomous choice about whether they will follow their parents' path or not. Education is the place most liberals look, and education certainly matters a lot (see the next chapter), but as long as parents have a large influence over their children and private schools exist, education will not by itself ensure that children will become vigorously autonomous. Liberals rarely address the economic barriers to exit; the Hutterites' condition is the exception in this regard, not the rule.

The right to exit from insular communities suggests some limits to what these communities can do. They cannot prevent members from leaving their community, which means they must educate their children—both girls and boys—to a large enough degree so they can leave their community if they wish. This does not mean calculus and French lessons (the sorts of things taught in the public schools many liberals wish existed in large numbers); it means reading and rudimentary knowledge in math and science. Members of insular communities should have the basic skills to join the larger community if they wish.

To ensure that members can leave, children of these communities also cannot be purposely physically harmed by community members. Children should not be considered full-fledged members of a particular community, since they may want to exercise their option to leave when they become an adult. Physical harm may reduce the opportunity of exit or, what is more likely, it may reduce the chances of someone taking advantage of one's liberty in the mainstream society. While parents can influence their children's decisions, they cannot permanently make it impossible for their children to exercise their liberty.

This suggests some answers to some apparently difficult cases that arise in a pluralistic society. What about groups that practice female circumcision? Or try to deny their children standard medical treatment, even if the alternative seems to be death? In these cases the solution is clear. Physical harm to children is simply not allowed in a liberal democracy, even in the name of diversity or tolerance. Children are entitled to basic health care; healing by prayer does not meet this minimal standard if there are generally accepted medical techniques available. Refusing children basic medical care is the sort of harm that will unnecessarily give children permanent pain for the rest of their lives (if not early death). Women can opt for clitoridectomies and adults can choose to forgo standard medical treatment. Liberal democracies should allow people to harm themselves, but not others, even their children. People that need not adhere to these standards are those that live in nonliberal sovereign communities.[27]

Similarly, marriages before the age of consent should be illegal. While such a marriage is not the same as physical harm, early marriages can make it nearly impossible to leave one's community. It is hard to leave an insular community in many circumstances. This difficulty becomes almost an impossibility for a girl who is married at age 15 and has children soon after. Leaving at the age of

18 or 19 and surviving in the outside world is hard. Leaving one's husband behind, and taking one's children into the outside world and trying to support oneself is nearly impossible. Alternatively, leaving one's children behind is hardly an attractive option. People should not have to make life commitments like marriages until they are ready to join the community in which the marriage takes place. That should not happen until adulthood.

Some might object to my example of the Hutterites and claim that they are an odd group that few will replicate. I agree that in many ways this is the case. But there are other groups that are less insular but still try to shield their members, particularly their children, from outside influences. Many fundamentalist churches typically shun cooperation with others. They won't join interfaith councils, for example, or even organizations for different Christian churches. They don't preach goodwill and friendship toward others. They do not want to cooperate with the heathens and heretics of the world. They only want to convert them. The rest of us are going to Hell and they see it as their job to try to save us, not cooperate with us in explorations of different faiths or in some sort of watery ecumenical service.

Such a fundamentalist church is exemplified by the Protestant fundamentalist school studied by Alan Peshkin. This school, and its mother church, try to become a moral community. Its pastor explained his school's pedagogical philosophy: "We come at it from an authoritarian point of view. The very first verse in the Bible doesn't endeavor to prove that God exists; it just assumes that God exists." Different kinds of living are not explored: "This is not a place where there are alternative world views, competing and confronting cosmologies. Christianity claims to be the only way." Questioning the teacher is often seen as a form of disobedience. Boys are supposed to learn skills, work habits, leadership, and economics, while girls learn cooking, housekeeping, household management, sewing, growing flowers, and child care. Girls are not allowed to have positions in school government that are higher than the positions that boys have. Fundamentalist schools do not try to teach just at school; they often try to become "total worlds." These schools are typically associated with a church; the church has social activities for the schoolchildren after school and on the weekends. Between the two they take up most of the time the students spend away from their family.[28] Churches like this one attempt to become an all-encompassing moral community.

Of course, children in the fundamentalist school do see the outside world. That's why the school's headmaster cruises the streets on the weekends: he wants to make sure his students are not out in the world.[29] But sometimes they are. My point here is that it is not just the atypical rural insular group that tries to shun others, but that many groups try to shield one's members, particularly one's children, from the influence of others. Their success, however, will almost always be limited.

The Right to Entrance

The right to exit places limits on the pluralism in a society with restrictive communities, limits that can be illustrated by a comparison with Chandran Kukathas. While many theorists of difference and liberals who recognize culture have a relatively narrow view of cultural diversity, this is not true for Chandran Kukathas. He believes in the importance of individual choice, but he does not think it is important to ensure that background conditions exist to make sure people are really making their own choices. While Kukathas does not support repression or subordination, he doesn't think the state has any right to combat them. Kukathas maintains that tolerance is the central liberal value, and argues that a tolerant society will consist of different kinds of communities, that are to a large extent self-governing and have little to do with one another.

Kukathas likens liberal societies to international society. He contends that this means we should take a "skeptical attitude towards established political authority, regarding it as (at best) not much more than the outcome of compromise among different peoples, with different ways, who have to find terms under which to co-exist." He wants to protect different communities and their practices from state interference, even if these practices physically harm their members or drastically restrict their members' life choices. In Kukathas's view, people live in different communities, and the state is there to define the "terms of association among the different groups." Since the state is only a settlement among different communities in Kukathas's account, there are no restrictions on what communities can do to their members. Kukathas explicitly says that communities can perform clitoridectomies on girls, or deny children blood transfusions. Presumably they can also deny their charges an education.[30] The state ensures that the groups do not interfere with one another too much, and perhaps concerns itself with a few collective goods like national security. Tolerance is paramount, and the state has no moral right to interfere with a community's practices.

While Kukathas takes oppression seriously, he argues that we should not presume that the state will be any less oppressive than various communities.

States, he notes, have been oppressive throughout history. Why presume that a particular community will be more oppressive than the state? Kukathas also contends if we want to change a community's practices—and he concedes that some practices should be changed—we should use persuasion and not force. Persuasion is morally preferable to force, it is more effective, and it is not as damaging to the people who are supposed to need to be changed.[31]

Kukathas's vision is a variant on the libertarian night watchman state, the difference being that Kukathas's basic unit is the group, not the individual. He talks about the "different peoples" in a state. The state, he says, is not just another community among communities. Rather, he says in language that is sometimes similar to Raz's, the state should be thought of as a "settlement among different groups."[32] (Unlike Raz, however, Kukathas has no conception of common institutions that also bring these communities together.) A society that consists of fundamentalist communities, a Catholic community, Jewish communities, and an atheist community might be the sort of state Kukathas envisions. Kukathas assumes that people are members of only one community or, if they inhabit several communities, that one is vastly more important than the others. Kukathas's vision—call it "group libertarianism"—assumes self-governing groups, with a state ensuring that the groups get along peacefully and fairly. Not much else beyond justice between groups is the state's concern.

Kukathas thinks that citizens need to allow one another to live peacefully in their own communities. Formal equality before the law is enough. He doesn't worry about people living in a community of obedience, and the social inequality that Fraser and Young want to reduce doesn't bother him much at all. Unlike theorists of difference, Kukathas doesn't emphasize an equality that undermines the group differences he wants to protect.

What is surprising, at least initially, about Kukathas's account is that he refuses to grant communities the institutional mechanisms needed to remain intact and to realize his vision of a society full of distinct communities. Kukathas argues *against* cultural rights.[33] He does not think that different cultural groups should have any legal mechanisms to maintain themselves. Rather, he says cultural groups are mutable historical associations, that may or may not survive, depending on the choices of their members. Kukathas suggests we think of cultural groups like voluntary associations, or perhaps as electoral minorities. People can stay within or leave them as they wish. Like voluntary associations, cultural communities may exist for a long time, or they may fade. It depends on how much support they have from their members. Kukathas also notes that the membership of a cultural group and its leaders may differ on important issues, or different groups with varying views within the cultural community may exist. Giving the group legal rights is to unfairly give those in charge of the group power over other members.

It is right to think that different communities, cultural and otherwise, will sometimes fade and sometimes increase in strength. Some may mesh with others. But Kukathas's vision of society is odd, and it doesn't reflect how liberal societies work in practice. His assumption that people have only one primary group or important membership is true for only some people. This may be true for people in subordinate groups, but many if not most people have multiple memberships, several of which may be quite important to them, while others are more trivial. Kukathas says cultural communities should exist only as long as their members support them, but what about people who do not want to only or mainly belong to a specific group? What about people who want to belong to several? Without granting communities control over their members, many people will choose to be part-time members.

One possibility for people who do not want to be part of one cultural group is to become members of the state. At one point Kukathas envisioned a society of different groups, along with a "wider society that is open to individuals wishing to leave their groups."[34] He has since changed his mind on this matter, however, and no longer envisions such a wider society. Now he specifically argues that the state is not another community but is a settlement among different groups. Being a member only of the state is not an option; the only members of the state are groups, not individuals. Perhaps Kukathas could say that people who refuse to belong to a particular cultural group are themselves a group. I doubt, however, that these people would have the traditions and forms of authority that a group needs to govern itself. These people might form an aggregate, not a group, and they would almost inevitably rely on the state to provide authority and regulate interactions among individuals. Kukathas does not, however, leave room for this possibility, since there are only cultural groups in Kukathas's state, not unaffiliated individuals.

It would appear that Kukathas's community of communities is more pluralistic than my argument for a liberal mainstream society, surrounded by a variety of communities, communities that must respect the right to exit. The communities with internal restrictions that I have defended here do not have the right to forcibly restrict their adult members. They cannot forcibly violate the civil rights of their members. These communities can perhaps punish or expel people who break their rules. They can punish those who exercise their civil rights, if they speak ill about the community in a public setting, for example. Yet these members can always avoid punishment by leaving the community and entering another community or the mainstream society, where their rights are protected. Since communities cannot forcibly violate the basic civil rights protected in a liberal society, difference is limited.

Kukathas, however, limits difference in another way because he does not grant people the right to enter into a community. Though Kukathas argues against giving cultures specific rights, he does grant them the right to establish their own rules, including the rules of membership. This is surely important, since communities that cannot establish these rules cannot control their own character.[35] Yet this means that in a state of different groups that control entrance, the right to exit is curtailed. The right to exit only makes sense if there is somewhere to go. If every community refuses a person, then that person's right to exit isn't very meaningful. Under Kukathas's scheme, no community must accept everyone. Kukathas's claim that he is against cultural rights is deceptive. If members cannot leave a community, then a cultural community has rights and powers over its members.

The best way to ensure that people have a right to exit is to have a liberal mainstream society with few requirements for entrance. In Kukathas's model, however, there is no mainstream society. Any right to exit is circumscribed by this lack of this right to entrance. If other communities can refuse to accept someone, as they can in Kukathas's society, and there is no mainstream society to go to, then there is no right to entrance. Since Kukathas makes no provision for a liberal mainstream society, his argument against cultural rights should be viewed skeptically.

That he does nothing to ensure that people can live a liberal life is certainly cause for alarm. Because Kukathas does not insist on a society or culture that is internally liberal, there is no way to ensure that one has a right to live in a society that lacks internal restrictions. While Kukathas defends his vision in the name of liberalism, it may be that no one can live a liberal life in his society. The idea that toleration must be set at the level of community means that there is no assurance of toleration of individuals. It is hard to see what is liberal about tolerating the torture of girls (clitoridectomy), or the denial of a basic education to children, or even the right to leave one's community. The ability or desire of people to live as they please (without harming others) is absent in Kukathas's society, unless they happen to find a community they like. If they do not find such a community, then their way of life is not tolerated. While Kukathas argues that tolerance should be placed at the center of liberalism, he willingly forgoes tolerance of individuals for tolerance of groups.

Kukathas's state protects group differences more than I would, because he doesn't ensure that people could live a liberal life. Yet I am hesitant to call his vision more diverse than one rooted in the idea of autonomy. He protects group differences at the expense of individual autonomy, individual diversity, and tolerance. If people can't live an unrestricted life, then Kukathas's argument narrows diversity in its own way.

It would be wrong to suggest that my argument allows for a limitless pluralism. The right to exit exacts certain limitations on difference. A society that is both pluralistic and liberal has a mainstream and a variety of communities, some on its periphery and some closer to center. Some of these communities can meet two of the conditions of autonomy rather minimally and its third condition—range of options—not at all. This presumes, however, a mainstream society that contains a range of options. It presumes a mainstream society that encourages autonomy in a fairly robust manner. Explaining this means entering the terrain of citizenship.

4 | Morality and Citizenship

RESTRICTIVE COMMUNITIES pose two important problems for a liberal democracy, problems that have similar solutions. First, if relatively insular groups were to increase in size, and the mainstream society was to begin to capsize, then the rights of exit and entrance would begin to lose their meaning. My argument for pluralism, and for allowing people to live a nonautonomous life, is predicated on a diverse mainstream society that supports autonomy. When insular and relatively closed communities become too large, then people's range of options begin to narrow, and autonomy becomes threatened.

The second problem is similar but is a concern of citizenship. If too many communities eschew the autonomous life, if many citizens are raised to be primarily members of insular or relatively closed communities, if they are raised to obey blindly their religious authority, then the virtues of citizenship (civic virtue) needed to sustain liberal democratic institutions become scarce.

Citizenship is a secondary matter in liberal theory, but it is still important. Liberals have recently become preoccupied with citizenship, but Kymlicka is right to note that we liberals need to be careful that our new preoccupation with civic virtue does not displace the more central liberal concern for justice. Civic virtue is important, but mostly as an instrumental value: "the main reason to be concerned about the erosion of civic virtue is that it may over time diminish the ability of the state to secure justice."[1]

This means that groups that reject autonomy cannot simply be outlawed or undermined by the state. The primary value in liberalism is autonomy, not citizenship, and people can choose to be bad citizens. Yet the concern about citizenship remains. Kymlicka asks what happens when the number of members of insular groups begins to grow. The possibility of their growth, he argues, is "not a happy prospect," because we do not want to have too many people adopting a way of life that is inherently in conflict with the norms of liberal citizenship.[2] This is not much of a worry with the most insular groups, like the Amish and the Hutterites, groups that I have elsewhere termed "partial citizens."[3] They are fairly removed from mainstream society, and the costs of membership in these kinds of groups is very high since their withdrawal from mainstream society is so large.

The real problem comes with less-insular conservative religions: some Hasidic and Ultraorthodox Jews, Protestant fundamentalists, and some Mormons and Catholics. Members of these groups do withdraw from mainstream life, but often only in a partial manner. Unlike the Hutterites and the Amish, these groups actively recruit new members and try to influence the political process. These groups are sometimes a danger to liberal citizenship. If groups that threaten liberal citizenship become too large and influential, then autonomy and the institutions of a liberal state become threatened.

The idea that religion can subvert citizenship is hardly obvious, though, with many religious conservatives contending that liberalism is often reliant on virtues inculcated in the church. These advocates argue that a state hostile to religion undermines that very values that undergird the state. While liberals are sometimes skeptical that any benefits can come from religion, religion can sometimes buttress liberal morality. But it's not always or even mostly the case. The relationship between religion and the liberal virtues remains a mixed one.

A Common Citizenship

One issue that theorists of diversity face is that of citizenship. How can a common citizenship be encouraged in a diverse society? This is the sort of question that Chandran Kukathas dismisses. In addition to resting on the odd idea that liberal society is like international society, Kukathas's society undervalues the importance of a common citizenship. By assuming that people are members of more or less self-contained communities, Kukathas can assume away the importance of a common citizenship. Few common decisions have to be made if people live in self-contained groups; there is little worry about how to ensure a common life together if there is not much that ties people together. There is no need to figure out to encourage diverse people to make common political decisions if there are few common decisions to be made. Kukathas's thin view of citizenship also allows for considerable discrimination to continue. It means men can discriminate against women, and whites against blacks, with impunity. It means that members of certain groups can dominate political and economic life. This does not matter, of course, if you assume that people live in groups and there are few common institutions. It matters little if members from different groups discriminate against one another if they have little contact.

These things matter, however, if there is a common life among members of the state and a common citizenship. Since people do not live in the self-contained groups that Kukathas assumes they do, the need for ways to sustain a common citizenship becomes more important. If a liberal society has a set of common institutions, then these societies must figure out how their citizens can inhabit them on an equal basis. If these societies are also diverse, then this project becomes harder. Indeed, I take part of the multicultural project to be a way to construct a common citizenship in the light of diversity. In their own ways, this is true for Raz, Kymlicka, Young, and Fraser. They all place an importance on a common citizenship, that people from different groups should respect one another, and that equality is an important goal. While my opinion differs from some of their conclusions, I share their concern for constructing a common citizenship in a diverse society.

Liberal citizenship is not self-perpetuating. Fulfilling the tenets of liberal citizenship is often hard to do, and there is no reason to think that it will occur without effort. Unsurprisingly, liberals speak of the need for liberal citizens to have certain virtues.[4] If citizens, at least if many citizens do not have the virtues needed to sustain liberal institutions, these institutions will become corrupted or collapse over time. If liberal citizens are not publicly spirited at all, then politicians will be able to do what they please. If liberal citizens are not willing to discuss, cooperate, and compromise, then politics is in danger of becoming bloody. If liberal citizens do not trust one another, then the societal cohesion needed to discuss and cooperate is absent.

This is harder to accomplish in a diverse society. A diverse society with common institutions has to figure out ways for different kinds of people to work, study, and live together or near one another. This is particularly true for immigrant societies, and it is increasingly the case that most Western democracies are becoming immigrant societies. In these kinds of societies, the immigrants and their children need to learn about the practices, laws, and institutions of their new country. While they may not like it, many of the people already living in this country have to learn about the practices of the new immigrants. If this doesn't happen, if different people do not understand one another at all, tensions and sometimes bloodshed arises. Trust between different people declines; the hope for equality that immigrants have is lost in what seems like perpetual intolerance and subordination. In liberal democracies the people have power, and they need to figure out ways to use that power collectively and judiciously. Getting people to respect one another enough to do this is not easy. We certainly shouldn't assume that respect will be forthcoming without effort.

Income and class are also at issue. In a society with a weak sense of citizenship and a market economy, the poor will often be left to their own devices. In this sort of society, one where wealthy people can withdraw from mainstream society with little worry about citizenship, weak public institutions are left behind for the poor and disadvantaged. For example, if we privatize public services like police and fire protection or street cleaning and snow plowing, then wealthy neighborhoods will enjoy good services while poor neighborhoods will not. If we privatize schooling, then the same effect will occur. A diverse society with only market institutions is not a recipe for a stable or just society.

A society with weak or no sense of citizenship also reduces the autonomy that people have. I have stated in the previous chapters that people living in restrictive communities typically choose to do so, but my position assumes that these communities exist alongside and are part of a larger liberal society that includes a mainstream with comparatively few restrictions. This society should be diverse and attractive: if it is merely a repository for poor people it can hardly be much of a choice for people living in restrictive communities. Instead, the mainstream society needs to support an adequate range of options for its members and potential members. This presumes a culture that supports a common citizenship; many of the characteristics of good citizens are the same of autonomous people.

Religion, Morality, and Citizenship

RESTRAINT

Some religious conservatives argue citizenship is, in fact, stronger when citizens are religious. Many contend that liberalism is parasitic on the morality that religion provides, or at least on a belief in God. Liberalism, the arguments runs, doesn't have much of a morality, yet liberal citizens need to have moral guidance. Religion tries to supply this morality. This is an argument with roots in Locke, which Tocqueville made famous, and is often repeated today.[5]

When religion is not successful in supplying the morality in the liberal state, the results are clear: moral breakdown, anomie, and social discord.

This argument has taken on renewed life in the late twentieth century as many observers claim a moral breakdown in the United States. Civility is being trampled upon, out-of-wedlock births and divorce rates are high, random and senseless violence is excessive, children are being neglected, and so on. If liberalism were to understand its reliance on religion, the argument runs, it could properly encourage religion to support the morality it needs. This is not an argument for a theological state, a state driven by a particular religion. Rather, it is an argument that public morality depends on private virtues, and government policies and pronouncements should aim at encouraging the institutions that encourage these virtues. Religion is one of the more important of these institutions.

For religious conservatives, religion (at least a certain kind) is crucial for a free society because it provides the moral backdrop needed for freedom by giving people a reason to follow the law and live by an ethical code. This morality is found in the Bible and is backed by a belief in God. What is crucial about biblical or Godly morality is its emphasis on self-denial. Without God there is no one to reward those who successfully deny their lusts in heaven. Human nature is always tempted toward sin, and a good society discourages this temptation. It is hard to get a detailed moral order from a belief in God, yet one main theme dominates in these arguments. People are driven toward self-interest at the expense of others, and so they need a belief in God to restrain their appetites.[6]

Locke, too, thought that people are frequently led by their lusts. It is the basis for his argument against an innate morality. If moral principles were inborn, we would see considerably more moral behavior than we do. "The great principle of morality, 'To do as one would be done to,' is more commended than practised." Men, Locke sighed over and over again, do not act morally. Still, something must done to curb men's desires. This is the job of moral laws. Attached to these laws must be rewards and punishments that are greater than the rewards men receive from following their desires. Men are self-interested, so the motivation to behave well must appeal to their interests: for Locke, self-interest and morality coincide.[7]

People should act morally, said Locke, and the way to ensure that is to get them to believe in God, heaven, and hell. The promise of heaven and the threat of hell will motivate self-interested people to behave well. What is crucial for Locke is that this belief assumes punishment for immoral behavior. Without a belief in everlasting punishment, people will take advantage of others whenever they can get away with it. They will try to figure out how they can use other people to advance their own interests. In such a world immoral behavior is rewarded. Locke didn't think that acting morally was reward in itself; it wouldn't convince people to act rightly. Men are too self-interested to view morality as its own reward. They need further rewards for moral behavior and punishments for acting immorally.

The theology that runs through these arguments may not be the best. Many devout Christians think that the Church is about God, not morality. Moreover, many Christians believe that salvation is a matter of grace, of accepting Christ as one's personal savior; salvation is often seen to be a matter of faith, not of works. It matters more that you accept Christ as your savior than what you do. My interest here, though, is less in Christian theology than in the political argument people make about God, religion, and morality. The idea that people are lustful creatures that can (only) be restrained by a belief in God is a common enough idea in many religious arguments today.

An important reason to be skeptical of the argument about morality and self-restraint was perceptively given by John Stuart Mill. Mill didn't think the idea of heaven and hell would motivate too many people to act morally, since the afterlife is too remote and too difficult for people to imagine for it to have much effect on behavior. It is also too uncertain a punishment to be very effective. Rewards and punishments in the afterlife, Mill noted, are supposedly awarded based "on a general survey of the person's life," and not because of any particular action.[8] Consequently, most people will easily convince themselves that despite some of their errors, the balance of their lives will be in their favor and they will end up in heaven. Someone who lies a little or steals a bit would hardly think their sins deserve everlasting hellfire. The choice of heaven or hell is simply too stark to motivate people to act morally. Few people think that what they do deserves hell. The threat of hell will affect the behavior of only a few, if any.

Even those who do more than lie or steal a little will not think they deserve hell: "Even the worst malefactor," Mill contended, "is hardly able to think that any crime he has had it in his power to commit, any evil he can have inflicted in this short space of existence, can have deserved torture extending through an eternity." Those who commit a deed that they admit was awful can always repent. The worst religions teach that "divine vengeance may be bought off."

The better ones do not want to drive sinners to despair and "dwell so much on divine mercy, that hardly any one is compelled to think of himself as irrevocably condemned."[9]

Mill didn't think that self-control was unimportant. Mill thought that autonomous people acted on their ideas, not merely on their desires. If someone simply followed his desires, he would not be acting on his considered reflections. He would not ask himself what he really wants to do and act upon it. An autonomous person reflects on his actions; he doesn't simply act. Denying our appetites is an important step toward autonomy. Self-denial in some ways can be seen as subsidiary to autonomy.

The way to reach self-denial was not, Mill argued, through heaven and hell. Mill thought that for people to be virtuous, they had to be taught to be so, and this education would best start at an early age. Self-control is unnatural to the undisciplined person. Like all virtues it must be taught. If people are to control their feelings, self-control must be habituated in them when they are young: "Now it is especially characteristic of the impressions of early education, that they possess what it is so much more difficult for later convictions to obtain — command over the feelings." When the virtues are fostered in the young, "the most elevated sentiments of which humanity is capable become a second nature, stronger than the first, and not so much subduing the original nature as merging it into itself."[10]

Self-restraint is important to autonomy: the autonomous person acts on her reason, not her appetite. If we can control our appetites, we can plan and pursue long-range plans. We can act on our considered reason, not our impulses. Training children to restrain their appetites is surely important, as Mill and religious conservatives both note. What is less clear in arguments about religion and morality is why early habituation in self-denial needs to be rooted in a belief in God. Why not simply argue that parents need to discipline their children and prevent them from getting everything they want?

This is what Locke ended up doing. Though Locke argued that a belief in God is important for morality, he placed the prime responsibility for teaching virtue with an education that takes place within the family, when the children are young. What is striking about this account of teaching morality is that God is barely in it. Locke mentioned God in his major work on education, but not until the second half of the book and there only briefly. Education is the family's business, and it is in educating their children that the parents (usually the father) can teach children how to deny their appetites. This denial is to be "got and improved by custom, made easy and familiar by an early practice." Children are easily impressionable, which makes the right kind of impression so important: "He that is not used to submit his will to the reason of others, when he is young, will scarce hearken or submit to his own reason, when he is of an age to make use of it."[11] Locke maintained that whether men are good or evil depends, nine times out of ten, on the sort of education they have. Habituate children when they are young to deny their appetites and they will become virtuous adults. Locke contended that if children are taught when they are older about good and evil in an abstract manner, their love of dominion and power already will be too strong to be combated. Instead, morality must be instilled from an early age.

It is not surprising that Locke's argument about how to teach self-restraint echoes Mill's by placing its importance in habituation at an early age, and not on God. Young children can be disciplined and trained to restrain their appetites, but two-, three-, and four-year-olds can hardly be expected to understand the idea of God or that of an afterlife. These are large and complicated ideas that are beyond the grasp of young children. It is the training of children to restrain themselves, not the belief in God, that is key to insuring self-denial. Those who maintain that self-denial is rooted in a belief in God and the afterlife and who argue for the importance of habituation at an early age do not do a good job explaining why God is necessary to instill the habits of self-restraint in children.

Discipline and self-restraint are important virtues, and there is no reason why liberals should concede their importance to conservatives. Liberals today do not talk much about self-restraint. Surely, the first five years of one's life are critical to one's morality. This makes the family an important place for moral education. When religious conservatives often argue this point, there is no reason for liberals to disagree. To be sure, too much discipline and too much self-restraint are not to be applauded. My argument here is not to help determine how parents should best teach self-restraint to their children, or how much self-restraint should be taught. Rather, I want to point out here that discussing habits and self-restraint within the family is something that liberalism has done since its inception, and is something that liberals should feel comfortable discussing today.

The concern of religious conservatives, however, is not the decline of the family, but the decline of the traditional family and religious observance. Families that teach moral education need not be religious; nor do they need to be traditional and patriarchal. The family that teaches self-restraint need not be a religious, patriarchal, two-parent family. Habit is the key to teaching children how to restrain themselves; religious beliefs can influence this habit but it is hardly crucial. Moreover, the line between self-restraint and unhealthy repression can be rather thin. The habit of self-restraint is an important one to learn, but it can easily be overemphasized.

Religious conservatives today often argue that government policy in the United States should do more to strengthen the family. Yet these same conservatives refuse to back many policy ideas that could fortify the family. The state can ensure more generous leaves for parents from their jobs after the birth of their children, and that all family members have decent health care. The state could do more to try to end poverty. To be sure, many impoverished families raise good children and many wealthy ones raise bad children. Good families with little money, however, will have a hard time raising their children well if they live in bad housing in dangerous neighborhoods. Reducing poverty is one way that liberal society can strengthen the family. The state should help strengthen the family when it can, though this should never mean allowing parents to harm their children or deny them an education. Stronger families, families where parents are able to spend more time with their children, may very well be more likely to teach liberal virtues, including self-restraint, to their children. Yet even the best of families will sometimes struggle to teach self-restraint in a society that is as aggressively materialist as the United States. Religion will sometimes help, but this won't always be the case, nor is being religious the only route to self-restraint.

If there is anything to the idea that religion encourages restraint, it may lie in the rules that religious communities lay down for their members. Some conservative religions are filled with rules that mandate self-restraint in a variety of settings. Some mandate that you cannot have sex with your wife or husband about half the time; obviously, sex before marriage is out of the question for most religious conservatives. In some religions, one cannot go to the table and eat; first, you must wash, say a prayer, or both. Certain religions prescribe the kinds of clothes you can and cannot wear. Many conservative religions are filled with rules. Instilled in the young, they can teach children that they must restrain their appetites on many occasions.

While one need not be religious to have rules and to instill a sense of self-discipline into children, many religions have a clear set of guidelines. The rules come from a long-standing community, and while these rules often change (slowly) over time, members can easily rely on the community to help them understand the rules; moreover, rules are often better enforced within a community. Rebellion is quite possible if only your child is not allowed to watch television. Forbidding your children to watch television is considerably easier, however, if you live in a community where few children are allowed to watch television. To the extent that religions do teach self-restraint, it is more likely to do with their rules than with their versions of heaven and hell. Too many rules, however, are not necessarily a good thing, and self-restraint is not the only virtue worth teaching. There is a fine line between healthy self-restraint and unhealthy repression, and some religious conservatives (and others) may very well go over it.

MEDIATING INSTITUTIONS

Some defenders of conservative religions use a version of the civil society argument to emphasize the importance of religion's political role. The argument here is religious institutions, not religious belief, helps liberalism. The point made by Richard John Neuhaus and Steven Carter is that religion is an important mediating institution between the individual and the government.[12] Individuals by themselves cannot oppose a government that threatens their liberty. Organizations are needed to check the government, keep an eye on it, and organize citizen opposition when necessary. Religions have a long history of opposing governments when liberty is threatened—their role in opposing the old communist regimes of Eastern Europe is well known—and so their presence is important to maintaining liberty. Neuhaus warns that once religion is pushed out of the public square and becomes nothing more than privatized conscience, then the naked public square arises. This is, however, "a transitional phenomenon. It is a vacuum begging to be filled."[13] The agent that will fill this vacuum is the state; but then, of course, there are no institutions available to oppose the state.

It is true that mediating institutions are needed to watch the state, to ensure that it does not abuse its power. And institutions that encourage the liberal virtues are important. On both counts the institutions of civil society are important, and the church is one of these institutions. Yet the argument that religion is an important mediating institution in a liberal democracy is easily exaggerated. While Neuhaus proclaims that once religion is pushed out of the public square then the state will take over—thus the "naked public square"—other mediating institutions fill the space of civil society, something that Neuhaus recognizes in other moments.[14] The media, corporations, the voluntary associations of the nonprofit sector, interest groups, labor unions, and universities are all mediating institutions. If religion were to disappear from the public sphere, liberty would not automatically be threatened by an overbearing state. This is not to say that religion plays no role as a mediating institution. Surely it does. But it is one institution among many that does so. If it were to disappear it is doubtful that disaster would strike.

If we are worried about mediating institutions, we might be concerned about the drop in union membership in the United States and look at changing laws in order to strengthen labor unions. Or we might be concerned that there are too many large media corporations and so work to break them up, the idea being the more independent news outlets there are to keep an eye on the government, the better. Civil society's health may be in decline because of too little interaction among citizens. Its decline may have to do with television and other forms of home entertainment, sprawling suburbs, and the interstate highway system. We may need to look at urban design to help shore up civil society. Religion is only one part of civil society. A strong religious presence may be one way to ensure an alternative mediating institution to the state, but it is not necessarily cause for concern if religion's voice in public is muted, as long as other voices and institutions in civil society remain strong. Only if the fading of religion's voice is accompanied by a general decline of civil society is there much cause for worry. This worry, however, would be general, about the health of civil society, and not specifically about religion.

RELIGION AND CIVIC SKILLS

Still, *some* church activity does support liberal virtues. Civic skills learned in the workplace are deeply stratified by class, race, and gender; in nonpolitical voluntary associations they are stratified by class and race. In churches, however, participation is not stratified: "The domain of equal access of opportunities to learn civic skills is in the church."[15] Participation here means not mere attendance. It means planning meetings, attending meetings where decisions are made, writing letters, and making a speech or presentation. Churches, some of which are moderate or lean toward the conservative end of the spectrum, have considerable participation by their African-American, female, and working-class members. These people do not learn civic skills at work or even at school. It is in church where they participate equally; in the church they are not silenced.

This is not true for all churches. Latino Catholics, for example, do not learn civic skills at church. This is probably due to the hierarchical structure of the Catholic Church.[16] Indeed, it is probably the case that other conservative churches with little room for participation do little for civic skills. Just as some religions support liberal morality, and others do not, so too do some churches foster democratic participatory skills and others do not. What matters is the structure of the church; some churches foster participation by a wide variety of members. From the point of view of encouraging civic skills, what is important is not what the minister teaches his or her flock, but what the church members do in church. Encouraging the liberal virtues is often not a matter of teaching someone the right belief; it is about engaging and habituating oneself to the right kind of practice.

Learning the liberal virtues is often not a matter of belief but of practice. One of the ways in which churches support the liberal virtues is by practice: by encouraging their members to participate in church activities. To be sure, beliefs matter when they encourage a church to become participatory. Not all churches believe that their members should participate much in church activities as equals, and their practices match this belief. When a church believes in having a participatory structure, and its practices follow from this belief, then the church will become one place, sometimes an important place, where its members learn civic skills.

The effect of churches on civic skills also depends on how insular the church is. Part of how the liberal virtues are encouraged is through interaction with others, with people who are different. In his well-known study, Robert Putnam has shown that it is within a dynamic civil society that citizens learn how to cooperate with one another in voluntary associations, to petition the government, and to read lively newspapers. When people, however, are members of different kinds of organizations they learn the qualities of "cooperation, solidarity, and public spiritedness."[17] When people are members of several groups—which need not be political—then their views tend to moderate, which makes compromise and cooperation more likely.

Joining organizations, usually the more the better, makes for good citizens in a liberal democracy. Many conservative religions, however, want to shield their members, and in particular their children, from the influence of others. They don't welcome multiple memberships; they are interested only in limited cooperation with others. If their members belong to different organizations, these organizations are often branches of the church. They may attend church camps, or church social organizations, or church Bible studies. Multiple membership in groups that all stem from the same branch, however, is not the way to have much interaction with those who are different. Some religious conservatives aspire to be an encompassing, moral community, one that has relatively little contact with others. After all, these communities want to perpetuate themselves. Yet to the extent that these communities remain insular, they undermine liberal citizenship.

PROGRESS

Both Mill and Dewey thought that religion was stagnant, that it held back believers from progress.[18] Yet these arguments against religion are too broad to be right. Sometimes religious traditions are full of vigorous debate, which Locke showed when he argued about the doctrines of Christianity. While the history of revealed religions sometimes display eras of uniformity and little dissent, other epochs are full of lively discussion and debate about the meaning of their relevant texts and social practices. These debates are not open-ended, if they take as a given that certain texts are divinely inspired. But many religious people today continue to debate vigorously the meaning of their texts, and take the skills learned from these debates when they discuss the political issues of the day. Few religions are the same today as they were at their inception.

Mill's complaint that the morality of Christianity is unchanging is too much of an exaggeration. Christian morality has changed considerably over the centuries; to be sure, some ideas of early Christianity are still with us in some form, but the Christian tradition (and other religious traditions) is rich and varied, and includes Christian socialism.[19] Some Christians might want to believe that Christian morality is unchanging but the history of their religion shows otherwise. Religions are often more dynamic than either Mill or Dewey give them credit for.

Still, one might say that those religious traditions that are full of vigorous debates are the liberal ones. Mill and Dewey's accusation may not be true for all religions, but it may be true enough for conservative ones. While it is wrong to think that conservative religions never have important debates within them, or that they never discuss some of their fundamental beliefs, Mill and Dewey's accusations are partly on target against some conservative religions. Some religions do prize obedience over thinking critically; some religions do insist that fidelity to one's religious leaders is more important than engaging with one's fellow citizens or evaluating one's political leaders. The tension between liberalism and religion is not as universal as Dewey and Mill make it out to be, but it is a real tension nonetheless.

Whether religion hinders or helps the liberal virtues is a contingent manner. It depends on the religion and the virtue at hand. The category of religion covers too many different kinds of beliefs to say anything definitive or anything close to definitive about the relationship between religion and morality. Liberals cannot automatically dismiss religion as a hindrance to civic engagement. It also means that liberals can't say that religions are always a help either. It depends on whether the church has a participatory structure or not and what the church teaches its flock. Sometimes, though, there are tensions between religion and liberalism; the more conservative and insular the religion, the more likely there will be fault lines between that religion and liberalism. The place to examine these tensions is where they tug at citizenship.

Reasonable Citizens

One of the more important problems that arise with religious conservatives is that they are so certain in their beliefs that it is hard to undertake a discussion with them. How can two people have a real discussion when one of them refuses to admit that she may be wrong? Religious people may change their minds about matters, but many religious conservatives look to their religious leaders for cues for this change. Religious leaders may change their views or develop new ones from time to time, but change is often very slow in coming. It may be hard to engage religious conservatives in discussions and debates if they are certain about their views or if they are dependent on religious leaders who think their beliefs are inerrant.

Eamonn Callan has in mind people like religious conservatives in his interpretation of Rawls's concepts of reasonableness and the burdens of judgment. Callan contends that reasonable people are committed to moral reciprocity. They will sincerely "propose principles intended to fix the rules of fair cooperation with others. They will discuss sincere proposals made by others, and they are willing to comply with such proposals if others are willing to do likewise." Reciprocity is meant to help people find mutually acceptable terms of cooperation where they initially disagree. When the norm of reciprocity governs, I put what I think is fair before you to consider and you take the proposal seriously. Similarly, I am ready to discuss your proposals seriously. We both hope that through dialogue we can converge on a common perspective.[20]

Reasonable people are also willing to recognize and accept the burdens of judgment when reasoning about public matters. The burdens of judgment are those "sources of divergent judgement that persist among us when all factors that signify a remediable failure to reason competently and to exhibit reciprocity are inoperative, such as logical bungling or inordinate self-interest."[21] Even when people deliberate reasonably, sincerely, and with the public interest in mind, disagreements are inevitable. One reason for these disagreements is that we come from diverse backgrounds, and our disparate experiences shape our judgments differently.

Reasonable people who recognize that they have sincere disagreements but want to come to a shared viewpoint or decision and are governed by the principle of reciprocity take the views of their interlocutors seriously. Since both interlocutors act in good conscience, both should think of each other's viewpoint to be as important as their own. Callan says that only through "empathic identification with your viewpoint can I appreciate what reason might commend in what you say." If I am to weigh your claims fairly, I cannot simply assume that you are wrong. Rather, I must "enter imaginatively into the moral perspective you occupy."[22]

The burdens of judgment are most grievous for those who are convinced of the truth of their arguments and think there is no reason to enter into debate about them. If you think your views are absolutely true, you won't engage in reciprocal discussion with others; you won't try to identify empathetically with the arguments of others. You may be unwilling to think of disagreements as reasonable or sincere, since this may be an admission that your views are mistaken.

Rawls thinks that the burdens of judgment are a public matter; they inform how we discuss public issues. Yet Rawls thinks we can retain our view of the truth in private. He suggests we can think one way as a citizen, where we have no one view of the truth, or accept that our view of the truth might be wrong, but act differently in private, where we retain our own view of the truth. Rawls argues that the arguments of "comprehensive liberals," who want all citizens to be autonomous in the way that Kant or Mill envisioned, narrow diversity too much. Instead, Rawls says people should be allowed to live a traditional life in the liberal polity. Callan rightly responds, however, that to believe in truths in private, yet suspend this belief in public, is "a high wire act." If one's beliefs about truth informs one's political judgment, which seems very likely, then one has fallen off the wire.[23] If one has a belief in the truth, suspending that belief when one acts as a citizen will be quite difficult.[24]

Moreover, Rawls's theory presupposes a "civic education which instills acceptance of the burdens of judgement."[25] The burdens of judgment surely thwart the efforts of conservative religions to instill in their members devotion to only their way of life. Rawls himself agrees when he discusses the importance of a civic education and remarks that it may very well undermine traditional communities.[26] Many religious conservatives, however, will object to such an education. They do not want their children educated to engage in reasonable public debates, to be told that there are sincere and reasonable views that differ from their own. The education that religious conservatives want for their children, and the lives they want for their members, "perpetuates a way of life in the particular form they cherish," and does not enhance liberal citizenship.[27]

Callan's account of citizenship is mostly right, though I am a bit skeptical of the moral psychology that informs his argument. The idea that we must be empathic with the arguments we oppose, that we must imaginatively enter into the moral perspective of people who we think are wrong is sometimes burdensome if not impossible. Sure, many people can do this on certain issues, for example, campaign finance reform. When someone tries to defend Serbian behavior in Bosnia or Kosovo, however, or South African apartheid because "it is good for the Blacks," I do not become empathic or try to enter into their moral perspective. I think see no reason why I should try, nor do I think I will be able to do so. Indeed, at times Callan himself recognizes that certain arguments—those corrupted by the "vices of unreason and domination"—need not be taken seriously.[28]

Furthermore, I think it is too easy to imply that because religious people believe in certain truths they cannot discuss matters reasonably. This is sometimes the case. Yet it also can easily be exaggerated. In chapter 6 I discuss religious arguments in public, but I want to briefly note here that not all religious views of the truth, even those that are moderate and conservative, threaten liberal citizenship. One may believe that it is true that one must keep kosher and the Sabbath to fulfill God's commandments, or that one can find grace and salvation only through Christ, but these beliefs say nothing about environmental policy, term limits, or campaign finance reform. The line from biblical truths to contemporary politics is rarely direct.

Still, Callan's account shows the need for liberal citizens to take the views of others seriously on many issues and to discuss issues sincerely and be willing to have their minds changed. Some religious conservatives take their views to be true and see little reason to debate or discuss them or to take seriously the views of others. Their separation from others means they have few chances to be confronted by others. These religious conservatives aren't reasonable citizens weighted by the burdens of judgment. Rather, they think they are right and want to use the political process to impose their views on others.

Other religious conservatives don't care that much about others. Their separation from others points to a different problem: it doesn't encourage people to think of the public good. People who have little contact with others will rarely think or care about them. Instead, they look at politics solely as a means to get more resources for their community. They rarely care about the health of the polity, except as it affects them. Socially separate people are rarely interested in discussing matters with their fellow citizens in a sincere matter. The give and take of everyday democratic politics is rarely embraced by people who live on the fringes of the political world.

Those on the fringe can still partake in politics; they can still vote. Citizens participate in politics and judge and vote for their elected officials. To use that power judiciously, citizens need to be taught how to judge political matters intelligently and critically. But some conservative religions do not want their members to be taught to think intelligently and critically. They want their members to be taught to obey the rules of the community. Yet many, if not most, people taught to think critically and intelligently about politics will take those skills home with them at the end of the day. It is hardly surprising that many religious people object to a state education. They worry, in part, that their children will be taught to think critically and will turn their critical eye toward their own traditions.

It should be clear by now that there is considerable overlap between the virtues of citizenship and the person who is autonomous in a robust way. The good liberal citizen is a critical thinker, able to consider different views and to talk sincerely to other citizens. These virtues map onto the autonomous person as well. Callan's (and Raz and Kymlicka's) idealized version of the good citizen is also the autonomous citizen. The difficulty with the account of citizenship I have given so far should be readily apparent. In chapters 2 and 3 I defended the choice of people to be nonautonomous, to choose to live a life of obedience. Here, however, I agree with other liberals that the good citizen is autonomous in a robust fashion. If this is the case, am I sneaking individuality back into liberalism under the rubric of citizenship? If so, how different is my account from Raz and Kymlicka?

Clearly, there are important similarities, as our version of the ideal citizen is similar. We also all support the idea of individual diversity, where people can fashion and refashion themselves as they like. Yet the differences between the opinions of Raz and Kymlicka (and Callan, Fraser, and Young) and my view are significant. I am quite willing to accept the idea that having some restrictions on people's lives is compatible with autonomy, and that such a life can be good. I certainly agree with Raz that the autonomous person has a range of options, but having this range is compatible with restrictions on one's options. This is particularly true for children, who may be given a way of life before they see and evaluate other ways. In some cases, the liberal virtues may even be encouraged by religious moderates. They may attend churches where they learn civic skills, and they may learn the important virtue of self-restraint through their communities. The religious institutions and rules of religious moderates may aid the liberal virtues in some ways.

Second, I am quite willing to admit that some people need not learn the virtues of liberal citizenship; some people can choose another kind of life. Some people will choose to disdain the virtues of citizenship. Most liberals will admit that this will happen as a matter of practice in a liberal state, and say this should be tolerated, but I want to protect this possibility as a matter of principle. People can choose to live a life of obedience, and they can give their children an illiberal education. To the contrary, Raz suggests that the liberal state might want to consider engaging in a "gradual transformation" of communities that do not prize autonomy.[29] It is one thing to allow people to choose to live in religious communities; it is quite another to suggest their gradual transformation.

Liberalism is not primarily about ensuring or encouraging good citizenship. It is primarily about giving people the freedom to pursue their lives as they see fit, within certain constraints (not harming others is the most notable). Liberalism is about enabling people to live the lives they choose. Citizenship is a significant matter in liberalism, but it is a secondary matter. There has been an important recent (re)discovery of citizenship by liberals, but there is an inherent tension between the autonomy at the center of liberalism and the demands of liberal citizenship. This explains the tensions in William Galston's argument against versions of liberalism that emphasize autonomy. He contends that doing so narrows "the range of possibilities available within liberal societies." Yet he makes this argument in a book that prescribes the virtues of good liberal citizens. Galston says that citizens should have the "capacity to discern the talent and character of candidates vying for public office, and to evaluate the performance of individuals who have attained office," and have a developed capacity to "engage in public discourse," which means taking seriously the ideas of others, even those one finds strange and obnoxious, and be willing to offer reasons for one's own views.[30] These virtues, however, narrow the range of options within liberal societies. They are indeed the virtues of an autonomous citizen. Galston wants it both ways: he criticizes those conceptions of liberalism that narrow the range of options a person can choose from, while he offers up a view of liberal citizenship that does exactly the same thing.

I don't mean to criticize Galston for not resolving the tension between allowing people to live the lives they want and the need for the state to encourage good citizenship. This tension is unavoidable; the main problem with Galston is that the tension runs through his book unacknowledged. This is better, however, than promoting citizenship over all other liberal values, as Richard Dagger does in his work on civic republicanism and liberalism. Dagger does recognize that autonomy and citizenship can pull in different directions,[31] but he notes this only in passing. He is mostly interested in how the two coincide. He then celebrates the "integrative experience" that citizenship gives people. Dagger says that one problem with contemporary life is that it is divided into many different compartments, allowing us to know few people well. We work with some people, shop at stores where we recognize people only as clerks and customers, we drive home in cars where we confront only other cars, not people. Our lives are now "split into many fragments," leaving many people suffering from "an identity crisis that leaves them unsure of who they are and what they want." The way to resolve this crisis is through citizenship.[32]

Making citizenship an integrative experience is a mistake for liberalism. The moral psychology of Dagger's argument is flawed, as is his conception of citizenship. It is not at all clear that many people do suffer from an identity crisis, or that they do not know what they want. Dagger states this without evidence. Moreover, even if it were true, and it is undoubtedly true for some people, it's hardly clear how a more robust sense of citizenship would solve these problems. There may be different reasons why different people have identity crises. It may be that people's sense of identity is suffering because they live in a mobile society, far from family; or that they are estranged from the religion of their childhood (and from all religions); or that they simply dislike their job; or that they have few friends. There may be other reasons, too, why some people's sense of self is suffering. The idea that if all the people suffering an identity crisis, regardless of the reason, should now view citizenship as an integrative experience to solve their problems is too easy a solution.

Moreover, it's hard to imagine how citizenship can be the integrative experience that Dagger wants it to be. People don't walk around every day thinking of themselves as citizens. Although this is what Rousseau wanted (and Dagger is inspired by Rousseau), it is hard to figure out how anything close to that can happen in the large, postindustrial Western democracies. People don't have the time, since they are busy working and spending time with their families, and many lack the inclination. Michael Walzer reminds us of Oscar Wilde's critique of socialism: it takes up too many evenings.[33] The criticism applies to Dagger's integrative citizenship as well.

People in a liberal society may be pulled in different directions by different commitments. Balancing these commitments is one of the things that liberal citizens need to do. A person's religious commitments may sometimes compete with a commitment to work, to school, or to citizenship. Making sense of how to balance one's life is up to the individual. This is what liberalism is all about: letting the individual decide for him- or herself how to live life. A liberalism that places citizenship first undercuts this crucial autonomy too much.

I agree with Dagger that citizenship is important. It is important that people think as citizens, that they think of the common good, and not merely of their own selfish interests. But they need to think of themselves as citizens only sometimes. Citizenship should remain a part-time affair for many. Dagger's relentless citizenship misses the tension between liberal autonomy and liberal citizenship. I will not solve this tension, mostly because this tension is inherent in the different ways each value pulls. This tension is something that liberals needs to recognize. The good citizen is fully autonomous, but the autonomous person is not necessarily a good citizen. Some people will fail the ideal of liberal citizenship, not because they are unable to think very well, but because they choose a nonliberal life. The tension between autonomy and citizenship becomes a problem only when so many people choose to eschew the virtues of citizenship that the stability of the state and the health of the mainstream society are threatened. Many, many citizens, however, must eschew the virtues of citizenship for this to happen.

While I want to defend the right of religious conservatives to avoid learning the liberal virtues, they are not the only ones who are not members of several organizations, publicly spirited, eager to debate and compromise, and willing to admit their errors. People that live within liberal institutions don't always come out as good liberals ready to engage their fellow citizens in a thoughtful and cooperative manner. Sometimes they emerge ready to spend time at the shopping mall. The liberal state can survive this failure, as long as it is not too widespread. This is the case even if some people purposefully avoid learning the liberal virtues.

Both autonomy and good citizenship fall across a wide range on the autonomy and citizenship scales. I don't think this necessarily threatens liberal democracy as long as enough citizens fall on the upper range of the scale and enough are politically interested. If liberals are to be attached to autonomy, as I think they should be, then they will have to admit that many people will not choose to be the ideal citizen. Some liberal citizens will have some liberal virtues, while a few may have nearly all, and still others will barely register at all when it comes to the liberal virtues. It is not the case that most or all citizens need to have all the liberal virtues. Liberal society will easily survive if a good portion of its members do not.

This doesn't mean the liberal state should admit that people can be more or less autonomous, more or less good citizens, and leave it at that. If we merely hope for the best, we should expect the worse. This is particularly true for immigrant societies. What idealized versions of citizens point to is how liberal institutions should encourage people to become good citizens. It is precisely because becoming an autonomous citizen is hard work that we need liberal institutions to encourage the liberal virtues in citizens. If too many citizens lack the liberal virtues, then liberal institutions are no longer sustainable. Liberal institutions should encourage the liberal virtues, expecting that some will learn them well, while others will not do quite as well.

Principles of Inclusion and Exclusion

As important as they are, the liberal virtues are not primary in the liberal state. As a matter of autonomy people should be allowed to belong to conservative and insular religions. Autonomy is primary here, but citizenship is an important secondary consideration, one that helps (or should help) direct public policy in the liberal state. Liberals should respect people's choices to belong to conservative and insular religions, though liberal citizenship should be supported as well. If liberal citizenship was to falter too much, then the choices within a liberal society would fade. Autonomy is primary in liberalism, but it is dependent on some civic virtues flourishing.

One could say that since conservative religious communities threaten liberal citizenship, they should be opposed as much as possible by the liberal state, even if this harms the more moderate or liberal communities that help sustain autonomy and the liberal virtues. A liberal state could not outlaw religious communities or make it illegal to attend church, but it could, among other things, outlaw all private schooling, frown upon all forms of cooperation between the state and religious institutions, narrow the realm of legal discrimination as much as possible, and make suspect all forms of religious talk in the public square. At the other extreme, one could say that since some religions do sustain the liberal virtues, all religious institutions deserve public funding, encourage all kinds of cooperation between churches and the state, allow for a wide range of discrimination and encourage all forms of religious talk in the public sphere.

I have argued here that neither extreme is correct, so I must develop principles to help navigate policy matters. The first principle is one I discussed in the previous chapter, a principle of nonintervention in communities that sustain the minimal conditions of autonomy. Religious communities should be able to treat their members as they wish as long as they provide a decent education to their charges, do not physically harm their children, allow members the right to exit, and are not completely (or nearly so) cut off from other communities and mainstream society. The liberal state should not demand that these communities treat their members differently than the community wants, as long as they meet these minimal conditions.

The second principle is one of inclusion. Liberalism should follow a principle of inclusion of religious people in public life, except when doing so harms citizenship. A *general* principle of inclusion will usually — not always — work to support liberal citizenship. In other words, liberal institutions should typically try to include religious conservatives within them. The exception to this is when this inclusion will harm citizenship in some important way. This harm, however, is relatively infrequent, certainly much rarer than many contemporary liberals appear to believe.

Too often liberals want to exclude religious conservatives from public life and public institutions in the name of liberalism, but doing so often harms these religions and liberal citizenship. Some liberals, for example, argue that religious conservatives who demand some accommodation for their beliefs should be excluded from public schools. Other liberals maintain that any religious talk in the public square is illegitimate and should be excluded. These arguments do not enhance liberal citizenship; they undermine it. Excluding religious conservatives from liberal public life does little to spread liberal values, though it may further isolate religious conservatives, decreasing the chances that their beliefs will liberalize at all. This is only a sketch of how this principle works. In the next two chapters I work out this principle in the matters of education and public debate.

Religious conservatives don't always want to be included, and breaking down the barriers between them and public life will not always entice them in. Sometimes they want to exclude themselves and retreat to their own communities. The third principle is one of exclusion: the liberal state should allow for exclusion and discrimination, except when such discrimination harms the citizenship of nonmembers. The worry here is that while liberals want to exclude religious conservatives from public institutions and debate, they often want religious institutions themselves to become inclusive. This pressure for inclusion, however, often undermines the autonomy of religious people. Religious people should be able to attend religious services that discriminate against outsiders. They should be able to attend colleges and universities that abide by discriminatory religious rules. They should be able to belong to organizations of various kinds that discriminate. If they are not given this freedom, then their autonomy is wrongly curtailed. Only when citizenship is at stake should discrimination be curtailed. Citizenship is at stake in only a narrow range of cases and should be not used as an excuse to dismantle religious institutions. This argument, too, needs to be expanded and defended. That is the burden of chapter 7. I first attend to inclusion in education and the public sphere.

Educating Citizens and Educating Believers | 5

THE SPECTER hanging over this chapter is an elementary or high school where students work by themselves in cubicles separated by partitions, studying—or memorizing—their lessons. Class discussions are not held; group projects are not undertaken. Teachers do not ask the class any questions. Instead, silence permeates the school, broken only by the occasional question to an adult monitor, who is usually not a certified teacher or even a college graduate. Before taking an exam, which a student takes when he or she is ready, a monitor will kneel and pray with the student. When students pass the exam for one lesson, they go on to the next one.

This is a typical Accelerated Christian Education (ACE) school. ACE is a company in Texas that supplies schools with assignments and tests for students. These schools are inexpensive to maintain, since teachers are not needed and most work is done alone by students.[1] ACE schools are one kind of an increasing number of religiously affiliated and private schools in the United States. A little over 100,000 students attended evangelical and fundamentalist Protestant schools in 1964-65; by 1988-89 that number had increased to nearly one million. Enrollments in nondenominational private schools increased during the same time period from nearly 200,000 to over 900,000.[2]

ACE schools—and other religiously affiliated schools that emphasize memorization and obedience—should concern liberals on three grounds: what is taught in class, how it is taught, and to whom it is taught. Most liberal theorists of education emphasize the curriculum. Political theorists most often argue about what should be taught, and what—if any—exemptions should be allowed. The ACE schools, however, bring into sharp relief that *how* and *to whom* the curriculum is taught are also important. Schools that emphasize the memorization of facts and the importance of obedience to a relatively homogeneous student body fail both the students and the liberal democratic state. They fail the students by not teaching them to think for themselves; these students won't easily be able to develop and pursue their own plans and projects. The virtues that good liberal citizens have, virtues I outlined in chapter 4, are not inculcated in ACE schools. They fail liberal democracy because these students are less likely to become good liberal citizens than are better educated students.

It would be simple to say that schools like the ACE schools should be outlawed. The difficulty is that students are not only members of the state, to be educated to become good future citizens. Students are also daughters and sons of particular parents, some of whom have deeply felt commitments. These parents do not only want to raise good future citizens. They also want to raise their children with the particular commitments that they hold. Religious parents frequently want to pass their beliefs onto their children. Any account of religious diversity in schools should account for both common public schools and religiously affiliated schools. If religiously affiliated schools are allowed to exist, then that must have an effect on how we look at public schools.

Educating citizens and educating believers need not be at odds with one another, but the tensions between the two need sorting out. I will try to sort these tensions out by drawing on the principle of inclusion (see chapter 4): inclusion in education should be extended to the children of religious parents, as long as doing so does not harm citizenship. This means that public schools should cooperate with religiously affiliated schools and home-schooled children. Religious students and perspectives should be fairly included in the curriculum and life of common schools.[3] Finally, public schools should try to accommodate the special needs of religious students when possible. These forms of inclusion work to strengthen liberal citizenship.

Liberalism and the Problem of Children

Theorists argue about who is in charge of children: the state or parents? Most say that both have a claim. Children are both the children of particular adults and future citizens. Colin Macleod suggests that there are three interests worth considering when discussing parental autonomy: children's interests, parental interests, and societal interests. Children have an interest in living a good life, but since they are not able to form such a notion, they have an interest in acquiring the capacity to develop and live a good life. Adults, one hopes, are able to form a conception of the good, which may mean raising their children in a certain way. Parents have "an interest in including their children in some or all of the elements that constitute their conception of the good." This means they wish to pass onto their children their religious, moral, and cultural commitments.[4] Finally, the society has an interest in having children become good citizens. This means different things in different societies; in a liberal society it means having citizens who are able to think reflectively about politics and who are able and willing to cooperate with others and treat them with mutual respect. Autonomy may be something that parents encourage in their children, but this is not always the case. Frequently, parents will want their children to think critically about some matters but to accept uncritically certain aspects of the parents' conceptions of the good life. In any case, teaching children to reflect critically may lead children to think about the values and ideals their parents are trying to pass on to them. And some parents may not like that.

Liberals want to respect the choices of adults, yet they often argue that children should learn how to make choices so they are able to choose well as adults and become good citizens. Some liberals argue that the state needs to intervene in education to ensure that children are taught to be autonomous. Among the most crucial choices adults make, however, is how to raise their children. How can liberals emphasize the importance of making choices and being autonomous, yet restrict how parents choose to raise their children?

I don't think there is a clean solution to this dilemma. Clearly, liberalism is a theory made for adults, not children. Any good answer will have to balance in some imprecise way the three interests that Macleod points out. Macleod suggests that we give parents the "prerogative of provisionally privileging the conception of the good that they favor." This means that parents can advance their conception of the good life to their children, but cannot prevent their children from scrutinizing these ends; and as their children get older, the parents must accept the possibility of the children rejecting or revising their commitments. Macleod here is worried about parents who tightly insulate their children from "exposure and access to the social conditions of deliberation."[5]

I share this concern but I'm reluctant to force parents to expose children to other ways of life, except in extreme cases where children are not let out of the house or given a basic education. Rather, the liberal state should try to establish a culture where children are exposed to different ways of life, and where children confront different ideas that make them review at least some of their commitments. I say *some* commitments, because it is the rare person who reviews all of his or her commitments. Such an undertaking is extremely difficult. But children should be encouraged to think about the lives they want to live; they should also be encouraged to become more rather than less autonomous since autonomy is a key liberal virtue. Yet citizens have the right to shield their children from much in liberal society, as long as the right to exit exists. As I stated in chapter 3, it is the rare person with a minimal education who does not realize that he or she can choose another way of life. The liberal state should allow insular groups to exist, but it should not encourage this insularity. It should instead encourage a policy of inclusion, a policy that some may withstand if they choose.

The Case for Diverse Public Schools

A recent court case, *Mozert v Hawkins,* has been much discussed by liberals because it highlights a radical religious challenge to a liberal education.[6] In this case, fundamentalist parents were told by the court that the schools did not have to exempt their children from courses they found offensive. The fundamentalist parents objected to these courses because their children were being taught "role reversal," and were exposed to a variety of viewpoints and lifestyles without the school insisting that the fundamentalist interpretation of the biblical way of life was superior. The debate among liberal theorists about this case has centered around authority and curriculum in the public schools. Liberals argue about who should control a child's education, what kind of harm is done by exempting some children from certain classes, and what sorts of things should be included in the curriculum.[7]

These debates are important, yet they typically and oddly omit a crucial fact: fundamentalist parents are increasingly taking matters into their own hands by yanking their students out of public schools and sending them to private ones, or by home-schooling their children. When this happens, the debate between liberals about what exactly should be taught to students in public schools becomes meaningless, because few if any liberal virtues are taught in fundamentalist schools or by fundamentalist parents.[8] There is something curious in the lack of liberal concern about private schools and home-schooling. Liberals argue over how much responsibility the state and parents have to educate children, but if parents decide to opt out of public schools altogether, most liberals agree, the role of the state drastically decreases.[9] Parents can teach their children almost anything they want, with only a few restrictions, in private schools or at home. The much discussed case about the Amish, *Wisconsin v Yoder,* would probably not have taken place today. In that case, the state of Wisconsin wanted to force the Amish to send their teenagers to high school. The Amish refused because they were worried that the influence of a worldly high school might entice their children away from their way of life. The Supreme Court sided with the Amish. If the Amish were told by a state they had to send their children to school, the Amish might very well decide to home-school their children. Since the early 1980s most states have eased their restrictions on home-schooling, making this a possibility for most parents. While political theorists still argue about whether the Amish should have to send their children to public schools, the rise of home-schooling makes this issue purely academic. Today, the Amish do not need special exemptions to restrict their children's education.[10]

One problem with religiously affiliated schools (and to home-schooling, which I will presume to be part of the private school option) is that they are not diverse. I'm thinking here of diversity of ideas and ways of life. While it is true that many public schools have homogeneous student bodies in some ways — student bodies that are mostly white or black or middle class — these schools can and often do have a large diversity of ideas. Students will have different religious backgrounds and come from families with different political affiliations in common schools. These students will learn that there are other ways of thinking about the world than what their parents tell them. They will have to consider the practices and ideas of others. They will, liberals hope, learn to think for themselves and learn to respect those with whom they disagree. Diversity of ideas is one of the goods that common schools offer their students.

A racially diverse school is an even better idea, since it means that students from different backgrounds can learn from each other — but it must be noted that some desegregated schools are permeated by hatred between members of different groups, and so their diversity doesn't really benefit many people. Class diversity is similarly a good idea, but some schools are located in primarily poor or wealthy neighborhoods, and so mostly draw their student body from one income class. Sometimes the best we can expect is a public school with diverse ideas and practices. While a school with a student body that is diverse by both race and income would be better, a school with diverse ideas and practices could still encourage its students to think creatively and critically. It could encourage the virtues of liberal autonomy and citizenship.

Religiously affiliated schools that are established to preserve a community need not be homogeneous. They can allow for diverse ideas; they can encourage their students to think critically about many issues. Still, the diversity in this sort of school will be less than in a common school. A school where all the students come from the same community, whose parents share certain key organizing principles in their lives, will not get students to see a wide variety of lives up close. In principle, the variety in religiously affiliated schools that are meant to serve a particular community of believers will be less than in a common school that is meant to serve people with different beliefs. This should not be surprising, since the point of many religiously affiliated schools is to serve a particular community.

What common schools also show is that what matters in schools is not only what is taught, but also to whom it is taught. The same curriculum taught in a Jewish day school and in a common school does not mean students in both schools will emerge with the same sense and understanding of the lives of others. For students to see other ways of life up close, they must talk on a regular basis with people who are different; they must befriend those with different ideas. Schools with a diverse student population give children the opportunity to learn about others in a real way, not just through books. Diverse schools enable students to learn how to cooperate with others and the importance of compromising with those who are different. Part of the purpose of public schools is to get children from different backgrounds together.

Heterogeneous schools allow different students to learn about one another and to learn how to work together. When students learn these sorts of things they make for better citizens. The virtues that citizens have are learned in a complex world, which they learn when they confront people who are different from them. This is the idea behind Eamonn Callan's interpretation of the burdens of judgment, which I discussed in chapter 4. Learning about others is surely important. But learning *with* (and from) others is a better way to learn about other kinds of people and ideas. People who face others will, it is hoped, learn the liberal virtues of how to cooperate and compromise with people who are different; they will learn how to listen to others and how to respond to them. They will learn that others have different views from themselves, and that occasionally there are good reasons for these different convictions and so are worthy of respect. Good citizens do not only think of themselves or their primary group (if they have one) when they act as citizens. Rather, they think of the people who will be affected by different public policies and laws and consider them when taking a position on an issue. They learn that others have interests, and sometimes democracy calls for a compromise between those with different interests. Listening, negotiating and compromising, and thinking are all skills that are learned in diverse settings, including common schools.

Defending Religiously Affiliated Schools

Since exposure to diversity is an important component of a good school, and many religiously affiliated schools are not diverse, there is a case to be made that they should be prohibited in the liberal state. In the United States this suggestion will not go very far politically, but the reasons to support private schools are not simply pragmatic. In the nineteenth century Protestants used the public schools to marginalize Catholics by insisting on the use of the King James Bible in schools; segregated twentieth-century schools often meant black students received an inferior education, while the prejudices of all students were unchallenged. There is also the obvious concern that many public schools are in rather poor shape, but if all students had to attend public schools they would get more support as more parts of society had a clear stake in them. We would see a more concerted effort to make public schools better. Still, the history of the public schools in the United States suggests that having an escape route for dissenters is important.

But I want to give a defense of private schools that would stand up even if the educational history in the United States was a more defensible one, and if the public schools were in terrific shape. One obvious reason for religious parents to send their children to a private school is that they are unhappy with the public school curriculum, even a good public school curriculum. For many people religion permeates their life. Teachers in English, history, art, and politics touch upon religious matters. Religious conservatives often want these and other subjects taught from their religious perspective. To be sure, religion does not infuse every subject matter, but the wide reaches of both education and religion mean that there will be many points of contact.

Putting aside the curriculum, another reason to send children to a religious school is to situate them in a community. A minority community that wants to retain its identity may very well have good reason to establish its own school. This community may want to teach their children to be autonomous, good liberal citizens; but they also would like to increase the odds that their children will remain part of their community. To give minority children a real choice about what community they will be a part of when they are adults may mean to stack the deck in favor of the minority community early on. If they do not do so, the deck will certainly be stacked against them.

Arguments about education that only stress the importance of citizenship, like the one given by Richard Dagger, often fail to recognize that their overemphasis on citizenship makes it less likely for children to retain their family's identity. Dagger likes cultural pluralism only if it means exposing children to different beliefs and practices.[11] His view of citizenship blinds him to the way that diverse schools undercut cultural pluralism, as they lead children to live within the dominant culture, colored with perhaps a few strands of minority cultures. To protect minority cultures and religions, these communities must be able to teach their children within their communities. While doing so may harm citizenship, this is hardly inevitable.

I suggested in chapter 3 that members of restrictive communities may often be tempted to live a life with fewer restrictions, particularly when they see their neighbors and coworkers living such lives. This is the case for many adults. The pressure to give up one's restrictions is even more pronounced for children. If minority communities cannot provide their own education for their children, their opportunity to pass their way of life on to their children is severely diminished. This is one reason why I defend a life of some restrictions. This kind of life will give minority communities a reasonable chance of survival in the diverse and liberal state. Looking at common schools helps further explain why.

Religious communities are marked by rituals and celebrations of faith, but public schools make it harder for the children of some communities to participate in their celebrations. Celebrations and rituals are not always private matters that can be performed in the evening. Some of them are celebrated or observed among the relevant community. Jewish holidays, for example, come at several times during the year and children who want to celebrate them have to miss school to do so. Typically, only a few students will. Moreover, the restrictions of religious communities will often make their members stand out as different. Jewish students who keep kosher will not be able to eat at cafeterias in public schools. These students will also not be able to attend after-school events on Friday nights — football games, school dances, and so on.

Public schools are based on a weak Protestant model. The school calendar fits the needs of (some) Christians, as does the food. Recently there have been moves to accommodate minorities in public schools, but there are limits to these accommodations. Muslim students who want to skip lunch during the month of Ramadan will have a harder time keeping their daytime fast when they see their fellow students munching away at lunch time. These students *can* skip lunch if they choose, but it would surely be easier to do so in a school where all students skipped lunch, and where lunch hour was temporarily suspended during the month. Jewish students who cannot attend schools on Jewish holidays will probably feel more comfortable at a school where the school is closed down on the holidays. If a school has only a handful of Jewish students who keep kosher, it may be extremely expensive to accommodate their needs in the cafeteria. Moving the high school institution of football to a different night is like trying to move a mountain. Schools may not be able to close for every religious holiday celebrated by their students—in some places there will be too many of them.

Some students try to maintain their family religious practices despite their differences with the norms and practices of the public schools. For many, however, maintaining these differences is too hard, and conformity slowly sets in. Accommodating a minority doesn't change the fact that the minority will have different norms and practices than the majority. A community's practices are best kept up within the community. If Jewish students attend a Jewish school they will not constantly find themselves at odds with the practices and norms of their school or their classmates. Instead, they will fit in; they will be able to celebrate their traditions without the everyday threat of their community's boundaries corroding. Maintaining a community means having community institutions that are inhabited by the community's members.

The ideas of maintaining a community and of maintaining faith are surely connected. One could, however, want one's children to attend a religiously affiliated school not only because of a belief in God but also to give the children a sense of a belonging to a community enriched by a certain tradition. The default position in schools is the majority culture. Children may be taught in schools that they can lead many kinds of lives, but their choices will surely be shaped by those around them. The idea for some Jewish students that they cannot attend football games because they happen to occur on Friday night may cause them considerable distress and confusion. When most students talk about a popular television show that a Protestant fundamentalist is forbidden to watch because of its sexual nature, he will feel left out or perhaps be ridiculed. Children are particularly impressionable and the impressions they get in public schools will often lead them away from their minority community. The adults in these kinds of religious communities may rightly think that their children will have to figure out how to navigate between their faith and community and public norms when they are adults. The longer this navigation can be postponed, the better chance the community has to survive.

Here we see again how community restrictions are not inherently in conflict with liberalism and aid the pluralism of a society. Giving minority communities the right to educate their children on their own gives them a greater chance of surviving. This defense of religious schools assumes that these schools are not all encompassing—it assumes that these are moderate and not conservative religious communities. It means that their curriculum is diverse and provokes students to think about a variety of issues. It also presumes that these schools will allow for interaction with other students at some point. This may mean the school stops at the end of junior high or middle school, so students attend a common high school. The early years of religiously affiliated education would help secure for the students a deep understanding of their way of life. These students can then attend common schools and face other ways of life and ideas with a firm grounding in conception of the good; a conception that they may decide to alter or to retain. Or it means cooperation with common schools, an idea I explore more below. This "moderate separatist argument" that is willing to accept common schooling in the "culminating years" is attractive in some ways.[12] Certainly liberals should not feel too uneasy about such moderate separatists. A defense of religiously affiliated schools that is meant to defend moderate (and liberal) religious schools will, however, also encompass religious conservative schools. If I am right that religiously affiliated schools should be defended on the grounds that they help preserve minority communities, then some schools will help communities that are mostly compatible with liberal democracy and others will help those that are more antagonistic.

Financing Schools

Public funds should be used for things that are in the public interest. Encouraging citizenship is in the public interest and on this count common schools are important. There are two reasons for public resources to be directed toward public, common schools and not religiously affiliated schools. Public schools help encourage a diverse liberal citizenship that promotes autonomy, and they play an important role in equality of opportunity. Both of these obligations are particularly important in a pluralist society with an extensive immigrant tradition and large income disparities. In immigrant societies, support for citizenship cannot be taken for granted but must be encouraged. Common schools are one important (if inadequate) way to counteract the way large class differences work against equality of opportunity. In a pluralist society people have to work harder to understand one another and to act together politically. Cooperation and trust can't be assumed among citizens in an immigrant society; these virtues must be encouraged.

This is where the clash between liberal diversity and religious conservatives is apparent. Liberal diversity taps into the liberal virtues; diversity is usually grounded in the idea that people ought to be exposed to different ideas and different practices so they better understand their fellow citizens. Exposure to different ideas, though, is important in all liberal societies, homogeneous or not. This ideal is embodied in the idea of a liberal arts education; people receiving this kind of education learn about different ideas and different ways of thinking about the world.

It is not mere academic speculation to suggest that public funding for all private schools will mean funding illiberal schools that will teach values that threaten to undermine liberalism. Ultraorthodox Jews (the Haredim) in Israel receive state funding for their schools, and the success they have in teaching illiberal values to their students is all too apparent. Too many students are taught, and believe, that any compromise with the Palestinians is wrong. Too many of these students are taught that Israel should be a religious state, and many are ready to fight to realize this dream. Israel would be less fragile, and more liberal, if it gave less support to those who oppose the basic tenets of liberal democracy.

Still, some private schools, including certain religiously affiliated schools, are good schools. They teach their students well, and they teach the liberal virtues. This is not reason enough, however, to give private schools direct public funding. One reason, which I briefly expand on below, is that funding private schools means giving funds to some private schools that aim to undermine the liberal virtues. The liberal state should not fund illiberal institutions. More important, however, public funds for private schools will most likely hurt the most vulnerable in our society, the poor.

Support for public institutions is important in a society like the United States where this support is often tenuous, and where the wealthy often prefer to fund schools for their own children and not for others. If the state gave financial support to religiously affiliated schools, support for public support would probably decline dramatically. By support, I mean more than just financial support: many involved parents would transfer their energies to private schools, while good teachers might leave public schools for private ones. This would leave poor students, disabled students, and students with parents who did not care enough about them in public schools. Better funding for poorer public schools is not the magic elixir that would solve all or most of their problems and establish equality of opportunity in the United States. Good schools are more than a function of money: they also need good teachers and administrators, involved parents, and flexible rules. Good schools need support from different quarters if they will succeed. Common schools that draw on a wide public for support and for students will have a better chance of being good than schools that have mostly poor students. Privatizing more education would mean that all kinds of support for common public schools would decrease. Many parents would retreat into only supporting a private school. Of course, many schools are in poor neighborhoods and don't have a diverse student body. Yet these schools, too, need widespread public support: more money may not make them perfect, but it will probably make them better.

The problem of class is an important one when talking about public schools. Any move away from support for public schools will almost surely hurt lower-income people more than wealthy people. This is not to say that all public schools are in good shape. Some are not, including many that serve poorer students. What is needed are ways to strengthen public schools so we can come closer to equality of opportunity. Liberal society is far from reaching this important goal. It should not move further away from it.

That some public schools are not very good is a failure of practice, not principle. Their failure is a matter of bad planning, or scanty resources, too many bureaucratic rules, and so on. The reason to support religiously affiliated schools is that some of them encourage liberal citizenship and help maintain a community. Others do not, however, and the reason is not a failure of practice. Rather, some religiously affiliated schools purposefully do not teach the liberal virtues. They are animated by a different principle than what animates public schools. Many religiously affiliated schools do not aspire to encourage a diverse, liberal citizenship. This is why public schools and religiously affiliated schools are not both equally deserving of support: in principle public schools will support the liberal virtues, while only some religiously affiliated schools will do so. Supporting religiously affiliated schools will mean supporting schools that teach ideas that are antithetical to liberal citizenship. Because this will happen, religiously affiliated and public schools are not equally deserving of public support. This need not mean, however, that no support should be given religiously affiliated schools. Support that will encourage liberal citizenship can be given, even if this support will also help maintain (soft) community boundaries. To do this, avenues for cooperation with religious schools and accommodation for religious students in public schools should be sought. The animating principle is inclusion in a way that supports public schools, though it is also compatible with religiously affiliated schools.

Before I discuss cooperation and accommodation, I want to note that my argument against state funding for religiously affiliated schools is political, not philosophical or constitutional. While state funding to religiously affiliated schools is bad public policy in the United States, it does not violate U.S. constitutional principles. This, of course, raises the hackles of those who think that any state money that goes to churches violates the separation of church and state, and that somehow public funds to religiously affiliated schools begins the road to a public establishment of religion. But separation of church and state is neither a firmly established liberal principle nor in the American Constitution. John Locke, for example, argued that the state should tolerate dissenters, and even treat them equally to those belonging to the state church.[13] Locke wanted to ensure that church membership didn't affect anyone's "civil enjoyments," but this didn't preclude state support for one church.

The First Amendment says that Congress "shall make no law respecting an establishment of religion or prohibiting the free exercise thereof," but this does not say that there shouldn't be any connection between church and state. Indeed, when the Amendment became law some states had established churches, though state churches were on their way out. Over time the religious clause has come to mean that the state can use its funds for busing students to and from religiously affiliated schools at the beginning and end of the day, or for lending books to religiously affiliated school students, but public buses cannot be used to take religiously affiliated students on field trips. States can allow a deduction for private school tuition, though they cannot directly pay for religiously affiliated or private schools; public schools can have "release time" where students leave campus for religious instruction at a church, synagogue or mosque, but the priest, minister, rabbi, or imam cannot teach these same students on campus.

The principles guiding these decisions are hardly consistent—in fact, the jurisprudence in this area is a mess—but the more important point is that when it comes to education, church and state are not separate.[14] Nor need they be under liberal or constitutional principles. The liberal state should not promote a religion. Locke was wrong to think it acceptable for the state to support one church over another. When the trappings of state power are draped over one religion and not others, second-class citizenship may result for those in the unsupported religions. To say, however, that the state shouldn't support one religion doesn't mean that it cannot support *all* religions.[15] I think it is constitutional for the state to subsidize religiously affiliated schools directly, as long as it supports all religiously affiliated schools (or those that meet criteria that do not inherently favor one religion over another). The U.S. Supreme Court has declared otherwise, but this would not be the first time the Court erred in its interpretation of the Constitution. Funding religiously affiliated schools does not mean that government is establishing a religion — which is what the First Amendment is concerned with — particularly if it funds different kinds of religious schools and public schools. A government that funds Jewish, Mormon, Protestant, fundamentalist, Islamic, and Methodist schools is not establishing a religion. Rather, it is supporting many religions. If the government only funded Catholic schools, then there might a case that the government was establishing a religion. But if funding went to all schools that requested it or to all schools that met certain guidelines that didn't favor a particular denomination, then the government would not be establishing a religion. It would be supporting different religions, and what in the Constitution forbids that?

Funding many kinds of religiously affiliated schools is neither establishing a religion nor prohibiting the free exercise of religion. Some might object that this favors religion over nonreligion, but it simply means that the same support for religiously affiliated schools should be extended to nonreligious private schools. Such a scheme could also include public schools that are funded by the state. Parents could have a choice about what kind of school they would like to send their children. Some government money would go to pay for religious instruction in some schools (or atheist instruction in others), but this is not establishing a religion.

Some may object that this all looks fine in theory, but in practice it may be that one religion dominates in one country, so state funding to religiously affiliated schools will mostly benefit one religion. The logic of this arguments says that if the state of Utah began to fund religiously affiliated schools, the Mormons would benefit greatly, with the other religions gaining a relative small benefit. In these cases, though, the minority religions would have more to gain than the majority. Mormons dominate public schools in Utah; they don't need religiously affiliated schools to ensure their community boundaries. To be sure, the rules governing public schools will mean that Utah public schools cannot be overtly Mormon, but when the vast majority of students and teachers are of the same religion, surely the ethos of many public schools will be Mormon. The minorities are the ones that will suffer: they will seem strange and out of place. If they had a state-supported, religiously affiliated school, they could more readily protect their community boundaries. In their school they could celebrate their traditions and holidays; in their own schools, the children will not feel strange for being a Catholic or a Jew. These same students would also probably not feel so out of place in a diverse public school, one that had many Jews, Catholics, Mormon, Protestants, and atheists. But a couple of Jewish or Catholic children in an overwhelmingly Mormon school may very well feel out of place. Whether the school is public or private is immaterial. In places with large majorities, minorities may very well be more likely to want state-funded, religiously affiliated schools than in more diverse settings.

If the United States could fund religiously affiliated schools (supposing that the Supreme Court changed its mind on the matter) doesn't mean it should do so. While I have argued against such a policy, it seems to me that a scenario where liberals could support such funding is in a mostly homogeneous state. Imagine a mostly homogeneous state where, say, 97 percent of the population is Lutheran and a small, poor Muslim community exists. The only way the Muslims could support their own schools, which would be important to their survival, would be to have state funding. Such funding is compatible with but not mandated by liberalism. This would be a policy matter for the legislature, not a constitutional matter for the courts. The citizens of the country may decide that they would like to help the Muslim community maintain its identity. The people may think that the survival of the Muslim community will enrich their country in a variety of ways and that support for Muslim schools is one good way to help the Muslim community survive. Supporting the small Muslim community would not threaten liberal citizenship so much, since the community is so small; any small community has to learn the traditions and practices of the dominant liberal society if it is to thrive. I don't think that liberalism insists this support be given, but neither is it prohibited.

Cooperation between Public and Private Schools

In *Lemon v Kurtzman,* a well-known and controversial decision, the U.S. Supreme Court declared it unconstitutional to have public school teachers teaching secular subjects in church-related schools. Included in this case is the well-known three-part Lemon test. This test, drawn from previous court cases, is the Supreme Court's test to determine if a law violates the religious clauses of the First Amendment: the statute must have a valid secular purpose, it must neither advance nor inhibit religion, and it must not foster an excessive entanglement with religion. The Lemon test infuriates many constitutional scholars who accuse it of being too vague to be useful, but a more interesting criticism is made by Michael McConnell, who argues that the *Lemon* decision unfairly burdens families whose children attend religious schools.[16]

McConnell argues that because religiously affiliated schools have a legitimate place in the polity, and because religion should be accommodated, these schools should be given financial support by the state for their secular classes. McConnell is clear that there should not be support for the religious part of the religiously affiliated school's curriculum. McConnell gives two reasons for partial public financing for religious schools. First, the state has an interest in ensuring that children are well educated; whether they attend public or religiously affiliated schools is immaterial. What is material is a good education, and funding both kinds of schools would further this important end. Second, McConnell argues that it is unfair (and unconstitutional) to make religious parents pay for the secular education their children receive when they attend religiously affiliated schools. He complains that "if a family chooses to integrate a religious element into primary or secondary schooling, not only must they bear the costs of the religious education, but they also forfeit *all* public subsidy for education, including secular subjects."[17] Because of a few classes in Talmud or the gospels each day, religious schools lose public funding for courses in math, science, and English. McConnell maintains that taxpayers should be indifferent to private schools as long as they meet the same objective educational standards as public schools.

According to McConnell, some families prefer religiously affiliated to public schools since "secular knowledge cannot be rigidly separated from the religious without gravely distorting the child's education. To separate the secular from the religious is to suggest that religion is irrelevant to the things of this world."[18] While this is true, if the secular and the sacred cannot be separated out from one another, then public funding of their religiously affiliated schools will, in fact, fund religious courses. It may be hard to incorporate a religious perspective into math courses (using examples from religion to illustrate math problems is hardly incorporating a religious perspective into math), but courses in the physical sciences, social sciences, and humanities are another matter. Some religiously affiliated schools do separate out the sacred from the secular, but since many do not, as McConnell admits, global funding of religiously affiliated schools will result in funding religious courses. Unlike McConnell, however, I do not think this is a severe constitutional hurdle.

The state has an important interest in ensuring that its children are well educated, as McConnell notes, and giving public funds or lending public teachers to religiously affiliated schools will help with this end. The best argument for having public teachers in religiously affiliated schools is that for some of them the quality of teaching will improve. The teaching in many religiously affiliated schools is excellent, of course, and help from public school teachers is hardly needed, but in ACE schools, for example, this assistance will surely help the quality of the education. Why make the children suffer by refusing to give public assistance to them, either in the form of funds or public school teachers?

The problem with having public school teachers or public funds in religiously affiliated schools is that it deepens, rather than alleviates, one of the basic worries about them: the more religiously affiliated schools there are, the less students of different backgrounds will mix with one other, learn how to cooperate with one another, or understand that others with different views exist. This leaves the children in private schools hanging. Leaving them at the mercy of bad teachers because they are not in a diverse public school is hardly fair to them.

Instead of directly supporting religiously affiliated schools, the liberal state should try to entice parents to send their children to common schools. To further this inclusion, some type of cooperation between public and private schools is called for. My argument against McConnell is not an argument against cooperation between public and private schools. My objection is aimed against cooperation that takes place on the grounds of the private schools. Cooperation that allows for different children to get together in the same setting ought to be fostered by public school systems. Cooperation between religiously affiliated and public schools that do not foster this inclusion should be avoided. This sort of cooperation nicely illustrates the principle of inclusion. Cooperation between public and private schools will bolster citizenship by including more children educated in religiously affiliated schools in the public school system and so expose religiously affiliated school children to the diversity of common, public schools. It will also expose public school children to a wider diversity of students. Finally, cooperation will aid the pluralism of society by giving some financial support to minority communities.

Cooperation may satisfy minority students' parents who want to teach their children about their tradition, but who also want them to be educated in a diverse setting. Or it may satisfy their need to have their children learn about their tradition and about subjects that are less religious at a lower cost. This cooperation will allow for religious (and other) children to meet and interact with others. It will also add to the pluralism of public schools, since they now will probably have more religious students than they used to have.

Cooperation can take several forms. Students could be allowed to attend public schools in the morning and religiously affiliated schools in the afternoon or vice versa. Students attending both schools might end up taking two biology courses, or they may receive a secular education in the morning and learn theology in the afternoon. Parents who do not want to be penalized by having no state funding for their children's education merely because they want their children to receive a religious education can be accommodated by this scheme. The difference between a split-day program and funding teachers for secular subjects in religious schools is that the split-day program teaches students who attend religiously affiliated schools alongside public school students. It fosters the ideals of inclusion and diversity. It encourages students from different backgrounds to face another and examine the animating principles behind each other's lives. This is not only helpful to the religiously affiliated school students. Those who spend all day in public schools may very well be enriched by their encounters with students who are deeply rooted in a religious tradition.

Split-day programs will also alleviate some of the pressure felt to conform by some religious students. Having their religious identity and beliefs taught and reinforced during half the day, religious students will be better equipped to withstand the pressure of conformity in the other half than if they lacked this half day in a religiously affiliated school. Or they may feel pressure to conform in different ways during the day's two halves; then they will be confronted with the need to decide for themselves what to believe.

Cooperation should also take place with home-schooled children. Public schools should allow children who are taught at home to attend some courses or afterschool activities if they want. Being home-schooled is not the same as attending a private school, and not all home-schooled children are religious, but the principle of inclusion applies to all home-schooled children just as it does to private schools. Some home-schooled children want to attend one or two courses in public schools, because their parents do not think they can teach those courses well. Some school activities, like team sports or band, need to be done with others. The cost and time of field trips may be too much for a family, and so home-schooled children may want to join a public school's trips. The argument against this sort of cooperation seems to be motivated by spite: since these students do not enroll in public schools, they should be completely barred from them. This is hardly a matter of principle, however. More cooperation with children who are home-schooled will benefit them and probably benefit the schools as well by increasing their diversity.

One worry about cooperation between public and private schools is that it may lead some citizens to throw their support to the latter but not the former.

This worry does apply to direct funding to private schools, but it has considerably less bite when it comes to the sorts of arrangements I have suggested here. Allowing for split days may result in an indirect subsidy for religiously affiliated schools since their costs will be lower if they do not have to teach certain subjects. This may induce more parents to send their children to religiously affiliated schools. Parents who want their children to have both a public and a religious education may also be more apt to use religious schools under a split-day program. I don't see either one of these possibilities, however, as a cause for worry. First, these parents will still support public schools since their children attend them. Second, split days may also *encourage* parents who currently send their children to religiously affiliated schools for a full day to send their children to public schools for half a day. This will further increase support for public schools. As long as cooperation between public and private schools does not become mere financial subsidy for the private schools, I see little reason to worry that cooperation will decrease support for public schools.

Nor do I think cooperation will lead to a decline in the teaching of the liberal virtues. Cooperation may lead more students to attend religiously affiliated schools, since costs may decrease, but some also will attend diverse public schools, where the liberal virtues will presumably be taught, or private schools, where liberal virtues may be taught as well. Strengthening religious identity does not inherently undermine a common citizenship. It depends on the shape of that identity and the amount of exposure the person has to others. Further, students who currently only attend religiously affiliated schools might also attend public schools if there was more cooperation between the two, increasing the spread of liberal virtues.

Some religiously affiliated schools will be wary of cooperation with public schools. They may be afraid that cooperation will threaten the identity of their children. In some cases, this may be true. Indeed, some sorts of inclusion will not buttress pluralism; inclusion will sometimes lure people always from their minority community and decrease pluralism. The more antagonistic a community is to liberal values, the more inclusion will threaten their identity. Moderate communities, who are not so antagonistic to liberalism, may find that the tradeoff between exposure to public school students and more financial support for their schools a worthy one, since they already expose their children to other people. More conservative communities, however, may choose to limp along with no public cooperation, as they fear that a decent amount of exposure to outsiders will harm their community.

Cooperation with religiously affiliated schools will tend to increase pluralism in a way that doesn't support illiberal values and communities. The state can try to entice parents to use public schools, both by cooperating with religiously affiliated schools and by accommodating the beliefs of parents in public schools. Little can be done, however, about parents who refuse to be enticed. The policy of inclusion should be used to bolster liberal citizenship, but no one can be forced to be included in liberal institutions.

Multiculturalism in the Public Schools

Cooperation between religiously affiliated and public schools does not say much about how religion should be treated in public schools. Many religious parents will send their children to public school and will want religion to be discussed in the classroom; some will object to how some courses are taught. Education cannot be value neutral, so it won't do to say we should treat religion neutrally. The curriculum cannot be both secular and religious. It inevitably teaches some values, both directly through the curriculum and indirectly through how things are taught and to whom. But inclusion means treating religion more fairly in public schools, and some religious children should be accommodated if they or their parents object to parts of the curriculum, as long as doing so does not harm citizenship.

TEACHING ABOUT RELIGION

I want to briefly add my voice to the chorus that is now saying that religion should be taught in schools. Religion need not and should not be only taught in a separate course on religion. Religion will surely come up in history, social science, and literature courses. This seems like an obvious enough point, since the role of religion historically and in the modern world is rather large, but many schools shy away from any mention of religion.[19] This is partly because religion is so controversial it is easier to omit it than to discuss it openly and incur the wrath of parents who object to how it is taught. This does not, however, excuse writers on multicultural education who almost always pass over religion, yet who tackle other controversial subjects. At best, religion gets a passing nod from multiculturalists.[20] Any account of a multicultural society that omits any decent discussion of religion is surely severely flawed.

Religion is an important part of a well-rounded academic education. Learning about it will help students understand the history of the world and the world today. To the extent that a good, well-rounded education is important to good citizenship, students should be taught about religion. Studying another religion does not force students to engage in practices that violate their beliefs. Religions often allow the study of other religions, if only to point out to nonbelievers the error of their ways.

Schools should certainly teach about religion. Too often public school officials think that any mention of religion in public school violates the First Amendment. (I look at this fear from a different angle again in the next chapter.) I can explain what I mean by briefly looking at a court case, *Settle v Dickson County School Board*. In this case a teacher assigned a research paper on a topic of the students' choice; each student had to get the teacher's approval on the topic and use four sources in the paper. One student, Brittney Settle, wrote on Jesus Christ, which the teacher, Mrs. Ramsey, rejected. The case is complicated by the fact that Settle received permission to write on drama, but then decided to change topics without getting permission. This makes the case opaque enough that the court was probably right to say it didn't want to interfere in the teacher's decision. Yet Ramsey also indicated that one of the reasons she rejected the paper is that "we don't deal with personal religion—personal religious beliefs. It's just not an appropriate thing to do in a public school." Ramsey also added that she thought it would be hard to grade the paper since any criticisms might be taken too personally.[21]

What would happen, though, if a Muslim student wanted to write about Jesus Christ? That would not be dealing with personal religious beliefs. Or if Brittney Settle wanted to write about Muhammad? Another student may decide to write about the Reverend Martin Luther King Jr. He may not think King is divine, but he may certainly have strong feelings about him and think him above reproach. Should he be prevented from doing so since he may not take well to criticisms of his work? Christ is certainly an important historical figure, and a student should be able to write about him if doing so follows within the guidelines of the assignment.

Treating religion as an academic subject will not please all religious conservatives. Objectors may want some subjects taught from a religious perspective. They may object that teaching religion as an academic subject is treating religion within a liberal framework and not a religious one. They are certainly right about this. The real test for religious conservatives is the content of biology courses. Biology courses that emphasize evolution are proof for many that religion is not taken seriously. Teaching the biblical account of creation in a religion course, but not in science, separates the sacred from the secular. For many religious people, however, this is an artificial separation. The sacred permeates all aspects of life, biology included. If a student wrote a biology paper that tried to prove the Genesis account of Creation by quoting the Bible, he would probably receive a bad grade. The reason for the low grade should not be because religion has no place in public schools, but because the paper is bad science. Of course, if the paper gave a good account of the problems of evolutionary theory, then a bad grade would be inappropriate.

Science courses should teach the best account available on any particular subject. Most scientists believe that evolution is the best account we have for human origins, and some even place evolution as a central organizing principle in biology. Biology teachers can and probably should discuss the fact that some people do not believe in evolution, that the question of human origins is a controversial one in our society and that students may want to look elsewhere for alternative explanations. I don't think any liberal could object to letting students know that evolution is disputed by some, but it is important to explain how scientists test and falsify hypotheses. The biology teacher should note that because most scientists believe in evolution, and because the weight of scientific evidence supports the theory, he will teach evolution in his course. Exposing students who believe in the biblical account of creation in Genesis to the idea of evolution is not forcing students to engage in a practice that violates their faith; it merely exposes them to an alternative belief. Parents who object to this exposure, and who believe that the sacred permeates everything *and* want their children taught accordingly, will not receive satisfaction in the public schools. Their objection is not only to evolution, but to the idea of a secular education, even one that accommodates religion. These parents, and not all religious conservatives are like these parents, have to turn to religiously affiliated schools or home-schooling to have their children taught as they would like.

VALUES AND RESPECT

The harder issue with multiculturalism and religion comes with teaching about respect and appreciation for others, which are important themes for multiculturalists. Multiculturalists want students to appreciate that there is more than one way to see the world. They want students to appreciate that there is more than one truth in the world: "[Students] have to understand that there is not only one way of seeing things, nor even two or three. A handy number to keep in mind, simply because it reflects how complex a process of reality is, is 17. There are at least 17 ways of understanding reality, and until we have learned to do that, we have only part of the truth."[22]

Part of what multicultural educators want is to "promote an understanding and appreciation of America's cultural diversity."[23] To multicultural educators (whom I will simply call multiculturalists here) *assimilation* is a dirty word. Education should promote understanding between groups, it should help students understand why some groups have power and others do not.[24] Education should not, however, help students lose their cultural identity and become assimilated Americans. Take the matter of the family. Multiculturalists want to teach that different kinds of family are equally acceptable: "Through contrasts and comparisons of alternative family structures and educational patterns, for instance, students can come to appreciate and accept the wide diversity of life-styles, value systems, and communication patterns which characterize many members of differing cultural and racial backgrounds."[25]

Few multiculturalists actually mean that all assimilation is bad, and they often qualify their arguments against assimilation by noting that all groups must conform to democratic ideals and "major school and societal goals."[26] These are huge qualifications, of course, the importance of which is rarely noted by multiculturalists. They don't explain what are major school or societal goals. Since most societies in the world are not democratic, most immigrants in the United States will come from cultures that have at least some antidemocratic practices. Most cultures are patriarchal, many are racist, and few are egalitarian. A multicultural education that is predicated on democratic ideals like equality and respect for cultural diversity will find that much cultural diversity isn't worthy of respect. We need not expect immigrants and their progeny to assimilate completely, but we can rightly expect them to conform to democratic values. Many of their other cultural practices will be transformed in their interaction with the mainstream culture. Not surprisingly, few multiculturalists tackle this issue; few want to say directly that certain aspects of an oppressed culture are not worthy of respect. Until multiculturalists do so, the argument that students should learn to respect and appreciate cultural diversity will be rather hollow.

This argument also leaves multiculturalists vulnerable to the charge of relativism. Schools should not teach that everyone's values are worthy of respect, since in a liberal society many values and beliefs are not worthy of respect. I can easily respect your values if I believe one of two things. First, that our different values are dependent on idiosyncratic factors, like our talents and preferences. I want to spend as much time gardening as possible, and you want to spend time biking. We recognize that neither is inherently superior to the other, but that each of us prefers one activity over the other. We wish each other well in our endeavors. Second, we may think our values are right, but we may not be certain about this. Implicit in this remark is the idea that people should have a certain humility about their values and their conception of the good life. Here I am returning to Rawls, Callan, and the burdens of judgment I discussed in chapter 4. We accept the possibility that there are reasonable disagreements about many issues and that we may even be wrong about some matters. Our uncertainty allows us to think that other people may have gotten the good life correct, though we may doubt it. Still, our humility tells us that we should respect and affirm their version of the good life.

Respect for the values of others becomes harder, however, for even the humble person who thinks that while she can't be certain about the true or best way of life among certain options, she may think that some ways of life are obviously wrong. Someone may be certain that the true good life includes a belief in God, but she might be uncertain about what form that belief takes. She knows, however, that someone who lacks this belief is mistaken about the good life. Or someone may think that there are several ways of living a good life, but that a life devoted solely to making more money is not one of them. It is not that this person knows which life is the good life, but he does know that certain lives can't be good.

Why should we respect the choices of others? It may be that some people's version of the good life is wrong-headed, perhaps mean-spirited, and should not be respected. To say that we should respect all forms of cultural diversity says too much and doesn't allow us to take our beliefs seriously. This is not just the case for religious conservatives; others, too, will find that the kinds of lives some people want to lead are not worthy of respect. The person who thinks that the goal of only making money is a sign of a superficial person should not have to respect the ends of the greedy person. I will not make a list of possible ends that some people will find so unworthy that they can't respect them: most of us can think of ends that people we know have picked that we cannot respect.

I can sharpen here my modest disagreement with Callan that I noted in the previous chapter. Callan argues that we should identify with the viewpoint of our interlocutors; we should imaginatively enter into the moral perspective of those we talk to.[27] This demands too much of us, and not only because some people are moral monsters who we can't or shouldn't identify with. I am not going to try to enter into the moral perspective of someone whose main goal in life is to earn a lot of money. I doubt I could if I tried. I also know I'm not going to respect their choices very much. It is not as if this is a new and surprising goal that someone has; rather, it's a common enough goal for me to understand that I dislike it. Other people have values that I cannot simply fathom, much less empathize with. In a diverse society, where people have many different values, we should expect that some people will have values that we can't understand or respect. We might be able to be more understanding and give more respect in a society with a narrow range of values.

Yet mutual respect certainly is important. Mutual respect ensures that we can govern together and talk and listen to one another. If we are to listen to our fellow citizens sincerely, and engage in a moral dialogue where the interlocutors take each other's ideas seriously, then mutual respect is needed. Further, mutual respect ensures that citizens will treat each other fairly at work and at school. Without mutual respect, equality will be weakened. Not surprisingly, mutual respect is not always easy: "It requires a favorable attitude toward, and constructive interaction with, the persons with whom one disagrees. It consists in an excellence of character that permits a democracy to flourish in the face of fundamental moral disagreement."[28]

How do we teach mutual respect and appreciation for others while avoiding teaching that each way of life is equally acceptable to the others? Schools and teachers are in a particularly tough spot. If they teach values, they are bound to anger the parents who have different values. If they refuse to teach anyone's values, and teach instead that students should figure out for themselves what their values are, then schools will be accused of lacking any moral compass and teaching relativism. If they teach that everyone's perspective is valid and correct, as some multiculturalists advocate, and that we all have our own understanding of reality, then the accusation of relativism will once again be raised.

We shouldn't be expected to respect the values that everyone has. Yet we can expect citizens to affirm and respect the capacity of everyone to form their own values and beliefs. This Kantian formulation is different than saying we should respect people's beliefs. Having respect for your capacity to make decisions about the life you want to lead means I respect your ability to make informed and rational decisions. I can respect your ability to form a version of the good life, but I can also think that your conclusions are mistaken and not worthy of respect. I may also want to try to convince you of your mistakes. This doesn't take away my respect for you, but is instead a sign of respect of your rational capacities, of your ability to form your own beliefs: I respect your ability to look at evidence, think about it, and decide whether it is convincing or not. If I do so, I can talk to you about a variety of issues. I can try to persuade you that you are wrong about a variety of matters. If I respect your ability to form your own beliefs — if I respect your autonomy — I can work with you, even if I think you are mistaken about some matters. We don't have to teach that all beliefs are equally worthy for people to respect one another.

The fundamental presumptions of equality and autonomy in this idea of mutual respect will not be honored by some. If someone believes that it is wrong for a women to be in a position of authority over a man — like *some* religious conservatives believe — then they fail the test of mutual respect. If you think that nonbelievers are unimportant, and so you can lie and steal from them, then you fail the test of mutual respect. If you think that gay people live fundamentally immoral lives and that they do not deserve an equal place in the polity, then you do not meet the mandate of mutual respect. Some religious conservatives will undoubtedly find the liberal idea of mutual respect impossible to accept. Since the idea is crucial to liberal citizenship, though, schools should insist on teaching and practicing it.

There are other key liberal virtues that schools should teach in addition to mutual respect, even though this will anger some parents. Schools should not, though, be on an ideological tirade. Schools should teach democratic ideals and the liberal virtues, and if there is a clash between a particular culture or religion's values and these ideals, then so much the worse for the culture or religion. The school should not single out a particular religion or culture as undemocratic and so worthy of condemnation. It should let students come to their own conclusions about a clash involving liberal democratic ideals. This presumes that we respect students enough to help teach them to come to their own conclusions about their values and the good life.

It is important to note that the virtues of liberal citizenship are not all encompassing. The virtue of trust is, hopefully, rather uncontroversial. That politics should be used to pursue the common good won't be very contentious, as long as the content of the common good remains vague enough. Of course, the idea of mutual respect, and the idea of autonomy which is implicit in mutual respect, will be more controversial. Clearly, however, these are key liberal virtues and should be taught. These virtues are not all encompassing, however, and they leave plenty of values undetermined. Which beliefs will lead to salvation? How many children should one have? Is abortion murder?

How should the country balance the environment with pollution-creating industries? What about cloning?

Many questions remain after the liberal virtues are taught. In these areas schools need to tread carefully. They can teach about different beliefs about salvation, but they should avoid teaching that each answer is equally true. They should teach that people will come to different conclusions about salvation, and they should teach about some of these different conclusions. They should also teach that some people may be right about their beliefs and others wrong, and that one has to decide for oneself what is correct. The same is true about pollution and cloning. Teachers should, of course, provide students with relevant information about the subject at hand. They should also encourage students to discuss their ideas with others, including their parents, and provide evidence for their views. On some matters, of course—which is the best path to salvation—evidence is rather hard to come by. But evidence about pollution and jobs can be gathered and discussed. Teachers should teach students to respect the right and ability of their fellow students to form their own beliefs, but they need not respect the conclusions their fellow students reach.

Liberalism has certain core values that should be taught. The more controversial of these values, like the idea of mutual respect, are partly about how one goes about arguing, discussing, and figuring out various matters. Moral values are inherent in dialogue, and liberals are best off if they do not pretend otherwise. Yet these values are limited, and teaching them will leave many moral issues for students, often in consultation with their parents, to decide.

Accommodating Religious Beliefs

This sort of formula will not ease all tensions between religious conservatives and public schools. School that teach values will offend some people. (Schools that teach no values will offend other people.) Some religious conservatives will maintain that teaching that gay people deserve mutual respect, even if schools do not teach that any particular kind (or all kinds) of sexuality is correct, offends their values. When religious conservatives object to school practices and the curriculum, the school should try to accommodate them. Here again I rely on my principle of inclusion. Inclusion often bolsters citizenship; only when it clearly doesn't should it be rejected. I have in mind two kinds of accommodation. First, accommodation should almost always mean that religious students should not have to engage in any practice that violates their beliefs. This is the easy kind of accommodation. Second, accommodation should be granted even when it means exempting students from being exposed to beliefs that are at odds with their own faith when it is feasible to do so. Accommodation in these sorts of cases need not be granted as readily as in the first instance.

Public schools often refuse to accommodate religion sometimes because of a slippery-slope argument: if one person objects to a rule for a religious reason, why won't others object for other reasons? School officials sometimes avoid accommodating religious practices because they think doing so violates the First Amendment. In many cases, however, these worries are not enough to avoid accommodation of religion. Other times, they may think important values are at stake, and they should be taught. How can a school exempt a student from a course that teaches equality or mutual respect? This is at the heart of the concern that most political theorists have about accommodation.

Steve Macedo and Amy Gutmann disagree about the nature of liberal education, but they both agree that the school district rightly decided to refuse the fundamentalist children to opt out of the courses that were in dispute in the *Mozert* case.[29] Along with Dennis Thompson, Gutmann says if the parents who sued the school district in the *Mozert* case were successful, "their children (and perhaps others) would fail to receive the education that is necessary for developing their capacities as democratic citizens."[30] Eamonn Callan agrees, saying that "children have a right to an education that includes an understanding of ethical diversity that the parents in *Mozert* wrongly wished to block."[31] Shelley Burtt, in her laudable attempt to argue for a more inclusive polity, rather surprisingly says that "religious parents and secular schools share the end of an education in the basic skills and virtues of a liberal democracy."[32] Because of these shared ends, Burtt argues, the children in *Mozert* should have been accommodated. Burtt's conclusion is correct, but for the wrong reason: it is particularly important to try to accommodate fundamentalist parents because they *don't* share many liberal beliefs. Many fundamentalist parents do not want their children to be autonomous citizens in any kind of robust way; having them attend public schools is one way to subvert their parents' wishes in a way that supports liberal citizenship.

I agree with Callan, Macedo, Gutmann, and Thompson that the education the parents wanted in *Mozert* was not a liberal education by any means. But their conclusion that the accommodation the parents sought was rightly denied is mistaken. These arguments reduce the number of students who receive a liberal education, rather than enlarge it. Gutmann and Thompson contend that if the parents in *Mozert* won, their children would fail to receive a liberal education. This is wrong, though: their children would fail to receive a liberal education in *one* class. The parents lost the case, and many of them sent their children to a religiously affiliated school, and now their children fail to receive a liberal education in *all* their classes. A relentless insistence that religious students never be accommodated does not aid liberal citizenship. It harms citizenship.

Arguments that focus on the curriculum — which characterizes most liberal arguments on education — note that what the parents objected to in *Mozert* are important liberal beliefs: equality and mutual respect were among them. This seems to me rather indisputable. Parents who object to girls being taught that they are equal to boys want to subvert a key tenet of liberal citizenship and autonomy. Yet if the refusal to accommodate leads the parents to pull their children out of the public schools and put them in ACE or similar schools, what has this tough line accomplished?

I will briefly look at easier cases first. One well-known case comes from France. There educators decided that Muslim school girls cannot wear head scarves in public schools. This supposedly violates the French view of republican citizenship and secular schools. Some of these girls, however, do not want to give up their head scarves and so are denied a public education. By refusing to accommodate the Muslim girls the French government has pushed many of them further into the arms of the Muslim community since some of them attend Muslim private schools, away from full French citizenship.

In the United States some religious students (or their parents) believe that looking at members of the opposite sex in "immodest dress" is against their beliefs. Though the rule in gym class might be that everyone needs to wear shorts and t-shirts, religious students with these beliefs should be exempt from gym courses or be put in an alternative course. There is little academic gain in goggling at one's scantily clad fellow classmates, and if doing so is against someone's religious practice they should be accommodated. A clothing rule that mandates shorts isn't designed to ensure good academic performance. If many students want to wear more modest clothing, then perhaps the clothing requirement needs to be rethought.[33]

Parents should be allowed to exempt their children from sex education classes, which are not academic courses; exposing students to birth-control pills and condoms is not an important part of a good education. Since premarital sex violates some people's religious beliefs, there is no reason to insist that their children take sex education courses. It's true that these courses do not condone premarital sex, but they often discuss sex graphically and teach students how to have sex without anyone getting pregnant or ill. Making an exception to this general rule will not hurt the academic education of any student.

There are a variety of other ways in which students may need to be accommodated so they do not violate their religious beliefs. For example, schools should not penalize any student for missing classes on a religious holiday; exams on holidays should be rescheduled for the believers who spent the day in church or synagogue. I cannot canvass all the possible accommodations, since this is too local a practice. Generally, schools need to have a very good reason to make a student violate a religious belief.

Students should also be accommodated if they or their parents object to the content of a particular assignment or course, even if this means exempting the student from learning about evolution or mutual respect. Liberals argue about the important of teaching liberal ideals like mutual respect or equality, but these ideals are lived as much—if not more—than taught. Learning does not only take place through teaching, through the curriculum. Habituation is one way to teach; surely, example is another important way to teach. A school whose ethos is one of mutual respect, where all students are treated respectfully by teachers, and teachers ensure that students treat one another respectfully in the classroom, is teaching mutual respect, not by books but by example. It is not so important if some students do not learn through a book that gay people deserve respect if they see their fellow students and teachers treating gays with respect. Students will learn a lot, though not from a book, if they see their teachers ridicule the Sikhs students who wear turbans. Conversely, students who are tempted to mock the Sikh students, but see others treating the Sikhs with respect, may be reluctant to engage in the ridicule. If parents do not want their children taught that women and men are equal, their children may learn the same lesson from the way girls are treated in school. They may even learn this lesson better through the ethos of a school than through books.

Mutual respect is, in part, about inclusion. A school characterized by mutual respect includes all students as respected members. When liberals argue that students must attend all classes that teach mutual respect, and that any accommodation or exemption of those who object to a class or two cannot be made, they are subverting their own values. Mutual respect isn't taught through exclusion. Sending fundamentalist children packing does little to teach these students about the value of inclusion. Accommodation in public schools should not and cannot be limitless, but it should be as widespread as possible.

Students won't learn about evolution by example, but I want to argue that students who want to be exempted from classes on evolution should still be accommodated. They should be given alternative materials and assignments. Students who do not learn about evolution will not then reject all the tenets of modern science. They may end up there if they take their beliefs to their logical conclusion, but how many students will do so? Many students will be able to believe in creationism and in carbon-14 dating. These beliefs may be incompatible, which is why they both should not be taught in public schools, but many people have contradictory beliefs that do not seem to inhibit their daily lives or their belief in science. Accommodating students who do not want to learn evolution will mean they may still be in public schools. They can still learn about science and its method, directly and indirectly, in their other courses. If the scientific method is a guiding force in the school, an exemption from one part of one course will not mean students will fail to learn about modern science and its method. They will simply not learn about one application of it.

Students are also more likely to confront different ideas and ways of life in common schools than in fundamentalist schools. This remains the case even if students are given an alternative assignment in one class each day. They would still remain in a diverse school; they would still learn about other ways of life from other students. They would be able to befriend children with different beliefs. Furthermore, they could learn from the method employed by their teachers. Good public school teachers do not ask their students simply to memorize; they goad their students to think and question. This is true in many kinds of classes, so if the students remained in the public school, even if they had alternative arrangements in the others, they could still be taught the liberal virtues. They might still be confronted in ways that would get them to think deeply about their and their parents' beliefs.

The dialogue between students that Gutmann, Thompson, and Callan (and I) want occurs many times during the school day. It takes place in classes, at lunch, and on the way home with one's fellow students. An exemption from one class might reduce the dialogue that takes place, but it hardly means that the students will no longer confront different beliefs from the ones they hold. Certainly a small reduction in the way a few students confront liberal ideas that depart from their own is considerably better than a complete reduction. I am not suggesting that the entire curriculum be changed to satisfy the illiberal values of a few parents. Rather I am recommending that some exemptions and accommodations for protesting parents be granted, instead of an immediate rejection of any deviation from the liberal curriculum.

Accommodation might decrease the pluralism of society. I argued above that cooperation between public and privates schools may work to support pluralism by indirectly giving public support to religiously affiliated schools. Accommodation, however, will sometimes have the opposite effect. If students of fundamentalist parents attend common public schools rather than fundamentalist schools, their differences from mainstream society will probably decrease rather than increase. This is hardly a reason to withhold support from accommodation, though. It is a positive development when illiberal communities are influenced by the mainstream liberal society.

Would such an accommodation satisfied the parents involved in *Mozert*? It mostly depends on how consistent the parents wanted to be with their beliefs. The ideas that the parents in *Mozert* objected to were actually taught in many classes, not just the one that became the focal point of the court case. Vicki Frost, the parent who was the main force behind the case, eventually admitted that she would have found many classes in the school objectionable. When parents like Frost come to that conclusion, they either enroll their children in private schools or try to force the public schools to change their curriculum. Many fundamentalist and evangelical parents have tried (some successfully) to change how public schools treat many subjects.[34] The fundamentalist parents in *Mozert* received help from organizations that often try to change the curriculum in public schools to better reflect the views of fundamentalists. This is why Burtt's comments that the parents in *Mozert* didn't want to impose their view of education on others has to be treated rather warily. Burtt is right that this is what some parents want, but other parents have an agenda that is more far-reaching than she admits.

Accommodation has its limits: if a mother wants her child to be given alternative assignments in four classes, then that mother is really asking for an alternative education for their child. When that happens, accommodation should be refused. I can't say exactly when accommodation is reasonable and when it should be refused. Public school officials will have to make that judgment. The point here is that they should make that judgment instead of assuming that every request for an accommodation is an attack on their school. They should try to accommodate reasonable requests for alternatives in classes. In a little-noticed part of the *Mozert* saga, some parents actually received the accommodation they wanted for their children in the one course that parents objected to. The school met their modest request with little difficulty.[35]

Inclusion should not mean telling religious parents that they either accept public schools and its curriculum or that they flee. Inclusion means that public schools should try to cooperate with religiously affiliated schools, and try to accommodate religious students when feasible. Inclusion isn't just a nice thing to do. It also helps bolster liberal citizenship; it helps expose students to different ideas and practices. This is true for religious and nonreligious students alike: in good common schools they will learn from one another and, it is hoped, will benefit. This is one of the reasons why the most conservative and insular religious groups shy away from most kinds of cooperation with public schools and why accommodation in public schools won't interest them. They do not want a partial exclusion, but an exclusion that runs very deep.

6 | The Public Squares

WHAT HAPPENS if religious people speak publicly in their own exclusive, sectarian language about public matters? Some worry that doing so will exclude others from public discussions. Sectarian languages should not be used in public since they are only spoken by a segment of the population. What is needed, some liberals argue, is a public language that is accessible to all, one that is based on reason instead of narrow sectarian languages.

I want to reject this account, that liberal discourse itself is exclusionary.[1] The principle I use here is the inclusive one: we should include people in public debates in a way that bolsters liberal citizenship. Relentless arguments against any role of religion in the public square are too sweeping, and too broad to do anything but foment an unfair exclusion that is bound to undermine liberal citizenship. Liberals should worry about people who want to base public policies on private religious beliefs, but excluding people from public debate (not through laws, but through social pressure) is exactly the way to make these beliefs more dangerous. It is better to include these beliefs in public debates, so they can perhaps be tamed. This is not to say that all arguments in the public square are fair game. My principle of inclusion ends where the subversion of liberal citizenship begins. Arguments that reject the idea of mutual respect among citizens, and want assertions to be accepted but not debated publicly, do not deserve the same respect as other arguments. This does not mean, however, that these arguments can simply be dismissed.

Sectarian Influences

The statement that religion has no public place — or a very limited one — is usually based on two beliefs: that religion in public will serve to divide people in the liberal polity unnecessarily and dangerously; and that religious arguments in the public square may lead to imposing a particular version of the good life on others. Neither argument advocates putting legal limits on what can be publicly said; rather, they offer ethical guidelines to citizens on what counts as a legitimate public reason and what is not. Both arguments assume that religion in public will divide the polity, that there is something particularly divisive about religion. Bruce Ackerman expresses this worry about the divisiveness of religion when he says that religion in the public square

will drive us apart. American Christianity is riven with factions. The political implications of this have been only suppressed by the liberal taboo [on religion in the public square]. If that taboo were broken, the idea of a Christian coalition would soon reveal itself to be a secular construct. . . . Different Christians think and believe different things about politics and everything else. And would mobilize in ways that would emphasize these differences. All of which would provoke Jews, and Muslims and Buddhists and atheists into an energetic and bitter counter-mobilization in self-defense.[2]

Ackerman maintains that civic order calls for us to leave questions and answers about salvation at home. In public, we must speak a common civic language: "If we are to survive as a polity—and I do not take that for granted—I can see only one way out. And that is to cultivate a distinctive civic culture, which self-consciously recognizes that it is not the job of the state to save our souls."[3]

Robert Audi also sees something particularly dangerous about religion in the public square. He notes that democratic government and religious liberty are worth preserving, but says that their preservation is "far from easy, particularly when politically active religious groups are passionately convinced that certain freedoms are religiously forbidden or are immoral or both." Audi claims that to preserve both democracy and religious liberty it is best for a society to have an institutional separation of church and state and for citizens to "seek a related separation between religious and political considerations."[4] Audi also maintains that we should speak in public using secular reason, though he goes farther than Ackerman when he argues that religious talk is best kept out of the public square. Audi also says that people should be motivated by secular reasons when they speak in the public square: "one should not advocate or promote any legal or public policy restriction on human conduct unless one . . . is *motivated by* adequate secular reason." By avoiding religious motivations, "the decisive principles and considerations can be shared by people of differing religious views, or even no religious convictions at all."[5]

According to Ackerman and Audi, keeping religion out of politics and out of political debate will ensure that civic and civil discussions can go forth.

People who act in the name of God tend to feel quite strongly about their beliefs. Rational debate and discussion followed by compromise are not necessarily possible for those who think homosexuality is a sin. Moreover, if some people see others inserting their religious views in politics, then they will respond in kind; with so many religions trying to insert their views into politics, discord will shortly follow. Ackerman and Audi maintain that we need a common language to talk about politics, and we have too many religious languages to use one for public and political purposes. So we must turn to a secular language.

It is true that many religious people are passionate about their beliefs. Yet many people are passionate about their nonreligious beliefs. There were religious wars in the West several hundred years ago, and religious wars still scar parts of the world today. Yet there are many nonreligious wars in the world as well. Moreover, Ackerman's argument assumes that religious languages are all competing. But that's hardly the case: many religions differ on specific doctrines but share certain political views. Religious conservatives tend to frown upon homosexuality and abortion and are skeptical of feminism; they worry about the disorder and permissiveness of society. Conservative Mormons, Orthodox Jews, Protestant fundamentalists, and many Catholics share these concerns. This alliance among religious conservatives is relatively new and, in light of their past antagonisms, somewhat surprising. But this alliance is certainly real and politically powerful. To say that religious voices in politics is acceptable does not pave the way for a theocracy. Many religious conservatives are quite aware of their differences — few Orthodox Jews marry Protestant fundamentalists — but this need not prevent them from pursuing a common social and political agenda.

It is also unclear that religion is a main cause for making public arguments incomprehensible to others. It is important to establish a common ground between public interlocutors, but why believe that arguments based only on secular reasons can be shared by all? Some secular reasons will be rather bewildering to some believers. Would an argument based on my understanding of Kant's categorical imperative, or Hegelian dialectics, or Rousseau's general will really be an argument that many could understand? A conversation between a Burkean conservative and a Marxist would probably begin, and end, with very few shared reasons. The problem of conversations that run past one another in public cannot be simply pinned on religion. In a society that is quite religious, where the Bible is read more than Kant, Hegel, or Rousseau, it is odd to claim that religiously influenced arguments are less accessible than ones influenced by secular philosophers.[6] It is more likely for nonbelievers to understand biblically based arguments than it is for non-Hegelians to understand Hegel. When believers point to what they believe is a biblical injunction against homosexuality, nonbelievers usually understand exactly what these believers mean. When Hegelians point to Hegel for a political position, most of us are completely confused.

The problems with Ackerman and Audi's arguments run deeper, however. Ackerman somehow thinks that religious talk in the public square will lead to the state trying to save people's souls.[7] The move from religious talk by some citizens to a theological state is a rather large leap and one Ackerman leaves begging for an explanation. More important, both Ackerman and Audi think that exclusion better unites people, since they believe that exclusion will bring about a common public language. This is mistaken: exclusion divides people. If people are told not to use their religious views in public, the polity will not somehow be united or find a common public language. Many people will surely chafe under this (moral) injunction; others will leave the public square. If social unity is to be strengthened, there needs to be fewer restrictions on talk in the public square, not more. I explain why this is so below.

A related objection to religion in the public square is that since religious views are "comprehensive views" their public role needs to be restricted in a diverse society with different comprehensive views. Comprehensive views encompass one's view of how to live a meaningful or good life; this necessarily touches upon moral and religious questions, not just political ones. Views that refer to particular conceptions of the good have no public role, since no one should be able to impose their morality on someone else.[8] If we want people to have different moral values, we must argue with them; we shouldn't try to get the state to force our values on others.

Certainly if some group decided that the United States should become a Protestant fundamentalist country, they would be trying to impose their comprehensive views on others. But many political issues call for people's moral views to come to bear on them. Abortion, family, homosexuality, and so on are all now political and moral matters. If morality and politics are intertwined, then it is hard to figure out how people's comprehensive views won't come to bear on political matters. If liberals want to avoid having some people impose their morality on others, they must figure out how to divorce morality from politics. Certainly, liberals do leave room for some moral questions to be decided by people for themselves. Yet other moral questions will also be political matters. There is no way for the liberal state to ignore moral issues; to some degree people will have to bring their comprehensive views, which for many people include religious views, to bear on these matters.

Furthermore, many people's political beliefs are influenced by religion, sometimes without them even being aware of it. To tell people that they cannot speak or act in the political arena if they are influenced by religion is to disenfranchise millions of people in the United States (if they take this ethical injunction seriously). If religious people speak in public using the language of secular reason they must be able to see the world through secular and sacred eyes. But religion informs the worldview of many religious people. They cannot look at issues only through a secular lens, since doing so means denying their religious views, something that is impossible for many religious people to do. Certainly religious liberty means being able to act on one's beliefs. It would be peculiar to say that this is true in private but not in public; such an argument presumes a neat division between public and private that does not exist.[9] People are properly guided by their religious beliefs in all kinds of ethical decisions, some of which inevitably spill over into politics. If someone is told that in the absence of a good secular reason he should not vote for a candidate who promises to vote for legislation that protects animals, even if that person's religious beliefs lead him to believe that animals need more protection, then his religious liberty is curtailed.

I don't see how liberals can argue that people's religious views have no public role. Imagine if a political movement arose which wanted to outlaw alcohol, make divorce nearly impossible to obtain, and made sodomy illegal, all because people interpreted the Bible to mandate these positions. Many liberals would object to the movement, saying that they are wrongly trying to impose their religious views on others. There certainly is something to this worry, but not nearly as much as appears at first blush.

How Religious Are Religious Arguments?

The statement that a person's religious views should not be imposed on others assumes that these views are, in fact, religious. I believe that many purportedly religious views actually have little to do with religion. Take polygamy, for example, something that most good Christians (and Jews) oppose. In 1878 the U.S. Supreme Court declared that Congress could outlaw polygamy. President Chester Arthur declared that polygamy violated the conscience of all of Christendom.[10] The Court implicitly agreed with this assessment: "Polygamy has always been odious among the Northern and Western

Nations of Europe, and, until the establishment of the Mormon Church, was almost exclusively a feature of the life of Asiatic and African people."[11] Indeed, many people in the United States at the time were sure that polygamy was a barbaric and un-Christian practice.[12] Yet polygamy is certainly biblical. It may be that God thought that Solomon's 900 wives were too many, but having a few wives was certainly acceptable to God. In the Old Testament, God does not condemn polygamy. There is every reason to believe that the nineteenth-century Mormon church understood the Bible quite well when it decided that polygamy was a Christian virtue.[13]

For many Christians today, of course, the defense of monogamous, heterosexual marriage is a cornerstone of their political agenda. Philip Johnson decries the "moral deficit" that permeates our society. In order to move toward moral renewal, he says, we need to reinforce duty, honor, and prudence. Such a responsible society is based "first and foremost on responsible parents who fulfill their obligations to each other and to their children." Children should be "nurtured and educated in moral behavior by loving parents, preferably by two parents."[14] Johnson's suggestions are perfectly sensible, though what they have to do with God or Christianity is rather mysterious. Written in a book about the flaws of evolutionary theory and the importance of a belief in God, these suggestions are driven by a belief in God, Johnson assumes, though he never explains why.

Some Christians, particularly if they are fundamentalist, also argue that drinking alcohol is sinful. But one must resort to Talmudic interpretations of the New Testament to show that the water that Jesus turned into "wine" wasn't really wine at all. Religious conservatives also frown on "unpatriotic" acts like flag-burning; they do not want textbooks to question the greatness of the United States. The connection that these doctrines have to the Bible is, of course, completely obscure. Many religious conservatives tend to dismiss welfare as a way to help people escape work, though Jesus's message was one of charity and help to the poor, not aid for two or three years and then you are on your own.

My point here should be clear: many social and political positions taken by religious conservatives are not rooted in religion. To be sure, some political positions taken by religious conservatives do have clear biblical roots. The biblical injunction against homosexuality is quite transparent. Yet even here it is possible to question the genesis of religious conservatives' virulent attitude toward homosexuality. God condemns many things in the Bible. He says, for example, that recalcitrant sons should be stoned to death.[15] How many Christians (or Jews) today echo this edict? Adultery, too, is a sin, but few Christians today have the same sort of attitude toward adulterers—or disobedient sons —as they do toward homosexuality. Clearly the greater opposition to homosexuality can be traced to the cultural and political climate of the times. Yet even the virulent opposition to homosexuality that many religious conservatives have is tempered by the modern idea of tolerance, since few Christians today call for putting lesbians and gays to death.

Many Christians have many beliefs that are odds with their church. It is no longer news that many church members ignore church teachings on many issues. It is well known that many Catholics oppose the church's teaching on abortion, the death penalty, and contraception. What is more interesting is that many Christians have pagan or New Age beliefs. Between one-fifth and one-half of all American Christians believe in clairvoyance, mental telepathy, astrology, and ESP. Ten percent of American Catholics believe in reincarnation.[16] These beliefs are largely incompatible with the creed of most Christian churches. Somehow, many people who believe in one God that affects the world also believe that the way the stars are aligned influences the world. The effort of Christian churches to stamp out beliefs in magic, which began hundreds of years ago, have clearly failed.[17]

The beliefs of many religious people are not always consistent. This is hardly surprising since many people have inconsistent beliefs. It is probable, however, that religious conservatives are less likely to believe in astrology and ESP. In any case, I am not questioning the integrity of religious conservatives or anyone religious. What is clear is that the beliefs of many religious people are connected, often deeply so, to the cultural and political context of the times in which they live. Many religious conservatives passionately believe that monogamy is better than polygamy, that making homosexuality acceptable will cause severe harm to our society, and that alcohol is the devil's drink. Many of them also believe that their positions on these matters come from the Bible or from God. But they are quite often wrong about the roots of their beliefs. Some beliefs have biblical roots, but the reason why these particular beliefs (homosexuality is a sin) and not others (disobedient sons should be stoned to death) are prominent on the political agenda of religious conservatives have to do with the current cultural and political movements.

Many arguments made by religious conservatives can and are made without any reference to the Bible (or the Torah or Koran). It seems obvious enough that some people have their political and social views first, and then find support for them in their sacred text. The Bible is a large book, open to many different interpretations. To be sure, religious conversions do affect some people's views and behavior. Having joined a church, they change to conform to the rules of the church, as well as take on many of the church's beliefs. Conformity to at least some of the rules is often an important way to ensure membership in the church. The views of their church will sometimes have biblical roots; often they will not. In either case, the standards of behavior demanded by the church and their social and political views will be shaped by the larger culture surrounding them.

Religion, Truth, and Reason

One worry about some religious conservatives is that they have beliefs that are "true with an assurance that self-consciously goes beyond the limits of the reasonable," and so dialogue with them seems fruitless.[18] Liberals should not be so quick, however, to dismiss the idea of talking to religious conservatives. The connection between religion and politics is often a serpentine one. It is too easy to exaggerate the idea that religious conservatives cannot engage in dialogue. Many positions taken by religious people do not have clear biblical roots. When the Bible is a murky guide, as will often be the case, then dialogue with religious conservative may very well be worthwhile. Religious people may believe in certain truths, but there are times when one's religious truths will shed little light on politics.

Sometimes the Bible is a hazy political guide; other times it is not much of a guide at all. There are many issues that do not map onto religious beliefs. Should certain cities in New Jersey slow down their development? Should Congress pass campaign finance reform? Should health insurance pay for experimental bone-marrow transplants for cancer patients? Should interest rates be raised? One's belief that Christ died for our sins says little about these matters. Sometimes one's religious truth will appear to have straightforward political consequences, but often this will not be the case. On these and other issues, many people will have to look at sources other than their religious beliefs for guidance. They may still be willing to engage others on the issues where they do draw upon their religious beliefs for guidance and inspiration, since their religious beliefs on many of these issues will often not be definitive.

Having faith need not mean giving up one's reason. Certainly believers can argue about scripture, as many do. Even Mill praised Protestant churches for encouraging discussion among its members. One of the great effects of Protestantism is that it cultivates the "intelligence and conscience of the individual believer." Protestantism expects the mind to be active, not passive. Even the poorest Protestant peasant expounded the Bible to his family, Mill noted, and discussed all points of his religion. Mill is not concerned with the doctrines discussed, but that there was discussion was important: "The food may not have been the most nourishing, but we cannot be blind to the sharpening and strengthening exercise which such great topics gave to the understanding."[19]

People who think and argue about scripture may do the same when it comes to politics. When the directions of scripture on current-day political issues is vague, then people have to figure out for themselves what to think. People who think they must follow God's truth may often use their reason. It is not just that their reason may lead them to believe in God, but that a belief in God or in scripture is not a blueprint on what to think about every or even most issues of the day. A religious belief in the truth may still leave many questions unanswered, allowing for dialogue with the believer. This is not to say that there is no issue when it comes to religious views in public. It does mean that the connection between one's religion and one's political views is sometimes clear, but other times it is not.

The real problem comes either when religious people claim to know what God's will is or when they believe they must follow the lead of their religious leader. Dialogue is hard to accomplish when a person decides that he will no longer think about social or political issues for himself, but merely follow the lead of another. Dialogue is also difficult when someone simply announces she knows what God's will is, and what we all need to do is follow it, not discuss it. I don't know what can be done about these problems, but excluding religious people from the public square certainly does not help. Including religious people in public debate may even provide a partial and indirect way to help solve this difficulty.

The Danger of Exclusion

Because conservative Christians mischaracterize many of their positions as "Christian," liberalism would probably be better off if there was *more* religious dialogue about politics than there currently is. (The same is true for other religious conservatives.) I am not suggesting that liberals begin to dust off their Bibles and engage in theological arguments with Christian conservatives. But liberals make matters worse when they proclaim that religion should be completely kept out of the public. The problem here is political, but it is caused by many liberals' theoretical commitments. The argument that religious conservatives should keep their religious views to themselves in public will be proof to many that the liberal political culture is biased against them; they think a politics without religion is an immoral politics. They also find that their religious views permeate their outlook on most if not all things. The idea that the secular and sacred be separate is a liberal idea, one that most religious conservatives and moderates reject.

Religious liberals, however, have a hard time being heard publicly. Some subscribe to the idea that separation of church and state or the idea that they should keep their religious ideas and arguments to themselves. Others are silent for fear of being treated derisively by their secular friends.[20] This gives religious conservatives more opportunity to dominate the discussion of religion and politics. These religious conservatives need to be engaged about their assumptions. Those who think that religious conservatives misinterpret Jesus's message for crass political purposes to help the rich and powerful should be able to say so without being embarrassed or looked down upon by their secular friends. There are evangelical liberals, but their public role in society is more muted than their conservative counterparts. We have all heard of Pat Robertson and Jerry Falwell, but how many liberals have heard of Jim Wallis, a leading liberal evangelical thinker?[21]

Excluding religious conservatives (and others) from liberal institutions will not make them more eager to compromise and negotiate. If we exclude religious conservatives, just the opposite is likely to happen. Excluded groups are more likely to become passionate (and perhaps paranoid) about their beliefs than included groups. Any exclusion cannot be a legal one, but if liberals ridicule religious conservatives whenever they make an argument in public, the conservatives will rarely venture out to the wider public. They will remain in their smaller circles, talking mostly to one another, where similar private truths are widely accepted and rarely challenged. It is in these smaller publics that private truths can become dangerous. Exclusion does not bolster citizenship; it threatens citizenship. Ackerman and Audi rightly worry about how to prevent the polity from becoming too divisive, but their strategy of exclusion exacerbates the problem instead of solving it.

That there are smaller publics means that the idea that there is one public square, which is frequently implied by people who write about it, is mistaken. The idea of the public square recalls the image of the New England town square, filled with farmers and townspeople discussing the news of the day. In these towns, perhaps, there was a public square. Today, however, there are many small public squares that tie particular communities together. Many different communities have their own smaller public squares. The Jewish communities and black communities, for example, have their own newspapers and magazines, as do many ethnic and religious groups. The separate publics have their parallels in the academy, where there are separate Judaic studies, African-American studies, Asian-American studies, programs, and departments. Along with these programs comes the requisite slew of separate journals.

The smaller publics do not exist in isolation. They typically have points of contact with the public square of the mainstream society. Conversations that take place among elected officials, in the major city newspapers, the national television and radio networks, and the major news magazines are part of a rather loose national conversation that may be considered the larger public square. The leaders of the smaller publics are often heard in this larger public. The members of the smaller publics sometimes follow the conversations in the larger public square. Liberals should want more points of contact between the national public square and the smaller publics, not less, even among those smaller publics that have widely shared private beliefs that many liberal consider dangerous. It is better to include people who want to base public policies on private beliefs in the larger public square.

By including religious conservatives in national debates, liberals can challenge them to provide evidence for their beliefs. This is how the principle of inclusion can buttress liberal citizenship. Sometimes secular liberals can engage religious conservatives in debate and discussion; other times, religious liberals should engage their more conservative counterparts. In either case, liberals can insist that religious conservatives try to persuade them of their beliefs. When the arguments of religious conservatives turn public, the nature of their arguments will change. Many will try to convince others of their beliefs; some will feel compelled to appeal to publicly available evidence to convince others. They will have to listen and respond to arguments made by others.

My suggestion is that dialogue itself may transform people and their arguments. It forces people to review and reconsider their arguments. It forces them to respond to the arguments of others. Getting people to engage with others forces them to recast their ideas in a way that will appeal to others. It forces them to leave their exclusive world and enter the wider, more inclusive mainstream society. This is one reason why liberals encourage such dialogue in schools. Why not try to encourage a similar kind of dialogue in the public sphere? There is, in fact, evidence to show that religious conservatives have changed as they have tried to convince others of their arguments.

Religious conservatives (and moderates) often try to use scientific arguments to buttress their biblical claims. Religious conservatives argue that homosexuality is not genetic, and that it contributes to the breakdown of the family. Rarely do they discuss Leviticus when they make their public argument explaining why homosexuality is dangerous to society. To convince others, they now use a shared public language, something they rarely did thirty years ago. Even the public debate about evolution is mostly couched in scientific terms. We now have "creation science" to discuss; those skeptical of evolution do not just talk about Genesis, but about gaps in the fossil record. To try to convince others that they are right, fundamentalists often take on the language of modern science.[22]

I do not want to exaggerate the influence of the public square on people's identity. There is a relationship, but it is a highly mediated one. That the fundamentalist Philip Johnson writes intelligent books criticizing the theory of evolution does not mean that all fundamentalists now speak the language of modern science. It does mean that Johnson's book will be taught in fundamentalist seminaries and reviewed in fundamentalist journals and magazines. Slowly it will filter down into the fundamentalist masses. This process will surely take some time.

The effect of the public sphere on religious conservatives will also depend on how often they stray into the more inclusive world around them. If religious conservatives limit these forays into the diverse world, they will be better able to protect their identity. If they only enter the national public square on occasion, the boundaries around their family and community will probably remain fairly robust. If, however, their children attend public schools, they own a business that has many employees and customers, or they play an active role in the national public square, then the boundaries around them will be fairly porous. Porous boundaries means that there is a greater chance of one's identity — or of one's children's identity — changing. The effects of entering the public square on one's identity will depend in part on whether this entrance is just an occasional incursion, or part of a larger pattern of entering inclusive institutions.

The best way for exclusive groups to protect their boundaries and identity is to remain exclusive, something that insular groups understand. Few groups, however, can completely shun the outside world. Those insular groups that want to shy away from the inclusive world around them often have leaders who are "bicultural" and "bilingual" — they act as mediators and translators between their community and the outside world. They talk to the national media, and visit with politicians. They might read secular newspapers and magazines. Most members of their communities, however, stay within the confines of their community. Hasidic leaders, for example, often meet with politicians, and then direct their followers how to vote. Certain Hasidic leaders may play a role in local politics, or regularly negotiate with leaders of other communities. These mediators and translators protect the majority of Hasidim, who have a more limited engagement with the outside world. This exclusion, about which not much can be directly done, is a problem for liberal democracy.

The public square can and should be more welcoming than liberals like Audi and Ackerman want. Yet this welcome is fraught with dangers for those who want to retain a distinct identity. If they enter the national public square, they must sculpt their arguments to appeal to a wide audience, and so speak in a more inclusive language, and the more they must meet, talk to, and perhaps learn from others. Religious conservatives may change when they enter the national public square, but they also may succeed in changing national debates to better reflect their concerns. Liberals may prefer that the idea of prayer in public schools no longer be discussed in public, but some religious conservatives are not willing to dismiss the idea. Many liberals think that the government has no business displaying religious symbols on public property, but others think differently. Sometimes religious conservatives will be able to shape debates to reflect their concerns. If the attempts by religious conservatives to fashion public debate disturbs liberals and, depending on the issue, it may, it won't do to say that religious arguments have no place in public. The better liberal response is to convince one's fellow citizens why the arguments of religious conservatives are flawed. Liberals should debate their opponents, not try to silence them.

I have said that many arguments by religious conservatives—like Protestant fundamentalists—have few biblical roots. I also maintain that it is acceptable for religious conservatives to be motivated by their religious concerns and to use religious language in public and in politics. But if the political views of fundamentalists aren't rooted in the Bible, then what is the problem with their role in politics? Sometimes their arguments are secular in nature. When religious conservatives claim that two-parent families are better for children than one-parent families, the evidence that backs them up does not come from God but from social science.[23] Religious conservatives trot out surveys and public opinions polls when it is to their advantage. Many of their arguments are often couched in a concern for the morality and order of society. This, in part, motivates their concern for violence in the media, for the consumption

of drugs and alcohol, teenage sex, and so on. They point out the bad consequences these things have for society; they don't simply say violence in the
media is against God's wishes and so should be outlawed.

Yet their religious and political views are intertwined. Under a religious ve-
neer, their arguments may be quite secular. An argument that God commands
us to be monogamous because polygamy violates the dignity of women and
the good order of society is an argument couched in religious packaging, but
at root it is a secular argument about dignity and order. Fundamentalists (and
other religious conservatives) who make this argument will not be able to separate the sacred and secular aspects of their beliefs easily. Some of their views
will have deep biblical roots; some will have shallow biblical roots; and some
will have none.

I want to emphasize here that engagement with religious people is typically
better than shunning them. Of course, some conversations with religious conservatives are fruitless. Generally, however, the more liberals — religious and
secular alike — engage in real dialogue with religious conservatives, the better
off the liberal polity will be. These conversations should go beyond conversations with the leaders of religious organizations and be held with the ordinary
religious believers. In these conversations it may become apparent that what
the religious conservative thought was true was not the case; the line between
the Bible (or the Torah or Koran) and politics may become murky. At the
least, these conversations might show the religious conservative that others
have legitimate and reasonable views, even if disagreements remain. These
conversations may result in the opposite, though: the liberal may be converted
by the religious conservative. This is the danger of dialogue; you may end up
convinced that the other person is right.

Conversion, though, will rarely happen because of one conversation. I'm
not recommending here that religious people be included in public debates so
that liberals can engage them on matters of faith or about whether God really
exists. I expect debates on narrower issues, to focus on the political matters at
hand. I generally agree with Dennis Thompson and Amy Gutmann's argument on what they call "moral economizing." In order to better come to
agreements on particular issues, we are better off narrowing the scope of the
conversation as much as possible.[24] While people do inevitably bring their
"comprehensive views" to bear on political matters, it would be a mistake to
begin a discussion on these comprehensive views in every political debate.
Doing so will surely prevent agreement or compromise on many issues. People with very different moral outlooks or comprehensive views may still be

able to agree or compromise on a particular issue. People with different worldviews may very well agree that it is important to reduce the amount of violence and sex on television shows and in the movies, but their reasons for doing so may be very different. Discussing those background reasons may serve only to prevent an agreement on the matter at hand.

Rarely, then, will one debate about one particular issue convert someone to liberalism. Over time, though, some conversions may take place. We should be clear, however, about the chances of dialogue between religious conservatives and liberals. We academics talk airily about conversations in the public square. As I suggested above, however, it is often not ordinary citizens who engage in these conversations. Elites are the actors in the public spheres. There are times when religious conservatives and liberals discuss politics, but most ordinary people typically spend their time with those who share their worldviews. The place where people are most likely to confront those with different beliefs is the classroom. But once people graduate from this captive arena, they are less likely to confront others with beliefs that are too different.

When people participate in national political discussions, they often do so as spectators: they read and listen about and watch these discussions. Engagement with religious conservatives is mostly an elite activity, not one that ordinary citizens often engage in. This doesn't reduce the importance of these discussions. People learn when they listen; this listening may spur conversations with neighbors, family members, and friends about complicated matters. It is worth remembering, though, that these discussions won't always have a direct or immediate impact on those listening. They don't even have to walk away to stop listening. They can simply change the channel.

This doesn't mean that liberals and religious conservatives never speak directly to one another. Certainly this dialogue takes place sometimes. Some political conversations take place at work or in voluntary associations. Still, we should be clear about the modest number of politically and morally meaningful and respectful conversations between liberals and religious conservatives.

Subverting Equality

Another objection to my principle of inclusion is that providing a respectful place to religious conservatives in public means giving their views, some of which are illiberal, a legitimacy that they would otherwise lack. I mean to take this objection seriously, but I also think it is important not to define what is illiberal or antidemocratic too expansively. Gutmann and Thompson argue that a deliberative democracy requires a commitment to affirmative action and to workfare, as long as it makes work available, guarantees child support, a living wage, and decent health and child care.[25] It is better to avoid mandating substantive policy positions as a requirement in fair and liberal democratic debate. If we insist that people should have certain views on particular policies for fair debate, then we are less interested in debate and more interested in figuring out the best policies. Fair debate means listening and responding to views that we may consider to be wrong or even repugnant.

This means that arguments that undercut debate and discussion itself should not be given the same respect as other arguments. The Southern Baptists in 1998, for example, declared that a woman should "submit herself graciously" to her husband's leadership; the husband should "provide for, protect and lead his family."[26] This sort of statement—which would subvert debate itself among citizens—does not deserve the same kind of respect that arguments compatible with equality deserve. Arguments that presume domination and subordination run counter to the basic liberal value of mutual respect. Just as schools should teach mutual respect, so liberals should be wary of public arguments that clearly run counter to the ideal of allowing debate and discussion among all citizens to flourish. Arguments that are antiegalitarian, that claim that blacks are inferior to whites, that contend that women do not deserve the same political rights as men, should not be given a warm public welcome. The principle of inclusion stops when inclusion undermines liberal citizenship.

Yet these arguments cannot simply be stricken from public discussion or wished away. The Southern Baptists are 16 million strong. If the Southern Baptists had 16,000 members, then their illiberal announcements could easily be ignored. Their cultural and political influence would be small, and responding to them might give them more publicity and influence than they otherwise would have. But when the leadership of a large religious group declares women to be subordinate to men, it deserves a response. This is a pragmatic decision, not a philosophical one, but a response is particularly needed from other Christians who can point out that they live a Christian life and believe in equality. Conversations in the national public square are needed so that the Southern Baptist membership knows that there are alternative views on Christianity and equality. A response to inegalitarian pronouncements is also needed to make sure that there is no mistake that the public ethos of a liberal society is one of equality.

One might say that I am calling less for dialogue and more for monologue here. I'm not supporting the idea that American citizens engage in "a national conversation" about patriarchy in the same way we discuss affirmative action or welfare. If liberal dialogue is to take place, it must do so in an atmosphere of mutual respect. Mutual respect cannot encompass everyone: those who reject the basic equality of mutual respect may receive less respect than others. Arguments in support of patriarchy beg for a response, but not for the same kind of fair hearing that an argument about affirmative action deserves. Arguments that subvert liberal citizenship should not be included in public on the same basis as other arguments.

Responding to inegalitarian pronouncements need not mean legitimizing them, since a response need not mean an engagement in the context of mutual respect. Responding to deeply illiberal arguments is important to ensure these ideas do not remain unchallenged. Other arguments, however, made by religious people do deserve a respectful hearing, which may legitimize these arguments. I do not see much wrong with this. Arguments compatible with mutual respect should often be taken seriously. Yet public pronouncements based on private beliefs should be discounted. Those announcements that people expect their fellow citizens to accept on faith instead of argument should be viewed with suspicion.

Publicity and Political Argument

The argument against making public claims based on private beliefs harks back to Thomas Hobbes. Hobbes argued that if a person received a revelation from God there was no reason for anyone else to believe him, so there was no way to verify that this was actually a revelation and not a dream or the result of an active imagination. Hobbes asked: "How can a man without supernatural revelation be assured of the revelation received by the declarer?" It is, Hobbes says, "evidently impossible" for "sanctity may be feigned; and the visible felicities of this world, are most often the work of God by natural, and ordinary causes." Similarly, we can't be sure that scripture is the word of God, since we can't know that God wrote the scriptures: "And consequently, when we believe that the scriptures are the word of God, having no immediate revelation from God himself, our belief, faith and trust is in the church; whose word we take and acquiesce therein."[27]

Hobbes wanted to deny alternative sources of authority to the sovereign. He wanted people to be unsure of revelation or scripture, so they wouldn't rely on these to justify opposing the sovereign. Hobbes maintained that a person could not be sure of anything that he could not confirm himself. This is an impossible standard, and one that we need not try to reach. Hobbes's insistence that public arguments should not rely on private faith, however, is more persuasive.

Many religions have private truths at their heart. Discovering Jesus to be your savior is a personal matter. This doesn't mean that Christians think that they can't persuade others to convert. The evidence that we live in a fallen world is easy enough to collect. It does mean, however, that empirical evidence will only take you so far for certain issues: at some point many religious beliefs are a matter of faith, not evidence. How can you prove to others that Jesus actually rose to heaven? Or if God actually gave the Ten Commandments to Moses? Or spoke to Moses as a burning bush? As Locke says, no one can know that Christianity (and presumably other religions) is true: it is belief, not knowledge.

Similarly, if someone claims special knowledge because she or he spoke to God, this is a private truth; it's not something to base public policy on. In 1897 the Indiana House of Representatives passed a bill that declared a new value of pi. According to the Indiana House, it was no longer 3.14.[28] The members were persuaded by a doctor who claimed he had supernatural information about how to square the circle, and so he had a new value for pi. Luckily for the people of Indiana, the bill died in the Senate, and the value of pi was left up to mathematicians and not the legislators. When the Indiana doctor claimed to have squared the circle, and found a new value for pi, his evidence needed to be debated. What should be debated is not whether the doctor actually talked to God or not — as Hobbes says, we can never know if that happened — but his ideas. There are enough reasons and evidence to test the doctor's ideas. Not everyone, however, has to look at the doctor's proof and evaluate it for him- or herself, as Hobbes might want us to do. Most of us don't have the mathematical skills to do that. What we want is the relevant public, the mathematicians, to debate the proof.

If most or all mathematicians, and those who understand math fairly well, agree that the evidence shows that the proof is mistaken, the rest of us can believe them as well. The public truth of the value of pi is probably not well understood by most of the public. Many people find complex scientific reasoning rather hard to follow. We can believe what mathematicians and scientists say in part because of the publicness of their method: their conclusions are verifiable by others, and will change in light of new evidence. To be sure, scientists are not always right; scientists can be resistant to new ideas and skeptical of new evidence. Some new scientific ideas have scanty evidence, yet may eventually be proven to be right when more evidence becomes available. The point is that these debates are public, and accepted ideas will eventually change if the evidence suggests they should.

If a religious person argues that God heals diseases, the proposition should be tested. If the proposition was found to be false, as I suspect it would be, then such an idea could be dismissed. While there may be a correlation between prayer and healing where modern medicine is also used, there is no evidence that prayer alone is better than proven modern drugs and treatments. Until and unless evidence to the contrary comes along, then prayer should not be the cornerstone of a state's health policy.

Some private announcements should be challenged and investigated. Yet some private beliefs cannot be empirically challenged or tested. There is no empirical challenge if someone declares that God gave the Jews the West Bank for all time. As with proclamations that denigrate mutual respect, announcements based solely on faith do not invite a respectful dialogue. If people refuse to listen to arguments based on evidence, there will not be much dialogue.

As with religious groups that denigrate mutual respect, if dangerous, faith-based pronouncements are made by small groups with little influence they can be safely ignored. Yet if the group has a large enough following to be influential, then silence is typically not the best reaction. These declarations are often dangerous, and need a response. There are often people who feel the pull of such faith-based announcements, but might be convinced to think otherwise. A response aimed at those in the middle is needed. There may be a religious challenge to faith-based announcements. Other religious Jews may point out that the evidence in the Torah and Talmud on Jewish "ownership" of the West Bank is ambiguous at best. There also may be a more secular challenge, with people pointing out the bloody consequences of the idea that God gave the West Bank to the Jews. Here there may even be a meeting between secular and religious arguments, since important strands of the Jewish tradition argue against the spilling of innocent blood.

Religion and Science

I have hinted here at a tension between religion and science. A cardinal rule of science is that any hypothesis must be falsifiable. Since many ideas rooted in the Bible can't be found to be false, many believe that there is a persistent tension between science and religion. One problem with private beliefs is that they cannot be falsified. There is no way to determine whether private beliefs are mistaken or not. This is why many scientists are skeptical of creationism: the basis of the belief is not falsifiable. If you take the Bible to be true, then any idea you think is biblical cannot be shown to be false. Stephen Carter both agrees and disagrees with this point. He charges that liberals wrongly view religious people as misplaced in a liberal democracy, and that religious arguments should have little hold in the public square. But then Carter argues that creationism has no role in science classes. He notes that the epistemologies of creationists and liberals are different, and he argues that creationism should not be taught in the public schools because it is "bad science."[29]

It is bad science, however, only to those who reject the epistemology of the creationists. For many religious conservatives, when the scientific evidence contradicts what they see as a biblical injunction, the evidence must be wrong. This is the point: creationists hold a view that cannot be falsified. Their views are based on private beliefs, and private beliefs are not the basis for good science or good public policy. It is strange that while agreeing with the point, Carter also criticizes liberal theorists who refuse to envision a public square where all are welcome.[30] Carter wants to have it both ways. He wants to welcome fundamentalists and other religious conservatives while he rejects their epistemology. Given their different epistemologies, any liberal welcome to fundamentalists would only be partial. When liberals (like Carter) call creationism "bad science," they are not giving a meaningful welcome to fundamentalists to the public square, despite Carter's claims that we ought to do so.

Despite the creationism controversy, the idea that science is based on reason and religious people base their lives on faith is much too simple a dichotomy. Few religious conservatives enter a medical operating room hoping their surgeon spent most of her time in medical school studying the Bible or Koran instead of her medical textbooks. Few religious conservatives believe that computer programmers gain their knowledge by meditating on the life of Jesus. Many religious conservatives are quite grateful for scientific progress and the benefits it brings. Religious inspiration is one thing, but many religious conservatives readily agree that the scientific method in its proper realm is the right method to be used.

It is wrong to think of a global clash between religion and science. Such a clash rarely exists. The more difficult tension between science and religion is over the scope of each. Few religious conservatives reject the tenets of modern science; they do say, however, that in certain spheres of life the strictures of modern science are subordinate to religious faith. A good example of how religious conservatives want to restrict the authority of publicly available evidence is the Jewish practice of circumcising infant boys. Debate exists in medical circles about the medical benefits and costs of the surgical procedure. Does circumcision reduce the risk of cancer? Help with hygiene? Or does it put eight-day-old infant boys at unnecessary risk with considerable pain? To observant Jews, however, this debate isn't meaningful. They are not concerned with the medical effects of circumcision. They are concerned about fulfilling the commandment of God that directs them to perform the circumcision.

Kosher food also highlights the issue of scope in religion and science. In some parts of Europe there is a call to ban the kosher method of slaughtering animals because it is unnecessarily cruel to the animals. At one point thousands of years ago killing animals according to the laws mandated by the rabbinic interpretation of keeping kosher was less painful to the animals than the alternatives. But scientific advances have given us ways of killing animals that some claim are even less brutal than killing them in a kosher way, and now some people maintain that slaughtering animals according to kosher laws is relatively cruel. The advancement of scientific methods is, however, meaningless to observant Jews. For them the issue is not one of how to reduce the pain to the animals, something that many liberals want to do. The issue is how to best fulfill God's wishes.

The matter of scope is not an easy one to resolve. On private matters religious people should be able to reject the tenets of modern science if they choose, as long as there is no harm to others. If there is much harm to others, however, the scope of scientific authority should trump the arguments of religious people. While most religious conservatives want their doctors to have studied their medical textbooks well, some religious people mostly avoid doctors. Many people are skeptical of the Christian Science belief that faith heals all diseases since we have a vast amount of empirical evidence that tells us that without the assistance of modern medicine many diseases will not be cured. Christian Science adults have the right to refuse medicine. Yet the state should (and often does) step in when these adults refuse to give medicine to their ill children.

When harm to other people is not an issue, the religious practice should be accepted.[31] If people who believe that God will heal their diseases do not push for public policies based on this belief, then there is no clash with liberalism—

except when children are involved. If people want to live their lives based on how the stars align, that is their business. When people constrict the scope of authority that modern science has in their private lives, it is not much of a direct public concern. There is no reason to blush if protecting children from harm means discounting the religious arguments of Christian Scientists in public. We should be concerned when a president seriously considers the advice of those who spend their times gazing at the stars. Religious (and other) arguments that are based on private beliefs should not be the basis of public policies. This is not because they are religious; it is because they cannot be debated, discussed, or evaluated.

I also want to note that science doesn't answer every question.[32] This may seem obvious enough, but those who think there is a clash between religion and science forget this point. Is the fetus a human being or not? Are humans too cruel to animals? Does the death penalty count as cruel and unusual punishment? There are no obvious answers to these questions. Some people searching for answers to these questions of morality will refer to their religious beliefs. Science can help us determine when the fetus is viable outside the womb, but this doesn't tell us when the fetus should be considered a person. Science may be able to help us understand how much pain animals can feel, but this will not tell us how much pain humans should inflict on animals. A person doesn't have to reject science to think that it can't answer many important questions. In the space where science is silent, and this space is rather large, religion will prove to be an important and valuable resource to many as they ponder important moral questions.

Institutions

LEGISLATURES

I have argued here for little exclusion on public debates. What if a member of Congress, though, who reads Catholic journals, announces on the floor of the House that he is against the death penalty because he is following Catholic natural law teaching on the subject? The member can announce this, of course, but it is generally best if legislators try to couch their arguments in ways that will engage as many citizens as possible.[33] Debate in the national public square should usually be as inclusive as possible. When there is both a secular and a sectarian language that can be used in a debate, it is best to use the secular language, since that language will involve the most people in the debate. This will rarely be a problem, since in many debates both languages are readily available.

Yet legislators can and should let their constituents know when their religious views affect their political views. This need not be done all the time, but neither does it need to be hidden from constituents. Part of the political process entails candidates speaking to the smaller publics in their districts; politicians attend religious events as a matter of course. It would not be surprising if at some of these events a politician discusses her religious views, and how it affects her political outlook. Such a discussion would allow voters to evaluate a candidate better than if they didn't know the source of many of the candidate's political views. If the candidate were to announce that she didn't care about scientific evidence, that she thought a certain biblical view of things was the only and best way to look at issues, then voters might not vote for this candidate. Things would be different, however, if the candidate said that on certain matters of status — the status of the fetus and of animals, for example — she consulted her religious beliefs, or that her concern for the poor was inspired by the teachings of Jesus. In the latter case, though, her mention of Jesus is really just the beginning of what citizens should expect from the candidate. They should want her to spell out his specific views on welfare. Who should be eligible for welfare? For how long? What is the role of food stamps? These questions and many more like them cannot be answered by simply consulting Jesus. The candidate may be inspired by Jesus in his concern for the poor, but she will have to go beyond Jesus to determine and explain her views on welfare. To say one's politics are inspired by one's religious commitments is really only the beginning of an explanation of one's politics. How one's religion maps onto one's politics is hardly a straightforward process, and it must be explained, not assumed.

CHURCHES

The legislator might turn to his church for guidance, but should the church give it? Churches discuss and give guidance on moral issues, so it would be odd to say that churches should never speak about political matters. Politics and morality sometimes coincide. The venerable argument is that churches should provide their members with moral guidelines and principles. Members of the church can then decide for themselves how these principles should guide their political decisions. If more technical information about a particular policy matter is needed, then the member should seek the information from the appropriate political body or interest group. The church, however, should avoid getting entangled in technical matters. Churches may also want to speak out directly on a few crucial moral issues, issues that have to do with life and death. Abortion, desegregation, and slavery all fit the category of crucial moral issues.[34]

The line between morality and politics is never a clear one, and a church may see many political issues as having important moral consequences. It is probably in the church's best long-term interest, however, to refrain from too much political involvement. There is no specific line that can be draw at "too much involvement," but a church that spends much of its times involved in politics may very well turn off its members. If the church has a lobbying office in Washington, D.C., is constantly urging its members to act on political matters, and has a minister that mostly preaches about politics, it will be seen by many as a political interest group, and not a church.[35] A church that spends most of its time building its community and discussing moral issues, and only a little on politics, may very well see itself growing. The church that can easily be mistaken for a political interest group will, I will hazard to guess, eventually see itself shrinking. People do not attend church to be told how to vote or to write to their senator.

Too much political involvement is probably not in the self-interest of churches. The venerable argument that churches should stick with articulating moral principles is a good strategy for churches. I see no reason, however, why they should avoid politics if they want to get involved, as long as their arguments are public in nature. There is no clear line between politics and morality, and a church's interest in the latter will bring them to the former. Yet if a church becomes intimately involved in politics and uses its resources to help specific candidates run for office, if it has phone banks set up in its basement, runs bingo fundraisers for the candidates, and so on, then there would be reason to revoke its tax-exempt status. This will not prevent them from helping the candidates or becoming politically involved; it just means that if a church acts like a political organization it should be treated like one.

7 | Identity and Discrimination

WHILE I HAVE URGED that liberals adopt a principle of inclusion toward exclusive groups, such as conservative religions, some of these groups will spurn the invitation to enter liberal institutions, at least some of the time. They often want to remain in their own exclusive institutions. They want external restrictions. People should be able to spend time with those who are like them if they wish. Doing so, however, means excluding and discriminating against others. Exclusion and discrimination are important ways in which groups maintain their boundaries and identities. The problem is that some people on the outside want to get in; they want to break down the barriers that keep them out. The exclusive nature of many organizations and small businesses, like that of the Boy Scouts, the Jaycees, religious social-service agencies, and private colleges and universities, is being questioned in the United States. These groups are told by various people and agencies that they must become inclusive; they must allow others in. Diversity here is no longer a guiding principle only for public institutions, but for institutions that are in some way private.

Inclusion, however, should not be mandated unless doing so is necessary for equal citizenship. In this chapter I explore my third principle: exclusion and discrimination are acceptable unless they harm the citizenship of others. The application of this principle is hardly straightforward, particularly in the age of a welfare state that touches many institutions. In many ways, churches and the government are partners in many welfare and charitable enterprises, complicating matters considerably. Still, the principle of exclusion must have some meaning if groups are going to be able to maintain their identity. Diversity and inclusion for their own sake are not enough of a reason to break down barriers of exclusion. Indeed, too much diversity typically undercuts pluralism.

Identity versus Diversity

The movement toward diversity has begun, at least in the United States, to take on a life of its own. Some people now believe that most sorts of discrimination are wrong. The idea often seems to be that discrimination and exclusion make people feel bad and therefore should be eliminated. I pointed out in chapter 2 that Joseph Raz and Will Kymlicka argue that all communities within a liberal state should be liberal, and that any internal restrictions they have are suspect. This idea has now filtered down so that some people think that many institutions, even churches and synagogues, should be internally liberal, that they should accept everyone who wants to enter, allow everyone the opportunity to stay, regardless of what they believe.

If the arguments of Raz, Kymlicka, Young, and Fraser that I discussed in previous chapters flattened out the different communities in a liberal society, this new movement (which I do not want to impute to these theorists) to make every institution inclusive and diverse will further reduce many differences, and get rid of the identity of many people and their communities. Communities should be allowed to retain restrictive organizations. Restrictive organizations do not necessarily harm liberal society, and can even help it. They give people opportunities to worship with like-minded people, to join associations with people with similar interests. Organizations with restrictions give people opportunities to pursue particular plans and projects.

Kymlicka argues that external restrictions help protect a societal culture from outsiders foisting unwelcome change on it. The analogous argument works for particular communities within a societal culture: external restrictions — or the right to discriminate — help the community protect itself from change by outsiders. Discrimination allows the community to retain its identity. Discrimination and exclusion should be outlawed only when citizenship is at stake. (Kymlicka's argument for external restrictions, which only applies to societal cultures, has no qualification for citizenship.) There are times when discrimination is morally wrong but people's private choices should still be protected. Too often, though, certain kinds of discrimination are decried simply because some people do not like to be excluded.

This is true for some members of the Catholic Church. The conservative Catholic bishop of Lincoln, Nebraska, Fabian Bruskewitz, excommunicated members of certain groups in 1996, including Planned Parenthood, Catholics for a Free Choice, and Call to Action, a Catholic group trying to reform the church in a more liberal direction. Call to Action maintained that the excommunication order violated "the most basic principles of justice." Call to Action believes that once a person is baptized into the church, that person is always a member: "Church members are given the gift of the Spirit at baptism and deserve fundamental human respect, communication, and participation in the life of the Church."[1] However, Bruskewitz maintains that belonging to the church involves accepting certain key beliefs. One cannot believe in anything one wants and still be a Catholic.

The Catholic Church does not want to be an inclusive organization. It wants to include everyone, but only as Catholics. Being Catholic is not only a matter of baptism, it is also a matter of belief. The Church believes that abortion is murder, so opposing abortion is a fundamental doctrine of the Church. Bruskewitz contends that one cannot oppose a fundamental doctrine of the Church and be a member of the Church in good standing. No one has a *right* to belong to a church.

Members of Call to Action apparently believe in the liberal ideas of antidiscrimination and diversity, however, and believe that they should be members of the Catholic Church in good standing regardless of their beliefs. They want the Church to be an inclusive organization, one that does not discriminate based on beliefs. But Bruskewitz thinks that the best way for the Church to remain Catholic is to ensure that most of its members agree — or at least do not actively oppose — its central doctrines. Bruskewitz rejects the idea that the Church should be all-inclusive, and certainly he is right to think that private organizations like the Church are under no obligation to be inclusive.[2]

Similarly, in some Reform and Reconstructionist synagogues in the United States debates rage about the role of non-Jews in their religious services.[3] As intermarriage among Jews has increased, many Jews attend religious services with their non-Jewish spouses. According to traditional Jewish doctrine, non-Jews cannot participate in leading the services or receive any of the honors that are given out at services. Many marriages today are conceived as equal partnerships, and the decision to attend Jewish services is often a joint one; it is a decision about how the family will participate in a community of faith. When the non-Jewish spouse cannot participate equally with the Jewish spouse in services, it strikes many as a form of discrimination. This discrimination can strike quite deeply on certain celebrations, like on a bar or bat mitzvah, when the Jewish parent can be called up to the Torah to be honored, but the non-Jewish parent cannot be. In the name of equality and nondiscrimination, some people have called for Jewish Reform and Reconstructionist synagogues to treat Jewish and non-Jewish members alike.

According to the lights of traditional Jewish practice this is a bizarre idea. If Jews cannot discriminate against non-Jews at services, what does it mean to be Jewish? I don't want to discuss the meaning of Judaism here, but I want to argue that discrimination against non-Jews in the synagogue, like discrimination against dissident Catholics in the Church, is perfectly understandable and acceptable.

No one is calling for legal action against churches and synagogues that discriminate in their membership, at least not yet, but the same moral impetus behind the calls for churches and synagogues to refrain from discrimination — the impetus that says that nearly all kinds of discrimination is wrong — is behind other lawsuits.[4] The trend in liberal practice to view all forms of discrimination as suspicious is perhaps most striking in attempts to make churches and synagogues all-inclusive. This trend, however, is easy to spot elsewhere. Too often, ethically questionable discrimination is seen as something that should be outlawed. Liberals normally think that discrimination within the home is acceptable — this is what traditional liberal doctrine dictates — even if it is ethically questionable. But this, it seems, is not always the case.

In the late 1980s two housemates in Madison, Wisconsin, advertised for a third housemate. A woman applied. Although the housemates originally told the applicant they would accept her as their housemate, they changed their minds when they found out she was a lesbian. The spurned applicant reported the case to the city's Equal Opportunity Commission, which found the two housemates guilty of discriminating on the basis of sexual orientation. The EOC originally fined the two women, insisted that they attend classes on gay and lesbian issues, and proposed to monitor them and their housing decisions for two years. While the EOC eventually backed away from some of these sanctions, the fine was upheld through the court system.[5]

The two housemates who refused to live with a lesbian may have irrational or unfounded fears about homosexuality, but that is not the point. People ought to be able to live with whom they want. The two housemates were not landlords who rented out many apartments to the public at large. They did not create an economic institution, nor did they have much effect on the market. Rather they simply wanted to find a compatible housemate, and perhaps a friend. The woman they rejected may have been hurt by this rejection, and she may have felt a loss of dignity. But the discrimination was not by an institution that serves the public or is important for equality of opportunity. Since the discrimination was not public and had no public effect, it should not be legally actionable.

It may be that the two women in the Madison housemate case exercised poor judgment based on prejudiced beliefs, but not all forms of prejudice and bad judgment should be legally actionable. People ought to be able to choose whomever they wish to share a house with, regardless of the reasons behind their choices. Unsurprisingly, the Boy Scouts have increasingly been sued for excluding girls, atheists, and gay men. The Boy Scouts claim to be a private religious organization, though they are not affiliated with any specific church. They maintain that all their members must believe in God. When a girl sued the Boy Scouts for discrimination in California, her lawyer, Gloria Allred, said this case was like a "junior Citadel."[6] But there is an important difference between the Citadel, the military academy in South Carolina that until recently excluded women until it was sued, and the Boy Scouts. While the courts have declared that the Citadel cannot discriminate, the Citadel is a public institution, directly supported with public funds. The Boy Scouts are not.

A twin trend is the idea that positive steps are needed to make many institutions diverse. Advocates for diversity often wrongly argue for diversity "all the way down." These advocates aspire to have all important institutions in society to be a mirror, more or less, of the population at large. This rationale is why the Middle States Association of Colleges and Schools, a college accreditation organization, ordered the Westminster Theological Seminary to include women on its governing board if it wanted to maintain its accreditation. Diversity for its own sake became the goal for Middle States. Middle States argued that the seminary's students would have to deal with women when they graduated (which is surely right), and so they needed to have women on the board to help them do so. Since most students rarely meet college board members, it is hard to follow this logic, and in the end Middle States rightly backed down.[7]

Westminster Theological Seminary should be allowed to administer itself according to its own beliefs. Accreditation should be based on the quality of its academic programs, not the composition of its board. The seminary maintains that its religious dictates mean that its board be composed of Presbyterian elders, who they believe can only be men. Their interpretation of scripture may be flawed, but that is no matter. We should allow religious people to live by their beliefs. They still can do so without accreditation, but accreditation is important for schools in many ways. Schools without accreditation are seen as academically inferior and students at unaccredited schools cannot receive funds from the federal government.

There are good reasons to want women involved in the upper levels of institutions of higher education, but why must every college or university be diverse? A relentless diversity flattens the pluralism of society. Here I recall my argument in chapter 2: a society that strives to make every community adhere to the same principles narrows group differences. A society that does the same with institutions is narrowing group differences even more. A pluralistic society is not a place where every institution mirrors the ethnic, racial, and gender composition of society. A pluralistic society has different kinds of groups with different kinds of memberships, including synagogues that cater to Jews and a Catholic Church that caters to Catholics. This kind of society will offer its members more choices than one that is diverse "all the way down." A society full of diverse and inclusive institutions will have little pluralism. If every institution is a mirror image of society, then there isn't much pluralism among the different institutions in society. This is the irony of a diversity that is taken too far: eventually it makes society more homogeneous rather than heterogeneous. A more pluralistic society will have some institutions that mirror society, and others that cater to a group, such as blacks, Catholics, Jews, men, or women. A society that has different institutions with different audiences, customers, clienteles, or students will be more pluralistic than a society where all the institutions are composed of the same people.

Discrimination and exclusion allow communities and groups — and individuals — to retain their identity as they see fit. It allows them to choose to live in particular communities with particular people. While this discrimination and exclusion will sometimes be morally wrong, this is not always the case. I will return to this issue below, but I must say that I see nothing wrong with barring non-Jews from Jewish services or insisting that Catholics in good standing believe in key Catholic doctrines if they want to remain Catholic.

It does matter which institutions are diverse and which are not. Institutions that are central to citizenship should be inclusive. This means that public institutions, which I presume to be central to citizenship, should be inclusive as well. Westminster Theological Seminary is not a public institution, nor is it central citizenship. Society will be most pluralistic when its diversity falls short of reaching into religious institutions, though it is not only religious institutions that should be shielded from the liberal urge to make all institutions diverse in the same manner. A diverse society will have some organizations that are internally monocultural. Together, these monocultural organizations, along with more diverse associations, will make up a pluralistic society.

Equal Citizenship and Discrimination

The best reason for putting pressure on nonpublic institutions to avoid discrimination and to become diverse is to enhance citizenship. Yet, to retain the idea of autonomy, liberals have to resist their tendency to think of all institutions as part of the public sphere and that every institution must be inclusive. The division between public and private is rather obscure. Some people argue that businesses and churches are private institutions, but this is not quite correct. Government and businesses cooperate on many levels, and not only because the U.S. government is a big consumer. Government economic policies and the tax code affect businesses, and businesses in turn lobby the government. But perhaps the most important moral reason why businesses should not be considered part of the private sphere is their large effects on public life. We have learned that economic monopolies can unfairly keep prices high for important goods. If businesses were left alone, pollution would be rampant and our environment destroyed; unsafe products would be commonplace. We have learned that while economic theory might say that economic discrimination against blacks and white women is irrational, in practice discrimination against black men, black women, and white women has been (and in many places still is) widespread. Discrimination itself is not the problem; the problem is when the discrimination is so widespread that victims of discrimination have nothing close to equal opportunity, which I take to be an important part of citizenship.[8] Many businesses have large amounts of power over people's lives, and this power sometimes must be regulated to ensure that it is not abused.

Church and government are also intertwined in many ways. Perhaps the most obvious is that churches are tax exempt in the United States. Tax exemption is defended as one way to ensure that church and state are kept separate, but this tax exemption can and is used as a threat by the government if it finds church policies offensive.[9] Churches and the government also cooperate to deliver social services to people in need. Many churches run programs to feed the homeless and to place children with foster or adoptive parents, and they frequently receive government money to do so. That 75 percent of the budget of the New York Catholic diocese comes from government sources reveals the degree of government funds that some churches receive.[10]

There are, in fact, few truly private institutions in the United States. Only a few institutions receive no government money or have little to do with the government. The division between public and private that seems so neat in Locke's *Letter Concerning Toleration* is so vague today because of the rise of the administrative state. When Locke wrote the *Letter,* the state had few functions. The state was important, to be sure, particularly in matters of religion, but it didn't employ millions of people, buy huge quantities of goods, and administer extensive programs like Western democracies do today. With the expansion of the state, it is hard to find many truly private institutions anymore. The family is an obvious example of a private institution, but public education, calls for publicly supported child care, and the need to intervene sometimes in families to protect children shows that here, too, the public plays a role.

With the state touching so many institutions, some liberals tend to see almost every institution as public. But this assumes too much. What we need is a test for when organizations should have to adhere to idea of nondiscrimination, and when they should not have to do so. The test here is my principle of exclusion: exclusion and discrimination are acceptable when access to the institution or organization is not important for equal citizenship. By equal citizenship I mean that discrimination should not unduly harm someone's economic opportunity or dignity as a citizen. If this determination is difficult to make, recourse can be made to a second test: discrimination is acceptable when it is crucial to the organization's purpose or identity. The first test is primary. The second test should only be used in hard cases. The idea behind these tests is to allow people to pursue their religious (and nonreligious) interests, which will often mean discrimination, while not infringing on equal citizenship. Generally, these tests will mean that economic and governmental organizations will not be able to engage in much discrimination, while noneconomic organizations will. A rough way to think of divisions is that government and market institutions cannot discriminate, while voluntary associations can. Matters complicate quickly, however, since many voluntary associations receive government funds and engage in market activities.[11]

MARKET INSTITUTIONS

One way to think about equal citizenship is to borrow the idea of primary goods from John Rawls. *Primary goods* are essential goods that "normally have a use whatever a person's rational plan of life." These goods are "rights and liberties, powers and opportunities, income and wealth" and include self-respect. Without primary goods, people will have a very difficult — or impossible — time pursuing their plans and projects. If someone's liberty is curtailed more than others, or someone does not have enough income to pay for essentials like housing, clothing, and food, then this person is not able to pursue a rational plan of life, but must simply try to survive. Primary goods, then, are a matter of justice: in a just society, everyone will have the primary goods necessary to form and pursue a rational plan of life. Self-respect is a primary good because without it "nothing may seem worth doing, or if some things have value for us, we lack the will to strive for them."[12]

It is easy enough to see why people denied the primary goods of housing and food are not equal citizens. Self-respect, however, is not as straightforward. Self-respect needs to be construed narrowly; otherwise it can be used to outlaw all discrimination and to insist that we all respect each others' ends, regardless of what they are. This is too global a reach. Instead, we need to focus on the standard of *losing respect and opportunity as a citizen*. This means looking at the political basis for self-respect in the matter of discrimination. The political basis for self-respect is located in public institutions and those institutions that serve the public. Citizenship is a public matter, and it should be supported by public institutions. These institutions should not wrongly discriminate against citizens. (By wrongful discrimination, I mean discrimination based on ascriptive characteristics. Discrimination based on merit is surely acceptable.) Self-respect should have little to do with respecting the ends people choose; it should have much to do with respecting the ability of people to achieve these ends.

To ensure that equal citizenship is not violated, discrimination by economic and government institutions should usually be made illegal. Public funds should not be used in a discriminatory fashion, to favor one group over another. Equal treatment by the government is an important statement of equal respect. If a class of people find themselves the victims of government discrimination, their citizenship is diminished. Similarly, a person with a public business should not be able to stigmatize certain people by refusing to serve them. If a class of people find they are often victims of discrimination in the marketplace, it is likely that their self-respect will decline.[13] When blacks could not use most hotels or motels in the United States, the problem wasn't only that they had to often sleep in their cars when traveling. The problem was also that their dignity was affronted; that a good that other citizens had access to was denied them for no good reason. Black Americans were humiliated, not because of their ideas or their arguments, but because of racism.

More directly, if a group of people cannot find housing because of discrimination, then they are denied an important primary good. Being refused the primary good of housing and denied the social basis of self-respect are violations of social justice. Discrimination prevents the realization of equality of opportunity and equal citizenship. In these kinds of circumstances, governmental intervention is needed to rectify the injustice and inequality.

The history of discrimination against certain groups of people in the United States colors my argument against discrimination by institutions that serve the public. African Americans and Asian Americans have faced considerable discrimination in this country (white women have as well, but to a lesser degree). If discrimination were random and occasional, then perhaps it would not harm the dignity or economic opportunities of citizens. If most of us found that once or twice a year a store would not serve us because of religion or ethnic background, we might be hurt or angry, but if our coreligionists or those that shared our ethnic identity did not face pervasive discrimination, then this occasional discrimination might not cause too much harm. Intermittent and random discrimination does not target out members of certain groups as people to be avoided; it does not single out certain groups in any way. It does not cause members of certain groups to feel their dignity is assaulted, nor does it undermine their economic opportunities.

Unfortunately, the history of discrimination in the United States is not random and sporadic, but specific and frequent. History establishes the context within which this discrimination takes place, and even if discrimination was no longer routine, when African Americans, Asian Americans, white women, and others face discrimination, it is hard — often impossible — to disentangle this discrimination from the history of discrimination that their fellow group members have faced. Members of minority groups and women would not have to separate the discrimination they face from historical discrimination. If discrimination was allowed, it is likely that those groups that have historically faced discrimination would be discriminated against in larger numbers than others. Discrimination would probably not be indiscriminate and intermittent. It would target members of certain groups, turning them into second-class citizens. We have enough testimony from black citizens to know that they still face discrimination in larger numbers than others do; allowing economic institutions to discriminate would not stop this discrimination but probably further it.

This does not mean that all discrimination is wrong. Anyone who faces discrimination, regardless of the setting, may find his or her dignity and self-respect diminishing. The excommunicated Catholics may have felt this, as do the non-Jews who attend synagogue. Colleagues who are not invited to a dinner party or even to lunch may feel slighted and a loss of dignity. These kinds of discrimination, however, are acceptable.

The dignity and economic interests of citizens are based in public institutions. Institutions that do not serve the public should be allowed to discriminate, regardless of its effects on one's dignity. Discrimination in these settings may make people feel bad, but does not affect their standing as citizens. The political basis for self-respect is found in public institutions and those that serve the public. These institutions can publicly humiliate citizens. It is when these institutions single out certain people or a group of people for discrimination that these people are publicly humiliated.

Institutions that serve the public cannot refuse to serve a certain group of people because of an ascriptive or irrelevant characteristic. Doing so would be treating them as less equal than others. It would be not respecting their ability to construct and pursue their plans and projects. To be sure, not all public humiliation is misguided. Someone's ideas can be criticized and even ridiculed. Criticism and ridicule of ideas, though, are compatible with respecting the person's ability to think of the ideas in the first place. Discrimination based on ascriptive characteristics, however, means publicly refusing to have anything to do with someone; it means not taking anything about that person seriously at all.

Applying for job after job only to be turned down because one is gay, or black, or Catholic harms one's citizenship because equality of opportunity is important to equal citizenship. Since these characteristics are irrelevant for most jobs, they should not be cause for being turned away from these jobs. Someone turned down for a job because a better qualified candidate exists may feel diminished self-respect, but this should not be considered public humiliation. Liberalism cannot ensure that everyone has self-respect and that one's dignity is never slighted, but it can try to ensure that no one should have his or her self-respect slighted publicly for the wrong reason. The standard of equal citizenship means that government institutions and economic transactions should be based on the principle of nondiscrimination.

The one exception to this can be made in the name of small employers. Some businesses are family affairs, and discrimination within them will happen as a matter of course. Further, in many small businesses the ongoing relationship between employer and employee may justify allowing the employer to find employees he is comfortable with. Being kicked out of a restaurant for living with a man who is not your husband is certainly more humiliating than quietly being turned down for a job for the same reason. Unlike large businesses, small businesses also have little effect on the economic opportunities of particular individuals, so they can be granted more leeway in their employment practices. (But not when it comes to their customers, since relationships with customers tend to more anonymous than with employees.) What counts as small is certainly going to be arbitrary, but some standard that ensures that business has a limited effect on economic opportunity can be found. (Current U.S. law states that employers with fewer than fifteen employees can discriminate.)

ROBERTS V JAYCEES

The economic opportunity rationale against discrimination explains why the U.S. Supreme Court was right to decide that the Jaycees could not discriminate against women, though its justification for the decision was partly misguided. The Jaycees call themselves the "Junior Chamber of Commerce" and were an organization for young men between the ages of 18 and 35 (now they are an organization for young women and men). The Jaycees engage in civic activities but, as befits their name, they are also interested in giving their members business experience and training. The Court reasoned that small, personal organizations and relationships, like the family, can discriminate. It is these organizations that "reflect the considerations that have led to an understanding of freedom of association as an intrinsic element of personal liberty."[14] The Court ruled that the Jaycees could not discriminate against women because it was not an intimate organization — its membership was neither small nor selective. The Court believes that large organizations are not part of our historical understanding that freedom of association is part of individual liberty. But this distinction between large and small, while sometimes useful, can only be taken so far. It is certainly the case that small organizations are more intimate than larger ones and so have a better case for discrimination, but large organizations should not be disqualified from discrimination simply because they are large. The Catholic Church is certainly large, discrimination is crucial to it, and most of us (including members of the U.S. Supreme Court) readily understand that allowing the Church to run its affairs as it likes, and allowing people to join or leave it as they wish, is an important part of personal liberty.

The Court was right to note, however, that gender discrimination was not central to the Jaycees' purpose. They could accept women as full members and still fulfill their goals. But this is not enough to make the Jaycees open their organization to women. If discrimination is irrational or nonrational, but does not affect the citizenship of others, it should be allowed. If someone wants to start a chess club for only women or only men in the neighborhood, that person should be allowed to do so, even if the club becomes very large. It would be a different matter, however, if membership in this originally casual organization became important for economic success.

A better reason for why the Jaycees should not be able to discriminate against women is their role in economic equality of opportunity. The Jaycees offer business training and, what is perhaps more important, connections to other business people, including current and former Jaycees. Membership in the Junior Chamber of Commerce, particularly but not only in smaller towns, gives one considerable help in the business world. The Jaycees are a commercial organization, as Justice Sandra Day O'Connor noted in her concurring opinion, and that is what should control the case, not the number of members it has. If the Jaycees can discriminate against women, the women will have a more difficult time than men in gaining success in business.[15] That over half of the membership of the Jaycees in the Minneapolis and St. Paul chapter were members of middle or upper management testifies to the strong business association of the Jaycees.[16]

Similar issues in the Jaycees were raised in another Supreme Court case involving the Rotaries.[17] The Rotary Club is made of business people whose stated goal is to provide humanitarian service and to help build world peace and good will. While there is every reason to believe that the Rotaries pursue these goals, the Rotary Club also provides its members important business contacts. In some cities the leaders of businesses and some nonprofit agencies are expected to belong; it is where these community leaders meet to discuss matters of mutual interest and to make business contacts. As a lower court noted, some Rotarians deduct their Rotary costs on their income tax as a business expense, while another court observed that "business concerns are a motivating factor in joining local clubs."[18] While the Supreme Court mentioned in passing the economic importance of Rotary Club membership, it again relied heavily — too heavily — on the fact that the Rotaries were not an intimate association in its ruling that the Rotary Clubs must open their doors to women. That the Rotaries and Jaycees are not intimate organizations, though, should not control the decision to open their doors to women. What is crucial is their importance in economic opportunity.

Nancy Rosenblum objects to the Court's ruling in these cases. She argues that the Jaycees are not a public accommodation, nor is the group broadly representative of the community at large. Further, Rosenblum points out that the Jaycees are "not the exclusive purveyors of career advantages; other associations were open to women."[19] The Jaycees are merely one association among many, and a liberal society should leave these associations alone. Rosenblum points out that people can join any group they wish, as long as they will be accepted as members. If they are barred from one association, they can simply try to join another.

Rosenblum, however, takes a different tact with the workplace. Workplaces are "quasi-public settings normally governed by at least some democratic norms." They are sites for "cultivating skills, exhibiting excellences, and garnering self-respect." Because it is in the workplace that we learn democratic norms, and the workplace serves much of the public, it is important that it abide by antidiscrimination laws and norms.[20] Much of Rosenblum's analysis of the Jaycees case, however, could apply to the workplace. There she argued that those barred from the Jaycees could join other associations. So, too, people excluded from one workplace could try to gain employment elsewhere.

Similarly, much of Rosenblum's analysis of the workplace could apply to the Jaycees. Just as certain democratic norms and skills are learned at work, so they are learned in many associations. Indeed, these skills are probably better learned in associations than at work. Many workplaces are hierarchical, not incubators of democratic virtues. Cooperation typically reigns more frequently in associations than at work, and is often more egalitarian in nature. Associations depend on the voluntary action of its members and frequently have an elected board to run the group. Corporations demand that workers perform to company standards or get fired, with elections having little to do with who is in charge. If the encouragement of liberal, democratic norms is our standard for where antidiscrimination laws should be enforced, then associations are more important than the workplace.

Rosenblum is right to suggest that not all associations must be internally democratic, but the comparison between associations and the workplace shows that her argument has, in part, the wrong basis. Whether organizations should be subject to antidiscrimination laws should not be a matter of how much the organization encourages democratic virtues or not, a test Rosenblum in fact often rejects.[21] Rather, what should matter is the organization's relationship to citizenship and its connection to public life. Since membership in the Jaycees and the Rotaries is so close to economic life in many places in this country, it makes sense to think of them as an extension of the workplace and of the business community, not apart from them. Since economic opportunities are closely tied to equal citizenship, so is membership in these business organizations.

VOLUNTARY ASSOCIATIONS

While the Rotary Club and the Jaycees have a weak claim to discriminate, other organizations or clubs that have little economic interests have a stronger claim. A slightly harder case involves the Boy Scouts, although I don't think the case is terribly difficult. The Boy Scouts claim to be a religious organization, although they are not attached to any specific religion. They believe that a moral society is one whose members believe in God. The Boy Scouts see part of their mission as helping to create moral citizens, and so they make a belief in God a prerequisite for members and leaders. The Boy Scouts believe that since gay men do not lead what they consider to be a moral life they should not be troop leaders or members. The Boy Scout leadership also claims that boys and girls develop differently and therefore are better off in troops segregated by sex. Unsurprisingly, local troops have been sued because of their discrimination based on religious belief, sexual orientation, and gender. The Scouts have a mixed record in their success with these cases.

I want to defend the Scouts' right to discriminate by beginning with an analogy. A church youth group might very well discriminate against atheists. (This is not an obvious point: a church group might welcome atheists in hopes of converting them.) They might insist that all group members be members of the church as well. Some might discriminate against lesbians and gays when they look for group leaders. The group might also segregate boys and girls. For example, they might go on camping trips and keep boys and girls apart to prevent anyone from giving into sexual temptation. Or they might decide that girls develop certain skills better and will build up their self-confidence when they are away from domineering boys.

If the government insisted that churches not discriminate, that their youth groups include both boys and girls, and that they allow anyone to become a member or leader who was qualified, churches would rightly be outraged. Churches don't have youth groups because they have a general interest in youth; rather, they have a particular interest in Methodist, or Baptist, or Jewish youth. They want to help these children understand and live by a certain religious ethic, and they want to encourage these children to meet and befriend others with a similar religious background. This is what building a community is all about. Churches and their affiliated social groups want to associate mainly with their co-religionists. Liberals may worry when these youth groups are part of a "total world" atmosphere that discourages contact with different believers at home, school, or other settings. But even in these cases, if civil society is to be made up of different kinds of communities, different kinds of voluntary societies, then church groups should be able to discriminate as they do.

If church groups are allowed to discriminate, then we should allow the Boy Scouts to do the same. In some ways, Boy Scouts pose less of a challenge to liberal democracy than do church groups. The membership of the Boy Scouts is usually more diverse than that of church groups. While a Methodist youth group will have mostly Methodist members, Boy Scouts welcome Methodists, Baptists, Jews, Muslims, and even theists. The Boy Scouts are not a conservative religious organization, but a moderate one. Even if a church group did welcome those from different faiths, this welcome would likely be ignored by most. Who wants to be the only Jew among a group of Baptists? The Boy Scouts are likely to teach believers of different faiths about one another, and to cooperate and work together. Indeed, it is because the Boy Scouts have been welcoming to people of different faiths that they have been so successful. The Boy Scouts show that a group can have some illiberal principles but still partially support the liberal virtues.

The Boy Scouts are not welcoming to all, but why should they be? Citizens do not have a right to join any voluntary group they want. Rather, voluntary associations have a right to regulate membership as they choose. Choosing who to hang out with is surely part of liberal autonomy. The important exception is when membership is an important requisite for equality of opportunity and citizenship. But it is hard to see how membership in the Boy Scouts is a matter of justice. If membership in the Boy Scouts was crucial to success later in life or to citizenship, then there would be a stronger case for intervening in their rules. While the Boy Scouts are a successful youth group, there are many youth groups in the United States. There are not only church groups, but other scouting organizations; there are sports leagues, 4-H clubs, and so on. Those who are not welcomed by the Boy Scouts can go elsewhere. Sometimes the choices a pluralistic society offers its citizens is one of its advantages.

The Boy Scouts also discriminate when they hire troop leaders, just as church groups discriminate when they hire youth group leaders. Here, too, the Scouts ought to be able to hire whom they want to make sure they have people whose values are consistent with their moral code. Like many people, I think the Scouts are simply wrong to argue that gay people cannot be good Scout leaders, but it is one thing to think that their rules are mistaken, another to think they should be illegal.

MAKING DISCRIMINATION PRIVATE

That the Boy Scouts discriminate but should not be forced to become more inclusive does not mean that nothing should be done in face of this discrimination. The problem is that many government institutions support the Boy Scouts. The Boy Scouts do have considerable prestige in our society, and many people think that the Boy Scouts are worth supporting because they instill morality into boys and teach them character. Since the Boy Scouts discriminate, however, they should not specially favored by public institutions. This support comes in a variety of ways. Many public institutions sponsor Scout troops, including schools, police and fire departments, and housing authorities. Some public schools let the Boy Scouts use their facilities for a nominal fee or for free. Indeed, the Boy Scouts are chartered by the U.S. Congress; the nominal "Commander in Chief" of the Boy Scouts is the U.S. president.

The president should resign from his position in the Boy Scouts. Public support and recognition of the Boy Scouts should stop. Unfair discrimination may exist in a liberal society, but this discrimination should not be publicly supported. When public funds and institutions discriminate against one group over another then the dictates of equal citizenship are violated. Public funds and institutions should be used to serve the public, not to the advantage of a group that discriminates against others. Public institutions should not add to the prestige and resources of institutions that discriminate. Perhaps by refusing their support, they may even pressure the Boy Scouts to change their ways. Ironically, the private sphere and the market sector may be leading the pressure on the Boy Scouts: some local branches of the United Way and some businesses have said they will stop contributing money to the Boy Scouts because they discriminate.

CHURCHES

I have stated all along that churches should be allowed to discriminate. If churches and synagogues and mosques are to keep their particular identity as religious institutions, it is reasonable to assume that they will have to discriminate against nonbelievers. Accepting discrimination within a church is easy if we assume they are not economic institutions. This assumption, however, is not so straightforward for at least two reasons. First, economic contacts are undoubtedly made in houses of worship. To be a member in good standing in the Mormon church in Utah will certainly help some Mormons in their business efforts. Similarly, synagogue membership, and membership in certain Jewish organizations, will help some Jewish businessmen. People may not talk business during services, but they will after services, or at other church or synagogue functions.

The primary function of the Mormon church and of synagogues is not pecuniary; they are not market institutions. Is membership in them important for equality of opportunity? This is a hard question, and since it is hard, discrimination is allowed under the second test. If churches and synagogues could not discriminate against nonmembers, they would no longer be churches and synagogues. By contrast, the Jaycees and Rotaries could stop discriminating and still serve their primary function. Discrimination against gays and women is a little harder, since some churches and synagogues have managed to end this discrimination without losing their identity. But this kind of discrimination appears to be central to some churches and synagogues that stick to traditional interpretations of sacred texts.

Getting kicked out of a church may also affect the dignity of some members, but it does not stigmatize them as unequal citizens, merely as unequal church members. In a pluralistic society like the United States, few people are seen as unequal or unworthy if they are excommunicated. They be looked down upon by some people in their community, but nothing in liberalism insists that everyone think of us highly. As long as excommunication is not done by a public institution or by an institution that serves the public, there is no liberal problem here.

The larger difficulty in thinking of churches as noneconomic institutions is that these organizations all have to hire people, and sometimes they offer goods and services to the general public. Churches not only hire priests and ministers, but also office staff, and sometimes child-care workers. What happens if a church owns a business open to the public but insists that the employees of the business be members of the church in good standing? The Mormons, who have large economic holdings, do in fact insist that their employees be members of the Mormon church in good standing. In one case, the Supreme Court agreed that the Mormons could make this a prerequisite to employment, when it said the Mormon church could fire the building engineer of a gymnasium that was owned by the church but open to the public. The engineer was a Mormon, but he was not a member in good standing.[22]

The Court was wrong in this decision, though, because it is hard to make the case that operating a gym that is open to the public is religious in nature. One could say, as Justice William Brennan did in his concurring opinion in the case, that we should give the benefit of the doubt to nonprofit organizations run by churches, and simply assume that they are an important part of the church's identity and community. This would be easier to see when it comes to child care: raising children to be part of a community faith is certainly part of the mission of many churches. That the office staff of a church be members of the church in good standing is also understandable, as people who help run the church are seen by others as its representatives.

But it is hard to see how the building engineer of a gym open to the public needs to be a church member of good standing. The worry here is that some churches—the Mormon church is a good example—own a large number of economic concerns, and these concerns have considerable economic power over others. The Mormon church is directly involved in many economic enterprises. It owns fifty ranches and farms around the country, including the top beef ranch in the United States. The real estate of the Desert Ranch in Florida alone is worth over $850 million. The Mormon church owns the Beneficial Life Insurance Company, 52 percent of ZCMI stores, the largest department store in Utah, along with other businesses.[23] Should the ZCMI stores be allowed to discriminate because they are partly owned by the Mormon church?

The answer is no. One could say that people could simply shop elsewhere. But things aren't that simple in Utah. The Mormon church is ubiquitous in Utah, and as a large economic institution its ability to discriminate will indeed harm the ability of many people to shop. It would also mark out publicly nonbelievers and members of the church in bad standing. If church-owned stores began to discriminate, and they included the largest stores in a city or a state, then the victims of this discrimination would be publicly characterized as people who are scorned by the church. Believers may take their cue from this discrimination and treat the rejected shoppers accordingly.

More important is the precedent that could be set by allowing church-owned, or partly church-owned, business enterprises the ability to discriminate. Their followers could easily have their church join their business as a minority partner, and then discriminate against whomever they wanted in their hiring practices and in whom they served: nonbelievers, women, and perhaps blacks would all be disadvantaged. Throughout much of American history people have hidden behind their religious principles to justify discrimination. There is no good reason to allow for such discrimination, though. Discrimination in business under the guise of religion is no better than other forms of discrimination.

The gymnasium case would be different if the gym was open only to Mormons; then perhaps the Mormons could make the case that the gym was part of the church. But since the gym was open to the public, like a grocery store or restaurant is open to the public, it should be subject to the public standards of nondiscrimination.

As I have implied, universities are another matter. Education certainly is important for economic opportunity, but universities are not another market institution. Students become part of an educational community. Education is not (or at least should not be) a consumer product like cars. Education is also about more than just money. It is often about teaching certain kinds of ideals and ideas, and so naturally it is important to many religions. Some religions want to have places of higher learning to train some of their members in their faith. They want to create a community of learning that is infused by their faith. If only private universities existed, then there might be a strong case to ensure that they served the public without discrimination. But we have public universities to ensure that access to higher education is equalized. Given that, there is no good public reason to make private universities adhere to the idea of nondiscrimination.

Social Services and the Church

Though it seems odd to suggest that many U.S. churches are extensions of the state, this description is partly accurate. Governments in the United States —federal, state, and local—give money to many community organizations that work in a variety of social-service settings. The government gives money to private agencies to house and feed the homeless, to place children in foster care, to provide after-school and summer activities for disadvantaged youth, to provide job training, to help the mentally ill, and so on. The government also gives money to individuals—student loans and Medicare are two prominent examples—who sometimes use this money at religious institutions, like universities and nursing homes.

The agencies that provide these services—and are partly funded by the government—are part of a church. This obviously brings up concerns about how closely tied church and state are. The law seems to be that government can give funds to a church for a generally secular purpose. The government cannot give money to a church to build a chapel, but it can give money to help run a homeless shelter. Government funds cannot be used to pay the salary of a minister, but can be used to help administer a church-sponsored foster-care agency. Furthermore, indirect aid is often acceptable. A student can use federally funded student loans to attend a religious college; direct funds to the religious college are another matter.[24]

Not surprisingly, the issue of discrimination arises in many cases where government funds are used by religious organizations. If a religious college receives indirect federal aid because its students receive federal funds or loans, then it must adhere to federal antidiscrimination standards. It is unclear, however, if a church can let its doctrine affect who it employs in its "secular" tasks that receive government funds. A Salvation Army post in Mississippi hired a manager for its domestic violence center who claimed to be a Catholic. It turned out that the manager didn't practice Catholicism at all, but thought of herself as a believer in the pagan religion of Wicca. The Army, which is a Christian charity, was unhappy when it discovered this and dismissed the employee. She sued, saying that she was improperly discriminated against. The court agreed with her, maintaining that since the Center received public funds —which meant the "government substantially, if not exclusively" funded the position—the Army could not discriminate based on religion in its hiring practices.[25]

In New York two teenage girls who were placed in a Catholic foster-care agency wanted access to contraceptives. The agency said no, since premarital sex is against Catholic doctrine. But the girls successfully sued in court, arguing that their lives should not be restricted by an agency that receives government money. The courts have also ruled that religious foster-care agencies cannot try to first care for and place children who are of the same faith as the agency.[26] Foster-care agencies cannot discriminate based on religion if they receive government funds. In some ways, this is a rather unusual arrangement. Religious foster-care agencies can receive government funds, but the fact that they are religious can have no bearing on how they operate. This odd state of affairs makes the church sometimes appear as an extension of the state.

Why use the church at all to deliver social services? The government could simply fund secular organizations or set up its own organizations to deliver social services. Indeed, it does both. It also uses the church, however, because churches can often offer the same services at less cost. Churches often have long-standing social-service programs in place and so the infrastructure to serve those in need is already there. Moreover, churches have long experience in reaching out to populations in need. Because churches are physically placed within different communities, they can easily reach out to these communities. The disadvantaged often turn to the church as a matter of course when they need help. This is the case for many immigrants. Russian Jews who have come to the United States frequently look to the Jewish community in their newly adopted city for help. Vietnamese immigrants look to churches in their new communities for many kinds of assistance. For the government to give money to churches to perform certain social services will be more effective and inexpensive than if it were to provide these services by itself.

Both secular and religious groups should be used by the government for social services (and the government should sometimes provide aid directly to those in need). People turn to the church for help because they understand that many religions have long-standing traditions of helping the poor. Other people turn to the church to help the poor because this is where they can most effectively fulfill an important religious obligation. But churches hardly have a monopoly on social-service expertise. Some secular groups provide these services as well. Yet if the church is to use government funds to help the disadvantaged, it must shed itself of many of its values. It cannot discriminate against nonbelievers when it hires people; it cannot restrict services because of its beliefs; and it must serve all people equally.

DIRECT AID

The reason for this nondiscrimination is that government funds should not directly support programs that discriminate. When government funds are used in a discriminatory fashion, equal citizenship is undermined. Some churches should be forced to decide what they want more, government funds or purity of doctrine. This does not mean that all doctrine must be thrown out the window when government funds arrive. Government funds should not directly support programs that discriminate in their hiring practices or in whom they serve. However, church-related agencies that receive direct government funds should be able to follow the strictures of their faith, as long as they refrain from discrimination.

The Salvation Army case was correctly decided. Since the liberal state should treat its citizens equally, its money should not be used to support discrimination. Certainly, a public university cannot decide that it will refuse to hire women, or gays, or witches, or atheists. A private university that receives government funds to pay its faculty should not be able to discriminate either; neither should the Salvation Army use public money to hire an employee in a discriminatory fashion. An institution that wants to discriminate in its hiring practices should not rely on public funds to hire its employees.

Yet religious-based social services should still be able to run their programs in accordance with their doctrine, as long as it does not further this kind of discrimination. This means that Catholic foster-care agencies should not be forced to distribute condoms to their wards. Foster-care agencies should provide a home that will care for the children, give them food and shelter, and help them with their school work. It is hard to figure why birth control needs to be part of this care. It can be, but teenagers do not have a right to birth control. If teenagers insist upon their foster-care agency giving them birth control, then they should be assigned to another agency that can accommodate their wishes. A homeless shelter run by a synagogue should not have to serve milk with its chicken dinner. It should provide good meals to its clientele, but no one has a right to nonkosher food. On the other hand, these programs should not makes their services contingent on their clients saying certain prayers or attending certain services. Religious organizations that receive government funds should be able to fulfill their religious dictates, as long as they do not force others to pretend to believe in church doctrine, or use the funds in a discriminatory way.

Religious organizations also ought to be able to advertise themselves as religious. Under current law a religious agency that accepts government money for social services can generally display only religious symbols — crosses, crucifixes, and the like — if these symbols are already in the building used before the government money was accepted. If, however, a building is built for social services after government money is accepted, then no religious symbols are allowed. That churches do not have to tear down their religious symbols if they already exist means that churches need not desecrate themselves if they receive government funds.[27] The idea here seems to be that a religious agency ought to appear to be a secular organization, short of desecration, if it accepts government money.

As long as the church gives assistance to all who qualify, however, and the government gives money to different churches and to nonsectarian organizations, allowing for religious symbolism does not mean that government endorses a religion or it is "excessive entanglement," as the Courts have claimed. Most adults will realize that a cross in a church-based program that receives some government funds does not mean that the government has begun financing religion. What matters is how effective the organization is in delivering social services to those in need. A Hispanic church in New York city that receives government funding to help the disadvantaged will help mostly Hispanics. A synagogue that helps train Russian Jews for new jobs which receives government money will not have to find new clientele with this new money. Rather, it should be given money because it can run an effective job-training program, whose clients are mostly Russian Jews. If, over time, the synagogue is successful, and the Russian Jews it trains have jobs, and there are few new immigrants, then the program needs to be rethought if it is to continue to receive government funds. If it finds a new clientele in need, then government support is warranted. This mean the synagogue program will have to reach out to others, perhaps to non-Jews, to continue to receive funding. If it is unsuccessful in doing this, the government support it receives should be dropped.

In larger urban areas, different agencies can target different populations in need. A myriad of social-service agencies, some sectarian, some not, will probably best reach the disadvantaged. In smaller cities and towns, however, religious agencies may have to reach out more than their counterparts in larger cities. If there is only one government-funded shelter for the homeless in a small town, then that shelter ought to reach out broadly; whether it is religious or not is immaterial. In this case, if its religious symbols make some people hesitant to use its facilities, the government ought to fund a program that has a broader outreach. The point here is that religious symbolism is not the issue: what is at stake is the effectiveness of the funded program. If religious symbols make the program less able to reach its target population, then the symbols ought to be taken down or the program rethought. Of course, there may be other avenues. The program can advertise in other communities or through other churches and synagogues. The government should not direct agencies on how to become more effective. Rather, it should award money for competent programs and refuse to renew grants to ineffectual agencies. The government should worry less about the crosses and crucifixes on church buildings that serve the public with government funds and worry more about the programs' effectiveness.

INDIRECT AID

I have emphasized here that religious organizations should be allowed to follow their doctrines even when directly receiving government funds, as long as these funds are not used in a discriminatory way. But this leaves open the issue of indirect funds. Take the following hypothetical example. A faculty member at a religious college receives a grant from the National Science Foundation. The college has some discriminatory practices; say, it will only allow men to serve on its Governing Board and it prefers to hire faculty that share the faith of the school, though this is only a preference and can be over-ridden for good reasons. It will, however, rarely hire non-Christians and all faculty must agree to go to Sunday services on campus on a regular basis. While the NSF money will pay for the professor's research, some of the money may very well indirectly help the college and so indirectly support dis-crimination. (He may, for example, fund graduate students to help him with his research.) Should the grant be given only if the college stop its discrimi-natory practices?

I want to argue that it should not. The money is given to an individual to conduct research that has been deemed worthy by a panel of experts. It is too easy to say that the individual should work at a different institution if he wants a NSF grant—academics have restricted mobility in what is for them a tight labor market. Yet that is not the only reason why the grant should be given; the money is given to the individual, and the benefits that college receives are indirect. If the state wants to make sure that every institution that indirectly benefits from its money refrains from discriminatory practices, then it will be treading on most institutions. Government funds find their way into many places; ensuring the money does not indirectly support discrimination is not only a large administrative burden, but it further ensures that the principle of nondiscrimination will be universal.

Another example of indirect money is student loans. Many students who attend religious colleges and universities receive government aid. Should these schools be allowed to discriminate? The money indirectly helps the college; students who pay tuition increase the college's budget. Fewer students means less money; perhaps fewer faculty or badly maintained buildings will be the re-sult. Colleges benefit from students who pay their tuition. When the federal government gives loans to students who attend religious schools that discrim-inate, it is indirectly supporting discrimination.

Congress passed a law in 1987 (commonly called the Grove City Bill) that makes it illegal for universities to discriminate if its students receive federal aid. Universities that are controlled by a religious organization can apply for an ex-emption. Universities that are closely related but not directly controlled by a religious organization, like Notre Dame or Georgetown, are not eligible for this exemption. Indirect aid makes for a hard case, but this aid can go to indi-viduals who use it at institutions that discriminate, whether they are directly controlled by a religious organization or not. I should be clear that by indirect aid I do not mean the Salvation Army can say the government funds it received paid for the food and shelter of its domestic violence center, but not for the director. Public funds that directly support a program should not be used to support a discriminatory program. Earmarking funds for this or that is simply paper shuffling. But it is another matter if funds go to individuals for their education, research, or medical care, and they use the money to attend an institution that discriminates.

In the case of student loans, the government has decided that eligible students should receive government aid to attend college. Higher education is important to opportunity in our society, and the government has rightly decided to help those who cannot afford a higher education receive one. Student loans are created to help students make a private choice about their education which they otherwise could not make. It gives poor students similar opportunities to those wealthy students have. The loans are meant to level the playing field, and allow poorer students to get an education. Students should be able to attend the institution of higher education of their choice; if they cannot afford this institution, the government should help them. Yet if the loan is contingent on the institution adhering to certain rules about its nonacademic practices, then the government is interfering with the private choice made by the student. It is telling the student that she cannot attend the college of her choice. Wealthy students can make that choice, but poorer students cannot. Student loans, though, are supposed to help poorer students have the same sorts of choices about their education as wealthier ones.[28] If we are to take the idea of equality of opportunity seriously, then students should be able to attend the college of their choice when given a government loan.

The distinction here between direct and indirect aid will still make many churches unhappy. The liberal state is now a large, administrative state. It is hard to be involved in social services and refuse government aid. Those who do will often be at a comparative disadvantage and may find their clientele leaving for more lucrative service agencies. A ban on discrimination by social-service agencies that receive government funds may have an unfortunate political effect: some churches may argue that the government should not support social services, should lower taxes, and should allow people to use their extra money to support the social-service agency of their choice. Of course such a solution will decrease total funds for social services, but it will level the playing field among the agencies, and it may increase the funds for those church-related agencies that refuse government money.

I do not know that there is a neat theoretical solution to this political problem. Luckily, there does not appear to be a large problem here, but it crops up here and there.[29] Many churches have no difficulty adhering to the idea of nondiscrimination, and others may find ways to comply. Still, some local compromises may be needed until the political will can be found in certain cases to keep social-service funding intact while following an antidiscrimination policy. To refuse to compromise on principle will mean hurting the poor in practice. The problem with this, of course, is that the poor cannot eat the principles of academic political theorists.

The Morality of Discrimination

I have defended here the legal right of religions (and other organizations) to discriminate under certain circumstances, but whether they are morally right to do so is another matter. One might say that Catholics have a legal right to discriminate within the Church against those who are pro-choice, or believe that women should become priests; one could say that Jews have a legal right to discriminate against non-Jews in services. But you might still want to condemn these Catholics and Jews as acting unethically. Liberalism allows people to act unethically, but liberals can still condemn unethical behavior. When is discrimination morally acceptable?

To answer that question, it is helpful to posit a distinction between internal and external discrimination, one that is similar to Kymlicka's distinction between internal and external restrictions. The ambiguity of these distinctions, though, will soon become apparent. I don't think the question about when discrimination is morally acceptable can be answered definitively in a general way. Much will depend on the particular form of discrimination. By "external discrimination," I mean discrimination against nonmembers: here I'm thinking of non-Jews at the Reconstructionist synagogues. By "internal discrimination" I mean discrimination that members of the church face because of its doctrines. The prime example is the discrimination that women face in many conservative religions.

Generally, external discrimination is more acceptable than internal discrimination, as long as this discrimination is not based on ascriptive characteristics. The basic idea is this. People must make discriminating distinctions all the time in their lives. If we want friends, we must discriminate against some in favor of others. If we have a dinner party, we must decide who to invite, since we can't invite everyone. If we want to pray with others, we might want to pray with those who have a similar conception of prayer and exclude those who do not. If a person believes that prayer should mostly be silent meditation with others, that person won't want to invite the person who believes that prayer should be accompanied by loud beating on drums. People wanting to have a like-minded community to spend time with must discriminate against those who do not share the key beliefs of the community.

There is nothing necessarily invidious about making these distinctions. These distinctions allow us to cherish certain people and things. The person who tries to be friends with everyone ends up befriending no one. Our time cannot be split indefinitely, and creating and sustaining worthwhile friendships means spending more time with some people than with others. Friendship is certainly a good that most people cherish, and it can only be cherished by discriminating. By inviting those with a similar conception of prayer to pray with us, we are creating a community that allows us to express ourselves in a satisfying and particular way. Inviting everyone to pray with us means we can't pray in the way we have chosen with like-minded people. To have the goods of friendship and community we must make discriminating distinctions; boundaries allow us to value certain things and people, and so they should not automatically be disparaged.

Kymlicka argues, rightly enough, that this sort of discrimination allows a culture to survive without being diluted or transformed by outsiders. Similarly, discrimination against outsiders allows a community to survive without being weakened or changed by others. Discriminating against outsiders, then, in an organization is morally acceptable (assuming, of course, that this discrimination has little effect on citizenship). If Jews do not discriminate against non-Jews in their services, then there may come a time when the service is no longer distinctively Jewish. This may be a long time coming, but its arrival is not far-fetched at all. If more and more non-Jews take part in the services, changes in the liturgy may be introduced to make them feel more comfortable. Allowing non-Jews equal participatory rights is motivated in part by the idea that these non-Jews should be more comfortable when they attend services. Slowly, the service may become less Jewish and more ecumenical. There is nothing wrong with this: an ecumenical service with traces of a Jewish service may nicely serve a particular community. But there is also nothing wrong with Jews saying that they want to distinguish between Jews and non-Jews in their services to ensure the services remain Jewish.

External discrimination becomes a problem when it permeates someone's life. This person avoids nonbelievers at home and at church, but also at work and at school. The moderate believer inhabits some institutions that practice external discrimination and some institutions that are more inclusive. The more conservative believer practices external discrimination on a wider scale. The same protections that help the moderate believer maintain an exclusive community will also be used by conservative believers. Laws that allow for the moderate religious person to discriminate will also help the conservative religious person.

Internal discrimination is usually more morally suspicious than external discrimination. Liberals may condemn the church that discriminates against gays or women. Churches that discriminate against some of their own members treat them unequally and unfairly.

Liberals will also condemn a church that doesn't allow gays as members. This is where the ambiguity of the distinction between internal and external discrimination becomes apparent. Furthermore, external restrictions will often — perhaps even typically — be used to protect internal restrictions. An objection to my argument might be that I'm arguing that the only morally acceptable religions are those that are internally egalitarian. I am saying something close to this. Yet the right to external discrimination gives communities the right to discriminate internally, even if it is morally suspect.

Still, I can here add another part of the meaning of religious moderates. I've said before that religious moderates tend to belong to some exclusive groups, but unlike their conservative counterparts they also belong to some inclusive ones. Now I want to add that the exclusive organizations of religious moderates also tend to be more egalitarian and internally inclusive than conservatives ones.

This does not necessarily mean that men and women are treated the same. Equality need not mean sameness. I don't think it's a disaster for equality if some parts of a ritual or a service are reserved only for men or only for women. This is the case even if certain positions of authority (like the rabbi or minister) are reserved only for men, if other positions of authority are open to women. It is true that many hierarchical churches and synagogues are also patriarchal. Women can't become rabbis in Hasidic circles or priests in the Catholic Church. Here, however, allowing women into the rabbinate or the priesthood doesn't really solve the problem at hand, the problem of hierarchy. Perhaps being hierarchical is made worse if you are also patriarchal, but how much worse?

I won't go over every possible form of suspicious discrimination that a church can undertake: there are too many. Generally, internal discrimination should disturb liberals from an ethical point of view, while external discrimination is usually less disturbing. Exceptions to these general rules certainly abound. My point here is that liberals should recognize that some forms of discrimination are morally acceptable. Discrimination is not a scourge that needs to be rooted out of society wherever it appears.

I want to be clear that my remarks on hierarchy do not mean it is always bad. It depends on how tight the hierarchy is, and how much people defer to it in an unthinking manner. Some Catholics take their religion's hierarchy seriously but think deeply about Catholic doctrine and how they should be interpreted. Others may simply do what their priest or pope says. Some religions may demand obedience, but only in a small sphere of life. Other religions may demand obedience in all spheres, regulating how one dresses, eats, earns money, and so on. The more encompassing the religion, the more demanding the hierarchy is, the more disturbing their power is from a liberal point of view. If one follows a church hierarchy critically, however, then there is less liberal worry.

One claim about religious practices of patriarchy is that it undermines equality. If many women are taught to obey their husbands, and many live subordinate lives and do not enter the workforce in great numbers, or work only at low-skilled jobs, then the equality of all women is undermined. If there are only a few women in the workforce, they will not be treated equally. If a profession has only a few women, they may feel isolated and powerless; they may feel unable to challenge the discrimination they face. Other women and younger girls will not think that the profession is friendly to women, and so they will avoid it. Some people now argue that for there to be real equality, the number of men and women in the workforce must be equal.

Equality, on this argument, is parity. Susan Moller Okin argues that equality and justice means "a future in which men and women participate in more or less equal numbers in every sphere of life, from infant care to different kinds of paid work to high-level politics." Judith Lorber is more precise in her argument for equality as parity:

In a world of scrupulous gender equality, equal numbers of girls and boys would be educated and trained for the liberal arts and for the sciences, for clerical and manual labor, and for all the professions. Among those with equal credentials, women and men would be hired in alternating fashion for the same type of job — or only men would be hired to do women's types of jobs and only women would be hired to do men's types of jobs until half of every workforce was made up of men and half, women.[30]

The problem with this argument is that it doesn't take the choices of people seriously enough. If a substantial minority of the population believes that women should be homemakers or that if they work outside the home their income is secondary, then it will not be easy to achieve parity at work and in higher education. Fewer women will attend college and pursue graduate degrees than men if they do not think they will pursue a professional career. If a quarter of all women refuse to consider a medical career or a career as a professor, how will equality be reached in these realms? As long as traditional religions hold sway over people, the only way to achieve parity at work and school is to compensate for the fewer women applicants. When 100 men and 75 women apply for 70 positions, 40 men and 30 women would get jobs if there was no discrimination and talents were equally distributed across gender. To try to achieve parity would mean discrimination against men among the pool of applicants. There is no way around this.

Equality in the workforce need not mean parity, though. If a particular profession consists of 40 percent women, they will be able to support each other and to fight discrimination along with their male allies. People will see many women in the particular profession, and realize that women can succeed in it without too many obstacles. The key here is power: when power is shared among men and women, discrimination is less of a problem. Feminists often discuss power, of course. My argument here is indebted to these discussions and is directed against the move from shared power to parity in all walks of life. Absolute parity is not necessary for shared power. Fighting for absolute parity does not take seriously the choices that some people make about their lives; it does not accept that some women want to spend more time at home than in the workforce.

It is possible, I suppose, to argue that women who choose to stay home to be homemakers, to raise their children full- or part-time and take care of the household, are deluded. It is also possible to argue that men and women who choose to have children that other people will then raise are also making a mistake. I don't want to enter into the debate here about how best to raise children and balance them with work commitments. (Such a discussion, I suspect, would lead into how the workplace might be restructured.) I do want to note that this is an important debate, and that when women decide to become homemakers they are not necessarily making a choice that only those in a patriarchal society would make. People who think that women should stay at home more than men to raise the family are not necessarily religious conservatives. Others, including the nonreligious, maintain that children are better off if a parent stays home, and that it is easier for women to do this than men. (Since breast feeding is considered to be better for the infant than bottles, the idea that mothers should spend more time with infants than husbands need not be rooted in patriarchal ideas.) This is not just a problem of religious conservatives blocking equality as parity, but it is true that religious conservatives are particularly likely to have traditional homes. If we are to respect the choice of mothers spending more time with their infants, and perhaps older children, and shy away from discrimination, we will have to back away from the idea of equality as parity.

One could say that some women may freely choose to stay home, but that women who are raised in patriarchal homes do not make such a free choice. The distinction is surely important. The women who choose to stay home are dividing up the household needs with their husbands in an equal manner. The women who seeing raising the family as an obligation may do so as a subordinate to their husbands.

The possibility that some women raise the family as a subordinate to men worries Okin. Okin criticizes many theorists of cultural recognition for not taking gender inequity seriously enough.[31] In the case of Chandran Kukathas, this criticism makes sense. She also takes Kymlicka to task for not taking gender inequality seriously enough. Kymlicka, however, is explicit about his support for autonomy for all people in his theory of cultural rights. While Kymlicka contends that there are issues in imposing liberal values on national minorities, he has no such compunction with other communities, as I said in chapter 2. In the United States and Canada, it is only the indigenous population that can avoid the imposition of liberal values. Other communities, including immigrant and religious communities, cannot claim such exemptions. Okin's examples include polygamy, enabling a rapist to escape criminal charges by marrying his victim, insisting that girls cover their faces in public, the killing of disobedient or overbearing wives, and the marriage of young girls to older men.[32] These inequitable gender practices would mostly or completely all be outlawed by Kymlicka—and Raz and myself—in liberal states with the exception of those communities that have claim to some kind of sovereignty status.

Since most liberal theorists readily agree that these practices should be illegal in liberal states, what is left of Okin's account is the matter of indigenous peoples and less overt kinds of discrimination. If Okin thinks the liberal state should ensure that indigenous peoples institute egalitarian governing structures, she needs to make that argument explicitly. She will need to show where liberal states get the moral authority to intervene in communities that they have historically oppressed and tried to destroy.[33]

Okin is also concerned about discrimination "practiced against women and girls within the household," even though their civil and political liberties may be formally assured.[34] It is no doubt true that many raised in patriarchal homes and communities have their choices influenced in ways that many liberals will find disturbing. This need not mean that liberals do nothing in the face of these choices. Most of the liberals I have discussed here want to create a society that supports autonomy for all citizens, men and women. Public schools should teach the importance of mutual respect and equality and all public institutions should practice it. An egalitarian public culture can do much to further equality. If public institutions are inclusive in the way I have argued in previous chapters, then equality will hopefully be furthered still. These suggestions are surely something that both Raz and Kymlicka agree with. An autonomy-based liberalism is engaged in a culture-changing project: it wants to change culture to encourage autonomy.

Okin's example of girls taught patriarchy points up to the success of this liberal public culture, though she does not recognize it. She complains how first-generation girls feel much more tied to their parents and their patriarchal wishes than boys do. Girls often feel that they must choose between respecting their parents' wishes—which often means submitting to an arranged marriage in the late teens—or furthering their own education and developing work skills that will enable them to have more control over their lives.[35] While Okin laments that the girls have to make this choice, it seems to me rather remarkable that after only one generation the egalitarianism of liberalism has encouraged these girls to question their parents' wishes. Sure, it would be better if they didn't have to choose between their pursuing their own wishes and their parents' wishes, but to expect that generations of patriarchy would disappear once immigrants walk on our shores is to expect the impossible. What is amazing, and what shows the power of a liberal public culture, is that after one generation here, centuries of patriarchy are questioned. If the first generation seriously questions patriarchy, it is likely that after one more generation most of the vestiges of patriarchy will be gone.

Still, if some women choose to live subordinate lives to men, and if some men acting "with the complicity of older women"[36] try to further teach their daughters to be subordinate to men, I'm not sure what can be done about this directly. Okin offers no suggestions of her own. She points out that patriarchy is taught at home, but leaves it to the reader to decide what should be done about it. That some people practice patriarchy is not a reason to invade people's homes and churches to ensure that they treat women equally to men.

Such would be a Jacobin state, not a liberal one. Liberalism allows people to make bad choices. Hopefully in a culture that supports an egalitarian liberal citizenship such choices will not be frequently made.

Discrimination against Religion

Although the general problem I have discussed here is discrimination by religious people against others, there is sometimes good reason to be concerned with discrimination against religion. Sometimes liberals think that any connection between religious groups and public institutions means the beginning of a theological state is around the corner. The cases that best illustrate this tendency take place in schools. The issue usually is: if a school opens its facilities to community or student groups, can and should it also do the same for religious groups?

Sometimes school officials think that if they do so they will violate the First Amendment. School officials would do better, however, if they treated religious student groups the same as other groups. If different students groups can use school facilities before or after school, then so too should student religious groups. If school officials follow a principle of inclusion to allow groups to use its facilities, it should not apply the principle in a discriminatory way. When public bodies discriminate, they undermine equal citizenship. Religious students should not have to work harder than others to be able to get together; the state merely should avoid facilitating religious groups more than others.

Both the Supreme Court and Congress support equal access to public school facilities, but some liberals see such a law as rather ominous.[37] Congress passed the Equal Access Act to ensure that religious groups are treated the same as other groups. Greg Ivers thinks this and the Supreme Court's efforts to uphold it are disastrous decisions. They "interfere with the special obligation of public schools to enforce the establishment clause. He says that allowing religious groups access to public school facilities "lends the government's prestige and support to religion in an unconstitutional manner."[38] Ivers claims that any religious activity on public grounds means giving active support to those religious activities. Ivers's argument here is hard to follow since the Equal Access Act does not promote religious activities. It says that if a school allows its building to be used by the chess club before or after school, then the Christian Students' Fellowship ought to be able to meet as well. If this promotes religion, it also promotes chess. But *promote* is the wrong word here. Schools are supposed to be neutral about what student groups use their facilities. The Equal Access Act means that schools have to treat religious clubs like other clubs. This is not promotion. It is neutrality.

This neutrality includes clubs of gay and lesbian students. Next to the Chess Club and the Christian Fellowship might be the Association of Gay and Lesbian Students. Though the Equal Access Act was passed with religious clubs in mind, in an ironic twist gay and lesbian clubs have successfully used the act to demand meeting space at schools. The school can forbid all clubs from meeting, as a school district in Salt Lake City did to deprive gay and lesbian students from having a forum to meet. This school district didn't violate the law, but schools ought to help out students who want to form clubs by letting them use their facilities. The students certainly thought this, as they marched to protest the banning of all student clubs. Students who want to decide voluntarily to join together to meet to discuss or practice a common interest are already learning the virtues of citizenship.

Preventing the government from establishing a religion does not mean that government and religion can never intertwine. Such a prohibition is surely impossible. What the Establishment Clause should mean is that the government does not promote one religion over another, or religion over nonreligion. It should treat student clubs, religious and nonreligious, in the same way. When teachers tell students they can write on any topic they choose, students should be allowed to write on religious or nonreligious topics. There is no reason for liberals to squirm every time they see a religious group in a public setting.

Surviving Diversity | 8

A LIBERAL SOCIETY that values and encourages autonomy will be pluralistic; it will give its members a range of options as they determine their life plans and projects. A pluralistic society can have both communities that do not value autonomy and communities and a mainstream society that do. There is no reason to think that every community within a liberal society must support autonomy, as some liberals argue. A liberal society should have different kinds of communities that value different things. This society provides its members with a range of options from which to choose what kind of life to lead, including the choice to live a life of faith. Some of these communities will be conservative religious ones, where members are not autonomous in any robust manner. However, some of these communities will be more moderate. They will still believe that their texts are sacred, but they won't aspire to the same kind of insularity as their more conservative counterparts do. Living partly in mainstream society, many will be as autonomous as secular liberals.

While liberals often say that religious freedom is a cardinal virtue of liberalism, it is hard to see that in much of today's liberalism. The kind of religion that liberals are comfortable with — the liberal religions — are precisely those religions that have the hardest time holding on to their members. To make the idea of religious freedom a real one, and to retain its promise to diversity, liberalism has to better accommodate conservative and moderate religions.

Liberalism and Religious Identity

Few liberals have written much about religion in a global fashion. Rather, they have looked at how religion applies in one matter — education, equality at home, public debate — or they have ignored religion, though their arguments have obvious implications for religious communities. When these arguments are taken together, however, they reveal a liberalism that is unduly hostile to religion. As I have shown in previous chapters, liberals invoke the idea of mutual respect when they assert that religious conservatives should not be accommodated in the public schools. In order to ensure that we all respect one another, some liberals want to exclude many religious people from public schools. Some liberals argue that religious groups should not be given access to public-school facilities after school hours, even though other groups have access. Others liberals argue that no religious argument—or even a religiously inspired argument—should have a role in public debate, in order to ensure that public arguments are accessible to all. Some liberals point to the inegalitarian practices that take place in religious homes and obliquely suggest that the liberal state is obligated to end these practices. Lawsuits and press releases from dissident religious groups increasingly argue that religions should not be able to discriminate in any way. The recent liberal interest in citizenship has sometimes elevated citizenship to the point where it trumps any other competing value, including the maintenance of minority communities. The leading liberal (and the leading nonliberal) arguments for cultural recognition maintain that every cultural community—which must include religious groups—must offer its members diverse and meaningful options.

These arguments are not completely misguided. Mutual respect is important to teach in public schools, and it will hopefully animate liberal practice. Certain religious arguments are inappropriate in public. A policy should not be passed just because some people think that it is dictated by the Bible. A liberal society should offer its members different kinds of meaningful options. Citizenship has an important, albeit secondary, role to play in a liberal democracy. An inclusive, diverse polity cannot include everyone. If an inclusive state is to be based on egalitarian principles—as a liberal state should be—then those who believe in domination and subordination will be on the outside looking in. Religious conservatives who want an entire public-school curriculum remade in their image should be disappointed in a liberal democracy.

Religious conservatives and liberal democracy cannot always readily coexist. Tensions between the two groups will frequently arise, and it will not always be incumbent on liberalism to become more accommodating to religion. My argument here is not that many of liberalism's ideas are without merit, but that many of the principles developed by liberals fail to take seriously the choice some people make to be religious. A religious conservative who wanted to follow many of contemporary liberalism's dictates would have to suffer through her children being taught matters in public school that contradict her most deeply held beliefs. She couldn't complain about it, though, since any argument stemming from religion in public would be considered unethical. She would have to teach her children the value of equality and inclusion, since she would have to open up her religion to dissidents who take issue with her church's core beliefs. Further, her attempts to teach her children to follow in her religious path or her way of life would be curbed, since her community is charged with providing a range of meaningful options to their members.

Of course, the religious conservative would not actually try to follow the dictates of liberalism in the way I just described. Few will allow public schools to subvert their most cherished beliefs without vigorously objecting. Few will allow dissidents to come into their church as equal members. They will not offer their own members diverse options. And they will fiercely protect their family life from state intrusion. Contemporary liberal ideas do, however, serve a purpose. They alienate religious conservatives from liberalism. The liberalism they see, in the name of toleration and diversity, makes it very hard to be a religious conservative. If religious conservatives find little attractive in contemporary liberalism, it is not all their fault.

My argument, though, is not only or mostly about the practical effects of liberal ideas. Central to my argument is a defense of autonomy: if someone wishes to be a religious conservative, liberalism should not stand in his or her way. It would be a mistake, though, to suggest that the choice to become part of a conservative religion is one that the state looks on neutrally. Just as parents and communities shape and even manipulate our choices, so too does the state. I have argued that the state has an important though secondary interest in sustaining liberal citizenship and its attendant virtues. This means that public institutions teach and practice mutual respect and autonomy. It means constructing a liberal public culture. This will encourage people from different backgrounds to encounter one another in meaningful ways. It will encourage people to examine and reexamine their own traditions and values and reinterpret them to better fit the plans and projects that they have constructed for themselves. People who encounter and learn from others, who reinterpret their own traditions, often leave their groups. They stretch their group boundaries, and sometimes break them. This may lead to an increase in individual diversity, as different people interpret and reinterpret their traditions in different ways. This is one outcome of liberal autonomy and liberal citizenship. This support for individual diversity will make it harder for groups to maintain their identity. Even the version of liberal diversity that I offer here makes it hard for some religious groups to survive.

Hard, but not impossible. If liberals learn to respect the role that restrictions can play in a meaningful life, and accept the idea that some people choose to live a moderate or conservative religious life, then liberalism will become more hospitable than it is currently to religious conservatives and other restrictive groups, liberal and illiberal. "More hospitable" means the arguments in this book will ease the tensions between liberalism and conservative religions, not end them. Further, my arguments here will not necessarily make it easier for religious conservatives to thrive in the liberal state. In some ways, they may make it harder than current liberal arguments. These arguments try to exclude religious conservatives from public schools, which insulates religious conservatives from liberal citizens. This helps religious conservatives maintain their identity more effectively than if they were better included in liberal institutions, as I've argued should be done.

Much of my discussion here, including my argument about autonomy, relies on a certain view of the Western liberal democracies. If I am right that the liberal democracies generally have a mainstream society within them, with smaller communities intermeshed with this society in varying degrees, then there is no reason to think that every community within the larger society must support autonomy in a robust manner. Indeed, assuming a healthy mainstream society, there is not much reason to worry about autonomy. Concerns about autonomy need only enter when the mainstream society becomes weak and society begins to break up into different groups, or when smaller groups become extremely insular, so their members are unaware or barely aware that other kinds of lives are lived within their society.

This makes the recent liberal argument that culture should be supported in order to support autonomy misguided. The mainstream society should be supported to ensure that people can live a life with few restrictions. This mainstream society should give people a variety of options, educate people to be independent, and ensure that people's choices are not coerced. Yet not all cultures and communities support autonomy, nor need they. Some communities restrict their members in such a way that doesn't necessarily inhibit autonomy, but that is because there is a mainstream society that they can go to if they wish. Supporting autonomy means allowing people to choose how they want to live their lives. It should not mean restricting the choices they can make by ensuring that every community and culture within a liberal state support autonomy.

Some might object that religious conservatives would be parasitic on the wider liberal state. That liberal citizenship can allow for exemptions means that those who are good liberal citizens are carrying much of the burden of the liberal state. I think this argument is mistaken for three reasons. First, religious conservatives often complain that they have to pay taxes for institutions, like public schools, that they do not use. They argue that they are double-taxed, since they must pay for their own schools as well. This extra burden is justified by the importance of citizenship, but that does not deny that it is an extra burden. Second, I think liberals need to be wary of putting citizenship first. Autonomy is a primary virtue of liberalism, while citizenship is a secondary virtue. Part of a just state is giving people the right to choose the kinds of lives they want to live, as long as these lives do not harm others.

Finally, a liberal state more hospitable to religion will also be more welcoming to religious moderates, who do not threaten liberalism. These moderates do not strive for the sort of social separation that many religious conservatives desire. Rather, religious moderates want some separation, they want some social space to themselves and some space to raise their children without the interference of others. Liberals today too often ignore the idea that religious moderates can live liberal lives. This may be partly due to a prejudice against religious people. It also may be because liberals typically undervalue the role that community restrictions can play in an autonomous life. Liberals like Raz and Kymlicka emphasize the role that cultures have in opening up opportunities and choices for their members. Yet these cultures also restrict their members in various ways. Some restrictions are needed if people are going to show their children the value of their particular community, before their children encounter the lives of others. I don't think this has to undermine autonomy. I have argued instead that these restrictions can sometimes enhance autonomy. Religious moderates aid liberal citizenship in other ways. Civic skills are often learned in their churches, and these religions sometimes teach a nonoppressive self-restraint that helps sustain the morality of the liberal regime.

The principles I have developed here support a healthy mainstream liberal society. The principle of nonintervention allows communities to raise their children and treat their members as they wish, as long as they do not physically harm their children and ensure that all members have the right to exit. The principle of inclusion fosters the use of public institutions by religious conservatives and moderates in ways that may bolster liberal citizenship. The principle of exclusion allows religious people to exclude outsiders from their institutions, as long as doing so does not harm citizenship.

These principles will sometimes transform the identity of religious people and will sometimes help deepen it. On the one hand, a principle of inclusion may work to support religious communities by giving them access to public resources or giving them a public legitimacy. On the other hand, a principle of inclusion may work to transform religious people (which is why some religious conservatives reject inclusion and want to exclude themselves from public life) in a more liberal direction by encouraging more interaction with liberal ideas and practices. I see no problem if a principle of inclusion transforms religious conservatives in a more liberal direction, even possibly undermining their community, as long as this transformation is voluntary. This transformation, if it happens, will decrease group differences in liberal society.

Yet inclusion will also bolster other group differences. A principle of inclusion will probably transform moderate religious communities to a lesser degree than conservative ones since moderate communities are already partly open. Inclusion will probably, in fact, support these moderate communities. While inclusion may decrease the group differences of conservative religions, it may support moderate group differences in society. Further, my principles of nonintervention and exclusion will often help communities maintain their differences. Unlike the arguments of Raz and Kymlicka, these principles allow communities to maintain restrictions on their members' way of life.

Still, the principle of inclusion may be used in contradictory ways. A community may decide that it wants to be included in certain ways to gain access to the state's resources, and yet want to be excluded in other ways to help protect its boundaries. Balancing the need to build and maintain a reasonably strong citizenship with the right of people to choose to live a life of obedience will sometimes lead to inconsistent trends in society. The principles themselves do not conflict. If people want to use them in a contradictory manner, that is their choice. Generally, exclusion and nonintervention will allow people to live in a restrictive community. Inclusion will generally best support liberal citizenship. Sometimes it will work to transform a group's identity, while at other times it will bolster the identity of the group.

Is Religion Special?

Joseph Raz argues that the government should try to ensure that its citizens have diverse and meaningful options in their lives. This may mean that the government should support educational institutions, museums, the arts, symphonies, science programs, and so on.[1] It could also mean direct support for groups, including religious ones. This does not have to mean financial support. The government could exempt religious people and institutions from laws that generally apply to others, giving religious groups more freedom to survive. As a matter of law, there are many religious exemptions in the United States. Michael McConnell notes some of them: "Employment discrimination laws conflict with the Roman Catholic priesthood; laws against serving alcoholic beverages to minors conflict with the celebration of communion; regulations requiring hard hats in construction areas effectively exclude Amish and Sikhs from the workplace." Presaging an important Supreme Court case, McConnell explains that without accommodation for religion "laws giving historic preservation commissions authority over changes in old buildings, if applied to churches, can result in official second-guessing of ecclesiastical decisions."[2]

We might want to exempt religions to help ensure society's pluralism, but this argument could be applied to many other groups, including ethnic groups and associations of all kinds. If we treat religion as a special source of exemption, why not other groups? One powerful argument for giving religion special treatment is that people who violate their religious conscience might believe they will go to hell, while people who violate their secular conscience don't believe they will face such drastic consequences. Making (or trying to make) the group violate their religious beliefs will cause a greater degree of "internal trauma" than those who are violating their conscience.[3] Certainly, if a person thinks doing an act will cause everlasting damnation, then doing so will clearly be very traumatic. It is not obvious, however, that nonbelievers cannot feel a similar trauma when acting against their conscience. The pain that someone with no belief in the afterlife may feel when violating a crucial dictate of his or her conscience may be just as painful as someone who violates a religious dictate. Thoreau was not the only nonreligious person willing to go to jail for his beliefs.

If we give religion special treatment as a matter of law or policy, then religious people will have more protection from laws than nonreligious people. Clearly, this violates the liberal ideal of treating everyone equally before the law. McConnell denies that accommodating religious beliefs, but not other beliefs, is giving the former an advantage.[4] But this is not the case. If religion was treated as special in the law, then religious people could smoke certain drugs in religious ceremonies, they could demand accommodation in schools, and they could claim to be conscientious objectors to war, while nonreligious people could not successfully make these same demands. Treating the religious to exemptions from the law that are denied the nonreligious would be giving a certain class of people more rights than others.

There are several other problems with the argument that religion should be treated differently than nonreligious beliefs. Religious beliefs often turn out to be quite malleable. Hasidic children can only attend schools segregated by sex, but a school for handicapped Hasidic children that was funded by the state received special dispensation to hold coeducational classes.[5] For years the Mormons declared that blacks were inferior and could not reach the final stage of heaven, but in the 1970s their leader received word that blacks were equal to whites. Mormons also believed that polygamy was ordered by God, but after considerable harassment by the U.S. government, their interpretation of God's order changed. Many churches sanctioned slavery before the U.S. Civil War, but hardly any do so today. Sometimes, the right kind of incentive can work changes in a church's doctrine.

This may partly be because it is not always easy to determine which religious doctrines can be violated only by risking eternal damnation and which cannot be. Few religions insist that heaven can be reached only by fulfilling *all* of its dictates. Many versions of Christianity, for example, assume that we are all sinners. If simply sinning is a ticket to hell, then we don't have to worry about pressuring anyone to sin, since we all have already. This means that if the government forces someone to rent an apartment to an unmarried couple the landlord is probably not on the way to hell.[6] Other versions of Christianity believe in predestination, so for them following government laws would have no effect on the afterlife. In Judaism the status of sin and how sin will affect the afterlife is hardly clearer. For example, to most devout Jews, the commandment to keep kosher means that one cannot eat milk with meat; that indeed, separate dishes are needed for milk and for meat. The commandment in the Torah, however, merely says that a calf should not be cooked in her mother's milk. The path from that commandment to the rules of keeping kosher is, of course, a matter of Talmudic interpretation.

Moreover, it is not clear why a person's view of the consequences of his or her beliefs should always matter. Some people may believe that interracial marriage is a sin, and so renting an apartment to such a couple would land a landlord in hell, but this should be of no matter when making laws. The government has a compelling interest in combating racism, regardless of some people's religious beliefs. As is well known, while the government often exempts religious organizations from its antidiscrimination statues, it took away Bob Jones University's tax-exempt status because of its racist policies, even though the university claimed its belief that blacks and whites should be separate was divinely sanctioned.

This does not mean there should be no accommodation of religion. It does mean that when there should be an accommodation that is particular to religion, others should probably be eligible for the accommodation as well. McConnell maintains that in a "night watchman state," accommodation for religion is hardly an issue. With an activist government, however, a government that extends its reach to a "wide variety of social objectives . . . the conflicts with religious practice become frequent and intense."[7] Accommodation of religion is needed if we want to have both an activist state and religious freedom.

McConnell is right that conflicts between religion and the activist state are bound to happen. If they do happen, however, and the conflict should be resolved in favor of religion, there is no reason why others similarly situated should not also benefit from a similar resolution. It may be that sometimes the activist state is too activist. If we think the state is trampling on the consciences or rights of religious people, then it is probably trampling on the consciences or rights of others as well. This means one of two things should happen. The law that was passed is a bad law and should be overturned. Or exemptions to the law are needed. I can explain what I mean by using examples that have come up in previous chapters.

The Grove City College Bill gave religious institutions an exemption from the general prohibition against discrimination that institutions that have students with federal loans must follow. The idea here seems to be that some religious institutions by their very nature discriminate and so deserve an exemption. By why shouldn't other private institutions be allowed to discriminate as well? Why should religious institutions be privileged in this regard? I have already argued that equality of opportunity means that student loans should not have a nondiscriminatory rider attached to them. If religious institutions are allowed to discriminate and others cannot, then some people — those comfortable attending religious institutions — have more benefits than others.

Similarly, my argument that people with religious objections to course materials in public schools should be accommodated if it is feasible also applies to people with nonreligious objections. Why make the distinction between religious and nonreligious objections? I argued that public schools should cooperate with parochial schools; they should also cooperate with nonreligious private schools. The principle of inclusion that animated my argument for cooperation and accommodation in education applies to both religious and nonreligious people. McConnell mentions other important exemptions and accommodations that he thinks are particular to religion but for the most part should either be generalized to fit nonreligious people or struck down to fit no one. Let me quickly respond to some of the issues he raises. Jobs that are not crucial to equal citizenship, like the priesthood or Boy Scout troop leaders, should not be open to all. All minors should be able to drink alcohol under the supervision of their parents, guardians, or close relatives, at communion and elsewhere. Rules that mandate hardhats are either crucial to the health of the worker and so should be mandatory for all, or should be made optional for all workers. If the latter option is chosen, it should be done with the understanding that any worker that chooses not to wear a hardhat must sign a waiver of liability so the employer is not liable for any injury due to the worker's stupid decision not to wear a hardhat. I am inclined to think that employees should be given the option to do the stupid thing, as long as it does not interfere with their ability to do their job.

The Supreme Court has ruled that generally applicable laws apply to religion as well. Special exemptions for religion and religious conscience are now not allowed on the federal level.[8] This is not the last word on the matter, though, as this is an extremely controversial decision. Some states may pass laws giving religion special exemptions; the struggle about this at the federal level is not over. I don't want to comment on the constitutionality of the decision, though I agree with the decision as a matter of policy. What I do want to look at briefly is the matter at hand in the court case. A church in Boerne, Texas, wanted to expand to accommodate its growing membership. The city denied it permission to do so, arguing that the church was in a historic district, and was itself a historic building that ought to be preserved. The church argued that denying it the right to expand was too much of a burden on religion. The Supreme Court ruled, however, that the general law about preserving historic buildings applied to religious buildings as well, that there was no special exemption for religions from generally applicable laws.

This is good policy, but in this case I think the law about historic buildings goes too far. The church ought to be able to expand. The city does not own the church. The church was built to serve its congregation, not to please those who happened to pass by. The congregation expanded, and so the church should be able to change the building to fit its needs. But not only religions should be allowed to change churches in historic districts. Zoning laws should not automatically prevent people and organizations from changing their buildings. A historic commission should work with those in charge of the building to ensure that the building is changed in a way that fits with the original building's structure, and the buildings nearby. This solution was available to those in Boerne. Indeed, after the litigation was over the two sides sat down and hammered out a compromise that allowed the church to expand and keep the facade that the city wanted to preserve.

The effect of treating religion the same as other matters of conscience will sometimes expand religious freedom and sometimes restrict it. If all colleges and universities are allowed to discriminate even though some of their students receive federal aid, then some institutions that are affiliated with a church though not operated by one, like Georgetown University and Notre Dame, will benefit. A rule that all groups, religious or not, can meet on a school's ground benefits religious groups that might otherwise be (mistakenly) banned in the name of the establishment clause. Yet a rule that economic institutions cannot discriminate will mean that churches that own businesses will not be able to discriminate in those businesses. McConnell is right to point out that sometimes the activist state squeezes religious freedom. But when religious freedom is wrongly trampled on, then we should be concerned that the state is squeezing the freedom of nonreligious people as well.

Some people object to churches receiving tax exemptions. These people might object to religion in general, or to a particular religion, and they do not want to subsidize religions they find offensive. Yet the tax-exempt status that churches receive is given to all nonprofit organizations. This means that if we think of a tax exemption as a tax subsidy, then we all are bound to support organizations we dislike. Handgun Control, Inc. and the National Rifle Association, the Christian-led Family Research Council and the American Civil Liberties Union are all tax-exempt organizations. Few people will support all four of these organizations. There is no special reason to single out the tax-exempt status of churches as objectionable, since so many kinds of organizations are tax exempt. This leaves the larger question of why any organization should be tax exempt.

I am inclined to support tax exemption for nonprofit organizations as an indirect way to support civil society. Some organizations within civil society will be small and poor. Taxing them will mean that some will be unable to survive, or will be unable to do very much. Some nonprofits, of course, are quite wealthy: Harvard University will not be put out of business if it begins to pay taxes.[9] Still, there are enough small churches, synagogues, mosques, clubs, unions, fraternal associations, and so on that benefit greatly from being tax exempt. This is a small way that the government can encourage a vibrant civil society, and since the cost of doing so is relatively low it should continue the tax-exempt status for nonprofit organizations.[10]

Religion should not be treated as special in law or in policy. So, why, then did I write this book? Because religion plays a large and important role in liberal societies, more so than many other associations. While religion should rarely be treated differently as a matter of law, its social and political role will be quite important. Socially and politically, religion matters a lot. Conservative religions have considerable staying power: their beliefs are not set in stone, but they are less flexible than many others. Unlike other communities, religious communities are better able to resist the tendency of liberalism to undermine longstanding communities. Religious conservatives have a wide set of practices and beliefs that deviate from liberal values.

Furthermore, many religions have an institutional infrastructure that few other communities have and that makes them an important force in society. Many religions operate schools, universities, nursing homes, child-care facilities, camps, social-service agencies, charities, and even, in the case of Hasidic Jews, private ambulance services. Few other groups in liberal societies can claim to have such an extensive network of agencies. This network, of course, means that there is considerable interaction between religion and the state. Even if the rules that guide the relationship between religions and the state should be applied to other groups, the need for these rules will often arise because of the interaction between religion and the state and will most often be applied to religious groups.

Moreover, liberals often assume that religious people subvert liberal values. The challenge that religion poses for liberalism is an important one. The lessons learned from investigating these challenges will tell us much about how liberalism should respond to those who deviate from accepted liberal principles, even if these answers should apply to more than just religious people. The largest challenge that religions have is to maintain their group boundaries. Liberalism is very good at encouraging individual diversity, as I hope I have shown, but it does less in helping groups maintain their particular boundaries. The groups that will be able to best sustain their boundaries in a liberal state will be religious, particularly conservative and perhaps moderate ones. Figuring out how religious groups can sustain their boundaries in the liberal state will teach us much about group difference and individual diversity.

Unfortunately, the many recent debates and discussions of difference and diversity rarely mention religion. This may be because many people do not consider religious groups to be oppressed, and it is a concern for ending oppression that motivates many people to want to bring issues raised by diversity and difference to the forefront. Many people look at the subordination of women and see religion as part of the problem, not part of the solution. Yet there is no question that many people choose to belong to religions, sometimes to patriarchal religions. While liberals and advocates of difference may not like this choice, that is hardly reason to ignore or dismiss it. Any discussion of diversity and group life surely must take religion into account, since it is religious groups that will remain among the most different in a liberal society.

I suspect that another reason why many liberals and multiculturalists don't discuss religion enough, at least not the conservative kinds, is that they have little sympathy for the reasons why people are religious. Many follow Mill and Dewey's view that revealed religion stands in the ways of progress and independent thinking.[11] Sometimes religion is an obstacle to progress; sometimes religious people have irrational fears of science; and sometimes religions stand in the way of liberal values. There is no reason to think well of all religious views or of every religion. But this is hardly *always* the case. Still, when liberals think that religion is the opiate of the masses, they would be better off if they were less angry with religion and more interested in improving liberal society.

Liberal societies have a variety of ills that may make some people rather disenchanted. The great economic uncertainty and insecurity, or the materialism, or the crime, or the poverty, or the cynicism that sometimes inflicts liberal society has led some people into the arms of religions, often conservative ones. I have not said much about the role of religious conservatives in contemporary politics in these pages. Clearly, some of the policies that they push for are worrisome. Yet when public schools cannot teach well, when random violence is on the increase, and greed becomes acceptable, it is no wonder that some people look to alternatives to liberalism to change society. To be sure, many of the problems of the United States cannot be traced to liberalism, but liberalism has not always articulated convincing responses to these problems.

These, of course, are not the only reasons why people seek out conservative religions, but they surely account for some of the reasons why many people are turning today to conservative religions.

As liberals try to figure out ways to improve liberal society, they should not cede important issues to religious conservatives. The family is an important institution, one that is crucial for the moral education of children. There is no reason why liberals should not say this, and try to figure out ways to bolster families. Sometimes schools are hostile to religion, and sometimes schools do teach a mindless relativism. Liberals should not accept this any more than conservatives do.

Liberals who are concerned about religious conservatives should worry less about their threat to liberalism and more about the state of liberal society. An improved liberal society will make conservative religions a less attractive option for many. I don't want to pretend that a better liberal society spells the demise of conservative religions. I suspect they will still survive, but probably with fewer members than they currently have. That they will survive is, in an odd way, testimony to the strength of liberalism.

Surviving Diversity

Not all religions present a challenge to liberalism. Liberalism shapes religion, and a liberal religion is compatible with membership in other communities. Liberal religions rarely insist that they have found the only way to salvation; they are able to cooperate with other religions, support the key liberal virtues of autonomy and diversity, and subscribe to the tenets of modern science. A liberal religion is ecumenical, one that sees many paths to salvation. It will seek cooperation with other churches. Its members will typically be members of other organizations, their lives not shaped by one moral community. It will have reconciled the Bible with modern science and with liberal values. A liberal religion will not disdain homosexuals or think of women as inferior to men. A liberal religion will also be compatible with the idea of liberal diversity, and sometimes even promote the idea. Driven by the idea of diversity, a liberal religion will strive to be inclusive, and treat all its members equally. It will also play down the differences between members and nonmembers. Liberal religions exist, of course. There are liberal Catholics, Reform Jews, and a variety of liberal Protestant churches. The seeds of many of these tenets of a liberal religion can be found in John Locke's writings on toleration and Christianity.

Since the Enlightenment, and particularly since Darwin, many people have not wanted to give up on their religious faith and yet want to adhere to liberal democratic principles. The results of this are easy enough to see. Some religions eschew the idea of patriarchy. There are women rabbis, priests, and ministers in the more liberal Protestant and Jewish denominations. Prayerbooks have been rewritten and religious services revamped to become more egalitarian. Some prayers and parts of the Bible seem rather bloodthirsty to the modern eye. Liberal religions try to explain away, change, or ignore these passages. Many liberal religions claim the Bible isn't to be taken literally but metaphorically. Many, too, have either softened or given up on the injunction to proselytize, thinking that this will offend others, or that conversion is unimportant since there are several paths to God.

The move toward inclusion is, of course, part of the reason why some Catholics support the right to abortion and women as priests in the church, and explains the call to include non-Jewish spouses in the services at Jewish synagogues and temples. Perhaps the most significant effect of the liberal norms of nondiscrimination and inclusion has been the increase of intermarriages. Intermarriages bring up a host of boundary problems. Can one family be both Lutheran and Jewish? How can the children believe in both faiths? Of course, many liberal religions do draw boundaries somewhere and not all recognize intermarriages. Nonetheless, liberal religions relax the rules of exclusion. Indeed, many religions in America face pressure to ease their rules. Instead of taking church rules as given by God, or as structured by a religious hierarchy, many people think that the ideals of liberal inclusion and liberal democracy fit not only politics, but also their church.

The democratization of religion is widespread and has affected conservative religions as well. This concerns the theologian Stanley Hauerwas, who complains that Christians want to make their church resemble the democratic polity. They think that the church should become internally democratic and inclusive and based on interests.[12] If the church has rules that its members do not want, Hauerwas says, the members seek to change their rules. This is certainly what Call to Action wants to do with the Catholic Church. But churches are not the same as a democratic polity. Hauerwas argues that it is not up to the members to decide when the rules change. God-given rules should not be subject to democratic pressures. Hauerwas complains that members of Protestant churches "now depend less on belief in the particular theological and ecclesial heritage of that denomination than on how that religious organization provides a means for individuals to express their particular interests."[13] He warns Catholics that if they are not careful they will become like Protestants — a number of denominations catering to the different interests and desires of people who claim to have the same core beliefs.

The American Catholic Church has not (yet?) become like mainline Protestantism, but it has been influenced by the larger liberal culture in other ways. Many Catholic dioceses now have altar girls. Similarly, some Orthodox Jewish girls celebrate their entry into the community as an adult with a bat mitzvah. To be sure, the requirements of the bat mitzvah are not as stringent as the bar mitzvah (the celebration for boys), and it is generally not as a festive occasion among the Orthodox as the bar mitzvah. Nonetheless, its existence among the Orthodox is a new phenomenon that shows the influence of liberal democracy on some varieties of Orthodox Judaism. Of course, the influence of liberalism has not been as far-reaching on conservative religions as it has been on liberal religions, but its influence is nonetheless easily seen.

The liberal emphasis on choice is bound to seep into some religions. Many people feel free to shape and reshape traditional beliefs so they are more to their liking.[14] When people reshape religion to their liking, however, it does not always have the same longstanding appeal as do less malleable religions. Liberal religions are often reshaped. They are also declining in membership.[15] The problem is that many people do not see much religious about liberal religions. It is not surprising that many liberal religions have turned to social and political action, an important way to cooperate with and help others. It is also an activity that can be inspired by the Bible. Yet a porous community that cooperates with others, that preaches that other ways of life and other ways of worshiping God are just as valid as theirs, and that participates in social and political action, does not have enough singularity to hold onto its membership. If a person participates in a church because of its activity in the nuclear freeze movement, he might be tempted one day to join a group whose main focus is the nuclear freeze. Or he may turn away from the church as its interest in the nuclear freeze declines and it turns to another issue he finds less interesting. His children may find that the church offers them little if they have little interest in its social or political agenda. They may very well marry or become partners with someone who is not a member of the church. Since they are taught that there are many legitimate ways to worship God or live a good life, why make the distinction between those in the church and those who are out?

Religions that are deeply shaped by liberalism will find that they often do not offer their members enough of an incentive to stay. This is probably even more true for a vague liberal religion like Mill and Dewey's Religion of Humanity or religious humanism. There is not much within them to retain many people's allegiance. I don't want to dismiss liberal religions as hollow. Unlike the Religion of Humanity, liberal religions based in longstanding traditions have certain rituals and beliefs that will attract some people. Liberal religions will offer their members a source of spirituality and community that many people will find important and satisfying. For many, their liberal religion is quite important. Yet there is still the problem of retaining their members' children, who may very well intermarry and find other sources of spirituality and community.

By emphasizing autonomy and inclusion, liberal diversity leads people to make their own choices about their lives, and to readily accept others. This doctrine, however, does little to help groups maintain their differences, since it leads to inclusion, not separation. Theorists of cultural recognition only give national minorities specific rights to exclusion and separation, which does little for the many groups, including most religious ones, which are not national minorities. It's not easy for groups to survive diversity, since to do so they must keep separate from others without state support. That liberal institutions usually encourage inclusion makes it even harder for groups to remain distinct within the liberal state. But conservative religions, more than most other groups, have a way to remain separate and retain their identity.

Liberal religions may find themselves competing with secular organizations that have liberal social and political commitments, but conservative religions declare that their way to heaven is the only way. This declaration will find few secular competitors. Moreover, these religions will tell their children that there is only one path to salvation and that whom they marry (and most assume that their children will marry someone of the opposite sex) matters a lot. Marrying outside the faith often results in severe condemnation or even shunning. The difference between insiders and outsiders for conservative religions is an important one. Conservative religions often try to ensure that their children are raised in rather closed worlds. The rules of a moral community keep the members together, providing clear boundaries to mark who is a member and who is not. These rules and the goods that conservative religions promise to people, like eternal salvation, give a very clear reason why people should join or remain a member of the religion. The amount of insularity — and number and scope of rules of the moral community — will depend on the particular religion. On balance conservative religions will have some amount of insularity, and liberal ones will have little. The more insular the religion, the less chance there is for the children to stray from the preferred path.

This all partly explains why conservative religions can retain their members and their members' children, but people can leave these religions if they wish. What is it about conservative religions that people find attractive? I can't touch upon all the reasons, but certainly it has something to do with the limits of liberalism. Liberalism is a moral doctrine, but it is purposefully not all-encompassing. It gives people space to find many of their own moral values. Some people are on a search for purity. They want to cleanse their souls and a strict religion provides them with the resources to do so.[16] Churches, particularly conservative religions, offer people a tight moral structure that many like. Other people are attracted to a particular religion simply because they think it is true. Others may join because they like a particular minister or rabbi. There are surely other reasons why people become or remain religious.

Whatever the reasons, conservative religions will be in constant tension with liberalism. Some people will leave their tightly structured moral communities because they want to live differently than the community prescribes. Obviously, the number of people who have left conservative religions over the past couple of centuries — or who have stayed only because their religion has become more liberal — is quite large. The people who leave conservative religions will sometimes become completely nonreligious. Many others, however, will still want some of the goods that religion offers, and will find a more liberal religion to join. What is liberal is relative to the religion that you leave: so people who leave Amish communities often become Mennonite, Orthodox Jews become Conservative Jews, Conservative Jews become Reformed, and so on. If this happens enough, liberal (and moderate) religions will find that they survive on the outcasts of their more conservative cousins. Another possibility is that as conservative churches become larger and more successful, the discipline they try to impose on their members begins to crumble, and they become more liberal as time goes on. There is some evidence that this happens to Christian churches.[17]

Then there is the counterreaction: the children of some religious liberals turn to a more conservative church.[18] How many will join conservative religions? Will it always be this way? I don't know and I want to stay away from the prophecy business. The tensions I have described between conservative religions and liberalism, and the difficulties liberal religions face in a liberal democracy, mean there is no clear way to predict how religion will fare in liberal societies. The culture of a liberal society makes it harder for conservative communities to remain partly closed, yet religious conservatives are often better than religious liberals at offering their members the distinctive benefits of a longstanding community. Moderate religions try to strike a balance between offering their members the good of community and the goods of liberal communities. How well religions do in a liberal society will depend on many factors, including the history of the religion in the particular country, the laws of the state, the charisma of the religious leaders, and the state of liberal society.

Regardless of whether religions grow or decline, liberalism must allow people to choose to live among religious conservatives. People in a liberal society should be able to choose the life they want to lead, even if it is illiberal, and even if it is a life that liberals find incomprehensible. The liberal state should protect people's choices as long as they do not harm others. Liberals should respect the choice of people to be religious if that is what they want.

Notes

1 | Introduction

1. I agree that since the two religions of the parents were starkly incompatible, the court had to decide which religion the children should be raised in. Since the parents originally agreed to raise their children as Jewish, and the mother had physical custody of the children (though the parents had joint custody), putting the children's religious upbringing in her hands seems to make the most sense. See *Kendall v Kendall* 426 MA 238 (1997).

2. Avishai Margalit, *The Decent Society* (Cambridge: Harvard University Press, 1996), 178.

3. John Stuart Mill, *On Liberty* (1859); reprinted in *On Liberty and Other Essays,* ed. John Gray (Oxford: Oxford University Press, 1991), 67, 65. Defining *culture* is notoriously difficult and I won't attempt to provide a definition here. I think it will be clear as this book unfolds that my starting point is a society that holds within it several kinds of communities, many of which overlap to different degrees. Some of these communities may also constitute a culture, while others may not.

4. Eamonn Callan, *Creating Citizens: Political Education and Liberal Democracy* (Oxford: Oxford University Press, 1997).

5. These arguments are made by Will Kymlicka in *Liberalism, Community and Culture* (Oxford: Oxford University Press, 1989) and *Multicultural Citizenship: A Liberal Theory of Minority Rights* (Oxford: Oxford University Press, 1995) and by Joseph Raz in *The Morality of Freedom* (Oxford: Clarendon, 1986) and *Ethics in the Public Domain: Essays in the Morality of Law and Politics* (Oxford: Oxford University Press, 1994).

6. Edited volumes include Will Kymlicka, ed., *The Rights of Minority Cultures* (Oxford: Oxford University Press, 1995); Seyla Benhabib, ed., *Democracy and Difference: Contesting the Boundaries of the Political* (Princeton: Princeton University Press, 1996); and Judith Baker, ed., *Group Rights* (Toronto: University of Toronto Press, 1994). Book-length treatments include Kymlicka, *Liberalism, Community, and Culture;* Iris Marion Young, *Justice and the Politics of Difference* (Princeton: Princeton University

Press, 1990); and my own *Boundaries of Citizenship: Race, Ethnicity and Nationality in the Liberal State* (Baltimore: Johns Hopkins University Press, 1994). Tariq Modood criticizes the lack of attention paid to religious groups in the literature on difference and diversity in "'Race' in Britain and the Politics of Difference," in *Philosophy and Pluralism,* ed. D. Archard (Cambridge: Cambridge University Press, 1996) and Modood, "Anti-Essentialism, Multiculturalism, and the 'Recognition' of Religious Groups," *Journal of Political Philosophy* 6, no. 4 (December 1998): 378–99.

7. Robert K. Fullinwider, *Public Education in a Multicultural Society: Policy, Theory, Critique* (Cambridge: Cambridge University Press, 1996), 15.

8. James Davison Hunter, *Culture Wars: The Struggle to Define America* (New York: Basic Books, 1991), 43–46.

9. There is a subtle distinction between Protestant evangelicalism and Protestant fundamentalism which is often overlooked. All fundamentalists are evangelicals, but not all evangelicals are fundamentalists. Both evangelicals and fundamentalists believe in the literal truth of the Bible, but evangelicals are less militant about their views. Evangelicals are more willing to entertain interpretive arguments about the Bible. Fundamentalists are less apt to cooperate with other churches in interfaith matters or attend mainstream universities than are evangelicals. Many fundamentalists dislike Billy Graham for his cooperation with nonevangelicals, for example. Fundamentalists are more apt to fight modernist theology and secular humanism.

10. The debate that classical liberals had about religion that resonates the most today is about the relationship between morality and religion. I return to this issue in chapter 4, where I look again at Locke, Mill, and Dewey.

11. Locke argued against toleration of those who were loyal to "another prince" (like the Pope).

12. *Letter Concerning Toleration* (1689; reprint, Indianapolis: Hackett, 1983), 51. Trust in Locke is a theme that looms large in the work of John Dunn. See his *The Political Thought of John Locke: An Historical Account of the Argument of the Two Treatises of Government* (Cambridge: Cambridge University Press, 1969) and *Rethinking Modern Political Theory* (Cambridge: Cambridge University Press, 1985).

13. Locke, *Letter Concerning Toleration,* 23, 35, 31.

14. Ibid., 31, 34.

15. John Locke, *An Essay Concerning Human Understanding* (1690); reprinted in 2 vols., ed. Alexander Campbell Fraser (New York: Dover Publications, 1959), vol. 2, book 4, chap. 19, paras. 4, 8, 10, 14; and Locke, *The Second Treatise of Government* (1690; reprint, ed. C. B. Macpherson, Indianapolis: Hackett, 1980), II, paras. 25, 26, 31–34.

16. Locke was clearly influenced by Socianism. Socians denied the Trinity (which is nowhere mentioned in the Bible; they refused to believe that Christ existed before the virgin birth), and refused to believe in original sin or predestination, because both denied man's responsibility for his actions. Socians insisted upon God's justice and

thought that Christ's resurrection showed that man could become immortal and be offered a moral law. On the relationship between Locke and Socianism see David Wooton, "John Locke: Socianian or Natural Law Theorist?," in *Religion, Secularization, and Political Thought: Thomas Hobbes to J. S. Mill,* ed. James E. Crimmins (London: Routledge, 1989). For Locke's questioning that original sin is charged upon all humans, see John Locke, *The Reasonableness of Christianity* (1695; reprint, Washington, D.C.: Regnery Gateway, 1965), 4-5.

17. Locke, *Essay Concerning Human Understanding,* 4.10. I should note that as he got older, Locke became less confident that people could use their reason to discover morality and the principles of justice. Locke, *Reasonableness of Christianity,* 170-76.

18. John Locke, *A Third Letter Concerning Toleration* (1797), reprinted in vol. 7 of *Works,* 10th ed. (London: T. Davison, 1801), 144; Locke, *A Second Letter Concerning Toleration* (1796), reprinted in vol. 7 of *Works,* 10th ed. (London: T. Davison, 1801), 62.

19. John Stuart Mill, "Utility of Religion," in *Three Essays on Religion* (New York: Henry Holt, 1874), 99-100.

20. Mill, *On Liberty and Other Essays,* 56-57.

21. Ibid., 55-56.

22. John Stuart Mill, "Theism," in *Three Essays on Religion,* 253, 255; Mill, *Blakey's History of Moral Science* (1833); reprinted in *Collected Works,* vol. 10, ed. J. M. Robson (Toronto: University of Toronto Press, 1969), 28; Mill, "Utility of Religion," 99, 97.

23. John Stuart Mill, *Coleridge* (1840), reprinted in *Utilitarianism and Other Essays,* ed. Alan Ryan (Harmondsworth: Penguin, 1987), 222, 178.

24. Mill, "Utility of Religion," 109.

25. John Dewey, *A Common Faith* (New Haven: Yale University Press, 1934), 9, 47.

26. Quoted in Steven C. Rockefeller, *John Dewey: Religious Faith and Democratic Humanism* (New York: Columbia University Press, 1991), 449.

27. Dewey, *Common Faith,* 53.

28. Ibid., 31; John Dewey, *The Quest for Certainty* (1929); reprinted in *The Later Works: 1925–1953,* 17 vols., ed. Jo Ann Boydston (Carbondale: University of Southern Illinois Press, 1984), vol. 4.

29. Rockefeller, *John Dewey,* 434.

30. To give a full account of Locke, Mill, and Dewey's views on religion would be to write another book. I have found the best sources on Locke and religion to be Dunn, *Political Thought of John Locke,* and the more ponderous though useful John Marshall, *John Locke: Resistance, Religion and Responsibility* (Cambridge: Cambridge University Press, 1994). Good sources on Dewey include Alan Ryan, *John Dewey and the High Tide of American Liberalism* (New York: Norton, 1995), and Robert B. Westbrook, *John Dewey and American Democracy* (Ithaca, N.Y.: Cornell University Press, 1991), but the best source on Dewey's religious views is Rockefeller, *John Dewey.* Most of the secondary literature on Mill gives scant attention to his views on religion. One

exception (which includes a discussion of Locke) is Eldon J. Eisenach, *Two Worlds of Liberalism: Religion and Politics in Hobbes, Locke and Mill* (Chicago: University of Chicago Press, 1981).

31. Mill, "Utility of Religion," 117-19.

2 | *The Limits of Cultural Recognition*

1. Susan D. Rose describes a community of Protestant charismatics, who are mostly college educated and who decided to become devout as adults, in *Keeping Them Out of the Hands of Satan* (New York: Routledge, 1988). Robert Eisenberg describes a variety of Hasidic Jews, some of whom join the Hasidim as adults in *Boychicks in the Hood: Travels in the Hasidic Underground* (San Francisco: Harper, 1995). Many of the people Eisenberg discusses were born into the Hasidic or Ultraorthodox communities and are obviously aware of the outside world.

2. Michael Sandel, *Democracy's Discontent: America in Search of a Public Philosophy* (Cambridge: Harvard University Press, 1996), 66-71.

3. Alexis de Tocqueville, *Democracy in America* (1835); reprint, ed. J. P. Mayer and Max Lerner, trans. George Lawrence (New York: Harper and Row, 1966), 291.

4. See Paul Johnson's brilliant little book, *A Shopkeeper's Millennium: Society and Revivals in Rochester, New York, 1815-1837* (New York: Hill and Wang, 1978).

5. Ibid.

6. George M. Marsden, *The Soul of the University: From Protestant Establishment to Established Nonbelief* (Oxford: Oxford University Press, 1994); Sarah Barringer Gordon, "The Second American Disestablishment: Blasphemy, Polygamy, and Church-State Relations in the Nineteenth Century," 1997, unpublished typescript, University of Pennsylvania, 1997.

7. For Protestantism's influence on society and its decline toward the end of the nineteenth century see George Marsden, *Fundamentalism and American Culture: The Shaping of Twentieth-Century Evangelicalism* (Oxford: Oxford University Press, 1980); Robert Handy, *Undermined Establishment: Church-State Relations in America, 1880-1920* (Princeton: Princeton University Press, 1991).

8. John Stuart Mill, *On Liberty* (1859); reprinted in *On Liberty and Other Essays*, ed. John Gray (Oxford: Oxford University Press, 1991), 64, 67.

9. Joseph Raz, *The Morality of Freedom* (Oxford: Clarendon, 1986), 373.

10. "We may indeed lament the limited space, as it were, of social worlds, and of ours in particular. . . . [T]here is no social world without loss; that is, no social world that does not exclude some ways of life." John Rawls, *Political Liberalism* (New York: Columbia University Press, 1993), 197. This admission that no state can be completely neutral is not as extensive as Raz's argument, which I describe presently. Rawls also argues that matters of citizenship constrain the state's neutrality, a matter I discuss further in chapter 4.

11. Raz, *Morality of Freedom,* 392.

12. Joseph Raz, *Ethics in the Public Domain: Essays in the Morality of Law and Politics* (Oxford: Oxford University Press, 1994), 120.

13. Raz, *Morality of Freedom,* 162.

14. Ibid., 374.

15. Ibid., 372–78.

16. Raz, *Ethics in the Public Domain,* 178.

17. Ibid., 177, 178.

18. Ibid., 120.

19. Raz, *Morality of Freedom,* 372, 424.

20. Raz, *Ethics in the Public Domain,* 190, 187, 184, 181.

21. Ibid., 187, 189, 182, 187.

22. Raz, *Morality of Freedom,* 424. Kymlicka has a similar view of tolerance toward illiberal communities.

23. Will Kymlicka, *Liberalism, Community, and Culture* (Oxford: Oxford University Press, 1989).

24. Ibid., 165.

25. Will Kymlicka, *Multicultural Citizenship: A Liberal Theory of Minority Rights* (Oxford: Oxford University Press, 1995), 76.

26. Ibid., 76, 79.

27. Kymlicka says indigenous peoples are an example of a societal culture, but it is not clear that they actually fit his criteria for one. Indigenous peoples are often very small, and usually do not have the people or the resources to be institutionally embodied in the way Kymlicka says societal cultures must be. See Kymlicka's comments on indigenous peoples in *Multicultural Citizenship,* 100.

It is worth noting that Kymlicka argues that all societal cultures should protect the civil rights of its members, but Kymlicka is sensitive to the problem of imposition. He is not willing to impose civil rights on national minorities. He thinks national minorities have to be the ones to decide to protect their civil rights. To explain this, he makes an analogy with sovereign communities. Just as the United States does not tell Saudi Arabia that it must protect the civil rights of its members, so the United States cannot tell its indigenous communities to protect their members' civil rights. Ibid., 164–65.

28. Ibid., 165.

29. Ibid., 41–42, 170; Will Kymlicka, "An Update from the Multiculturalism Wars: Comments on Shachar and Spinner-Halev," in *Multicultural Questions,* ed. Steve Lukes and Christian Joppke (Oxford: Oxford University Press, 1999).

30. Kymlicka, *Liberalism, Community, and Culture,* chap. 2; Kymlicka, *Multicultural Citizenship,* 159–60.

31. Kymlicka does say that certain religious groups have more rights than other polyethnic groups because historical agreements were made between these religious groups and the state. But Kymlicka doesn't like these agreements and suggests they are

regrettable, unjust, should be not repeated, and are not to be completely respected. He resolutely states that we should "draw a sharp distinction between the claims of older established religious groups, and the claims of newly emerging religious groups," accommodating the former but not the latter. As a matter of philosophical principle (rather than historical agreement), Kymlicka says religious groups do not deserve special group rights, and the state should do what it can to impress upon its members the norms of liberal citizenship. In any case, Kymlicka suggests that all insular religious groups should be forced to grant civil liberties to their members regardless of their historical agreements. (This is a little confusing, however, since religious groups in the societies that Kymlicka discusses, the United States and Canada, cannot restrict their members' civil rights. They may be able to pressure their members in various ways, but that is much different than denying them their civil rights.) Kymlicka, *Multicultural Citizenship,* 170, 235 n. 19, 161-62, 202 n. 1; Will Kymlicka, "Ethnic Associations and Democratic Citizenship," in *Freedom of Association,* ed. Amy Gutmann (Princeton: Princeton University Press, 1998), 191; Kymlicka, "Update from the Multiculturalism Wars."

32. Mark Blasius, "An Ethos of Lesbian and Gay Existence," *Political Theory* 20 (1992): 647. Blasius argues, however, that a gay and lesbian counterculture doesn't exist. Only some lesbians and gays live in gay ghettos; most live scattered throughout society. Without taking issue with Blasius, I only want to note that my argument does not presuppose a gay and lesbian counterculture; only that gays and lesbians have some specific cultural practices that are not shared with others in society. For a fuller account of gay life in America see Neil Miller, *In Search of Gay America* (New York: Atlantic Monthly Press, 1989).

33. Nancy Fraser, "Rethinking the Public Square: A Contribution to the Critique of Actually Existing Democracy," in *Rethinking the Public Square,* ed. Craig Calhoun (Cambridge: MIT Press, 1992), 127.

34. Nancy Fraser, *Justice Interruptus: Critical Reflections on the Postsocialist Condition* (New York: Routledge, 1997), 201-2.

35. Fraser, "Rethinking the Public Square," 123-24, 126.

36. Ibid., 126, 127.

37. Ibid., 127.

38. Fraser, *Justice Interruptus,* 189-205.

39. Fraser, "Rethinking the Public Square," 121, 125.

40. Fraser criticizes Young on these and other grounds in *Justice Interruptus,* 189-205.

41. Iris Marion Young, "Polity and Group Difference: A Critique of the Ideal of Universal Citizenship," *Ethics* 9, no. 2 (January 1989), 163, 40.

42. Ibid., 163.

43. Iris Marion Young, *Justice and the Politics of Difference* (Princeton: Princeton University Press, 1990), 48, 173.

44. Ibid., 86.

45. Ibid., 173.

46. I have given a similar account of inclusion and diversity in Jeff Spinner, *The Boundaries of Citizenship: Race, Ethnicity, and Nationality in the Liberal State* (Baltimore: Johns Hopkins University Press, 1994); and Jeff Spinner-Halev, "Difference and Diversity in an Egalitarian Democracy," *Journal of Political Philosophy* 3, no. 3 (September 1995): 259-79.

47. I discuss these limits in *Boundaries of Citizenship,* chap. 3.

48. Raz, *Ethics in the Public Domain,* 189.

49. Ibid., 189; see also 188.

50. Ibid., 188.

51. Geoff Levey points out how Kymlicka assumes too easily that all polyethnic rights are matters of inclusion instead of exclusion in "Equality, Autonomy, and Cultural Rights," *Political Theory* 25, no. 2 (April 1997): 221.

52. Kymlicka, *Multicultural Citizenship,* 176-81.

53. Social equality is another matter, and I return to it in chapter 7.

54. J. L. Mackie, "Can There Be a Rights-Based Moral Theory?" *Midwest Studies in Philosophy* 3 (1978): 354-55; quoted in Raz, *Morality of Freedom,* 370.

55. Raz, *Morality of Freedom,* 391, 394. My emphasis.

56. W. J. Norman notes this as well in his perceptive critique of Raz in "The Autonomy-Based Liberalism of Joseph Raz," *Canadian Journal of Law and Jurisprudence* 2, no. 2 (July 1989).

57. Rose, *Keeping Them Out of the Hands of Satan;* Eisenberg, *Boychicks in the Hood.*

58. Mill, *On Liberty and Other Essays,* 73, 58.

59. Levey, "Equality, Autonomy, and Cultural Rights," 227.

3 | *Autonomy and the Religious Life*

1. Joseph Raz, *The Morality of Freedom* (Oxford: Clarendon, 1986), 155.

2. Will Kymlicka, *Multicultural Citizenship: A Liberal Theory of Minority Rights* (Oxford: Oxford University Press, 1995), 35-44.

3. Avishai Margalit and Moshe Halbertal, "Liberalism and the Right to Culture," *Social Research* 61, no. 3 (Fall 1994): 505.

4. Will Kymlicka, *Liberalism, Community, and Culture* (Oxford: Oxford University Press, 1989), 189-92; Kymlicka, *Multicultural Citizenship,* 110.

5. Ibid., 41, 204 n. 11.

6. Raz, *Morality of Freedom,* 205.

7. Kymlicka, *Liberalism, Community, and Culture,* 165.

8. Joseph Raz, *Ethics in the Public Domain: Essays in the Morality of Law and Politics* (Oxford: Oxford University Press, 1994), 176.

9. I discuss these external restrictions in more depth in chapter 7. Here I concen-

trate on internal restrictions, though I also return to some discriminatory internal restrictions having to do with gender and equality in chapter 7.

10. I say "some," since many poor people have limited options in many liberal societies. Hopefully, this failure of liberal practice will one day be rectified.

11. Stephen G. Gilles, "On Educating Children: A Parentalist Manifesto," *University of Chicago Law Review* 63, no. 3 (Summer 1996): 971 (emphasis removed).

12. Gilles argues that strong communities can support autonomy, but he never suggests that some communities are so encompassing that they do not support autonomy very well. This seems obviously true, even if these communities are still compatible with liberalism. See ibid.

13. Raz, *Morality of Freedom*, 414.

14. It is common for the Amish, the Haredim, and other religious conservatives to boycott the stores of apostates.

15. Ibid., 206, 391.

16. Ibid., 377–78.

17. Eamonn Callan, *Creating Citizens: Political Education and Liberal Democracy* (Oxford: Oxford University Press, 1997), 35.

18. Jeremy Waldron also finds Raz's thin comments on manipulation to be oddly brief and unsatisfactory. He tries to redefine Raz's manipulation condition as purposefully inculcating a belief you know to be false into someone else. While I think Waldron's definition is often true, I'm skeptical that passing on false beliefs is always wrong. If in 1960 a three-year-old Black child says he wanted to be President of the United States, should his parents immediately squash this desire, and deflate their child's hopes and dreams? Or should they wait until he is older to tell him the reach of racism? Jeremy Waldron, "Autonomy and Perfectionism in Raz's *Morality of Freedom*," *Southern California Law Review* 62, nos. 3–4 (March–May 1989): 1097–1152.

19. Leslie Green, "Internal Minorities and Their Rights," in *Group Rights,* ed. Judith Baker (Toronto: University of Toronto Press, 1994), 111.

20. Ibid., 114.

21. Ibid., 111.

22. My account of the Hutterites comes from John Hostetler, *Hutterite Society* (Baltimore: Johns Hopkins University Press, 1975). The Hutterites don't own televisions or radios; each colony has a few cars and trucks so members can go into the city when needed. They wear simple clothes, live in community-built housing, and eat together in the common dining hall. They rarely take long trips. To a large degree, the colonies are self-sufficient. While they buy certain large items that they can't make themselves, they build their own housing and furnishing, weave their own clothes, and make their own wine.

23. *Hofer v Hofer* (1970) 13 DLR (3d) 1 (Supreme Court of Canada).

24. Although the colony should be treated like a corporation when it comes to its interactions with outsiders. For example, when it comes to liability issues if the colony

isn't treated like a corporation people with claims against a member of the colony wouldn't be able to collect anything. There would be no way to tax the colony's income. Other similar issues arise, meaning that in the colonies' external relations with others we should think of them as a corporation.

25. While Hutterites are aware of the outside world, this does not mean they have the necessary knowledge to navigate through it very well. How to find a place to stay for the night, how to look for a job, how to open up a bank account—mundane matters like these which are necessary to live in the world outside the colonies aren't known by most Hutterites.

26. Few groups hold property communally. One that does, Israeli kibbutzim, usually gives departing members some form of compensation.

27. I'm thinking here of national minorities, like native peoples in the United States and Canada that have a strong claim to be thought of as sovereign communities.

28. Alan Peshkin, *God's Choice: The Total World of a Fundamentalist Christian School* (Chicago: University of Chicago Press, 1986), 8, 9, 44, 127.

29. Ibid., 94.

30. Chandran Kukathas, "Cultural Toleration," in *Ethnicity and Group Rights,* ed. Will Kymlicka and Ian Shapiro (New York: New York University, 1996), 98, 97, 88.

31. Ibid., 88–89.

32. Ibid., 97.

33. Chandran Kukathas, "Are There Any Cultural Rights?," *Political Theory* 20, no. 1 (February 1992).

34. Ibid., 134.

35. I further defend the rights of communities to define their rules of membership in chapter 7.

4 | *Morality and Citizenship*

1. Will Kymlicka, "An Update from the Multiculturalism Wars: Comments on Shachar and Spinner-Halev," in *Multicultural Questions,* ed. Steve Lukes and Christian Joppke (Oxford: Oxford University Press, 1999).

2. Ibid.

3. Jeff Spinner, *The Boundaries of Citizenship: Race, Ethnicity, and Nationality in the Liberal State* (Baltimore: Johns Hopkins University Press, 1994), chap. 5; Jeff Spinner-Halev, "Cultural Pluralism and Partial Citizenship," in *Multicultural Questions,* ed. Lukes and Joppke, 65–86..

4. Eamonn Callan, *Creating Citizens: Political Education and Liberal Democracy* (Oxford: Oxford University Press, 1997); William Galston, *Liberal Purposes: Goods, Virtues, and Diversity in the Liberal State* (Cambridge: Cambridge University Press, 1991); Amy Gutmann and Dennis Thompson, *Democracy and Disagreement: Why Moral Conflict Cannot Be Avoided in Politics and What Should Be Done about It* (Cambridge: Harvard

University Press, 1996); Amy Gutmann, "Civic Education and Social Diversity," *Ethics* 105 (April 1995); Stephen Macedo, *Liberal Virtues: Citizenship, Virtue and Community in Liberal Constitutionalism* (Oxford: Oxford University Press, 1990).

5. Alexis de Tocqueville, *Democracy in America* (1835); reprint, ed. J. P. Mayer and Max Lerner, trans. George Lawrence (New York: Harper and Row, 1966), 290–93. Contemporary authors who echo Tocqueville's argument include A. James Reichley, *Religion in American Public Life* (Washington, D.C.: Brookings Institute, 1985) and Stephen Carter, *The Culture of Disbelief: How American Law and Politics Trivialize Religious Devotion* (New York: Basic Books, 1993). See also Philip Johnson, *Reason in the Balance: The Case Against Naturalism in Science, Law, and Education* (Downers Grove, Ill.: Intervarsity Press, 1995).

6. See Carter, *Culture of Disbelief,* 35-36 (where he relies on Tocqueville); Reichley, *Religion in American Public Life,* 359; Clarke E. Cochran, *Religion in Public and Private Life* (New York: Routledge, 1990), 56.

7. John Locke, *An Essay Concerning Human Understanding* (1690); reprinted in 2 vols., ed. Alexander Campbell Fraser (New York: Dover Publications, 1959), bk. 1, chap. 2, para. 7; Locke, *The Reasonableness of Christianity* (1695; reprint, Washington, D.C.: Regnery Gateway, 1965), 185.

8. John Stuart Mill, "Utility of Religion," in *Three Essays on Religion* (New York: Henry Holt, 1874), 90.

9. Ibid. David Hume made a slightly different argument against the idea of heaven and hell: "Heaven and hell suppose two distinct species of men, the good and the bad. But the greatest part of mankind float between virtue and vice." David Hume, *Essays: Moral, Political and Literary* (1777); reprint, ed. Eugene Miller (Indianapolis: Liberty Classics, 1985), 594.

10. John Stuart Mill, "Nature," in *Three Essays on Religion,* 50, 53; Mill, "Utility of Religion," 81.

11. John Locke, "Some Thoughts Concerning Education" (1693); reprinted in *The Educational Writings of John Locke,* ed. James L. Axtell (Cambridge: Cambridge University Press, 1968), 241-42, 143, 140.

12. Richard John Neuhaus, *The Naked Public Square: Religion and Democracy in America,* 2nd ed. (Grand Rapids, Mich.: Eerdmans, 1986), 82-86; Carter, *Culture of Disbelief,* 38.

13. Neuhaus, *Naked Public Square,* 86.

14. Ibid., 82, 84.

15. Sidney Verba, Kay Lehman Schlozman, and Henry E. Brady, *Voice and Equality: Civic Voluntarism in American Politics* (Cambridge: Harvard University Press, 1995), 320.

16. Ibid., 320-24. This corresponds to Robert Putnam's results, who found that civic engagement was negatively correlated with Catholic religiosity in Italy, because the Catholic church is hierarchal. See Robert Putnam, *Making Democracy Work: Civic Traditions in Modern Italy* (Princeton: Princeton University Press, 1993), 107.

17. Ibid., 107, 89-90.

18. I reviewed these arguments in chapter 1.

19. A recent argument for Christian socialism is Stephen Charles Mott, *A Christian Perspective on Political Thought* (Oxford: Oxford University Press, 1993).

20. Callan, *Creating Citizens,* 25-26.

21. Ibid., 25.

22. Ibid., 26.

23. Ibid., 37.

24. Rawls also assumes that one can understands when one acts as a citizen, and not in some other role. When you discuss politics with your spouse or children. are you acting as a citizen? How about when you have these discussions with your sisters or brothers, friends, coworkers, or neighbors?

25. Callan, *Creating Citizens,* 33.

26. John Rawls, *Political Liberalism* (New York: Columbia University Press, 1993), 199.

27. Callan, *Creating Citizens,* 33, 39. The account of citizenship I have given also shows how liberalism tends to encourage the fading of distinct cultural boundaries, as it encourages different people to confront and learn from one another.

28. Ibid., 217.

29. Joseph Raz, *The Morality of Freedom* (Oxford: Clarendon, 1986), 424.

30. Galston, *Liberal Purposes,* 329, 224, 227.

31. Richard Dagger, *Civic Virtues: Rights, Citizenship, and Republican Liberalism* (Oxford: Oxford University Press, 1997), 18.

32. Ibid., 102.

33. Michael Walzer, "A Day in the Life of a Socialist Citizen," *Obligations: Essays on Disobedience, War, and Citizenship* (New York: Basic Books, 1970).

5 | *Educating Citizens and Educating Believers*

1. One ACE school is described in Susan D. Rose, *Keeping Them Out of the Hands of Satan* (New York: Routledge, 1988).

2. Myron Lieberman, *Public Education: An Autopsy* (Cambridge: Harvard University Press, 1993), 19.

3. Eamonn Callan's definition of a common school explains it well: "Common schools have a distinctive ethos that makes them open to the pluralism of the larger society. Schools that lack this ethos are only de jure common schools." *Creating Citizens: Political Education and Liberal Democracy* (Oxford: Oxford University Press, 1997), 164. I use the terms *common school* and *public school* interchangeably here, but a private school can be a common school. A religiously affiliated school that welcomes students of different (or no) faith can be a common school, as can be a nonreligious private school. Of course, many private and religiously affiliated schools are exclusive in a variety of ways.

4. Colin M. Macleod, "Conceptions of Parental Autonomy," *Politics and Society* 25, no. 1 (March 1997): 121-22.

5. Ibid., 129-30. Emphasis removed.

6. *Mozert v Hawkins* 827 F2d 1058 (6th Cir 1987).

7. Stephen Macedo, "Liberal Civic Education: The Case of God V. John Rawls?," *Ethics* 105 (April 1995); Amy Gutmann, "Civic Education and Social Diversity," *Ethics* 105 (April 1995); Shelley Burtt, "Religious Parents, Secular Schools," *The Review of Politics* 56 (Winter 1994); Callan, *Creating Citizens,* 157-62.

8. Macedo mentions the private school option in passing in Macedo, "Liberal Civic Education."

9. Gutmann, for example, supports private schools but with the caveat that they teach democratic values to their students in *Democratic Education* (Princeton: Princeton University Press, 1989), 115-23.

10. The theoretical issues at stake in *Yoder* still remain important, though to make sense of today's political environment they must take into account the rationale behind home-schooling. More theorists than I can list have discussed the Yoder case. See my *Boundaries of Citizenship: Race, Ethnicity and Nationality in the Liberal State* (Baltimore: Johns Hopkins University Press, 1994), chap. 5; Macedo, "Liberal Civic Education"; Gutmann, "Civic Education"; Macleod, "Conceptions of Parental Autonomy"; Ian Shapiro with Richard Arneson, *Democracy's Place* (Ithaca, N.Y.: Cornell University Press, 1996); Richard Dagger, *Civic Virtues: Rights, Citizenship and Republican Liberalism* (Oxford: Oxford University Press, 1997). On the ease of restrictions on home schooling, see Neal Devins, "Fundamentalist Christian Educators v. State: An Inevitable Compromise," *George Washington Law Review* 60 (March 1992).

11. Dagger, *Civic Virtues,* 126.

12. Callan argues that the moderate separatist argument is compatible with liberalism. He maintains, however, that less moderate arguments that call for separatist schooling through all the years of schooling is not compatible with liberalism. *Creating Citizens,* chapter 7.

13. John Locke, *A Second Letter Concerning Toleration* (1796), reprinted in vol. 7 of *Works,* 10th ed. (London: T. Davison, 1801).

14. Frederick Mark Gedicks, *The Rhetoric of Church and State: A Critical Analysis of Religion Clause Jurisprudence* (Durham, N.C.: Duke University Press, 1995), well describes the jurisprudential mess on church-state issues and cites the many relevant cases.

15. For one classical liberal's argument who supported such a policy of funding all religions, see Benjamin Constant, *Principles of Politics Applicable to All Representative Governments* (1815; reprint, Cambridge: Cambridge University Press, 1988), 289.

16. Michael W. McConnell, "The Selective Funding Problem: Abortion and Religious Schools," *Harvard Law Review* 104 (1991).

17. Ibid., 1017.

18. Ibid.

19. This is a theme in Warren A. Nord, *Religion and American Education: Rethinking a National Dilemma* (Chapel Hill: University of North Carolina Press, 1995). Nord is one who calls for incorporating religion into the curriculum in the name of a liberal education.

20. Robert K. Fullinwider, *Public Education in a Multicultural Society: Policy, Theory, Critique* (Cambridge: Cambridge University Press, 1996).

21. *Settle v Dickson County School Board,* 53 F3d 152 (6th Cir).

22. Sonia Nieto, *Affirming Diversity: The Sociopolitical Context of Multicultural Education* (New York: Longman, 1992), 219.

23. Carl A. Grant and Christine E. Sleeter, *Turning on Learning: Five Approaches for Multicultural Teaching Plans for Race, Class, Gender and Disability* (Columbus: Merrill Publishing, 1989), 144.

24. Differences in power among groups is an important theme for multiculturalists. I won't say much about that here, except to note that dividing the United States into groups, the oppressed and the powerful as many multiculturalists do, is a sophomoric simplification.

25. Carl A. Grant and Susan L. Melnick, "In Praise of Diversity: Some Implications," in *In Praise of Diversity: A Resource Book for Multicultural Education,* ed. Milton J. Gold, Carl A. Grant, and Harry N. Rivlin (Washington, D.C.: Association of Teacher Educators, 1977), 220.

26. James A. Banks, "Curriculum Guidelines for Multicutural Education," *Social Education* 56, no. 5 (September 1992): 277, 280.

27. Callan, *Creating Citizens,* 26.

28. Amy Gutmann and Dennis Thompson, *Democracy and Disagreement: Why Moral Conflict Cannot Be Avoided in Politics and What Should Be Done about It* (Cambridge: Harvard University Press, 1996), 79.

29. See Macedo, "Liberal Civic Education"; Gutmann, "Civic Education." I did too in Spinner, *Boundaries of Citizenship,* 106-7.

30. Gutmann and Thompson, *Democracy and Disagreement,* 65.

31. Callan, *Creating Citizens,* 158.

32. Burtt, "Religious Parents, Secular Schools," 62.

33. A U.S. District Court agreed in *Moody v Cronin* 484 FSupp 270.

34. Eugene R. Provenzo, *Religious Fundamentalism and American Religion: The Battle for the Public Schools* (Albany: State University of New York Press, 1990).

35. Stephen Bates, *Battleground: One Mother's Crusade, the Religious Right, and the Struggle for Control of Our Classrooms* (New York: Poseidon Press, 1993).

6 | *The Public Squares*

1. There is a very large and still growing debate around this issue. I can't canvass all the arguments here. See Robert Audi, "The Separation of Church and State and the

Obligations of Citizenship," *Philosophy and Public Affairs* 18 (Summer 1989); Robert Audi and Nicholas Wolterstorff, *Religion in the Public Square: The Place of Religious Convictions in Political Debate* (Lanham, Md.: Rowman and Littlefield, 1997); Stephen Carter, *The Culture of Disbelief: How American Law and Politics Trivialize Religious Devotion* (New York: Basic Books, 1993); Clarke E. Cochran, *Religion in Public and Private Life* (New York: Routledge, 1990); Franklin I. Gamwell, *The Meaning of Religious Freedom: Modern Politics and the Democratic Resolution* (Albany: SUNY Press, 1995); Kent Greenawalt, *Private Consciences and Public Reasons* (Oxford: Oxford University Press, 1995); Kent Greenawalt, *Religious Convictions and Political Choice* (Oxford: Oxford University Press, 1988); Richard John Neuhaus, *The Naked Public Square: Religion and Democracy in America,* 2nd ed. (1984; reprint, Grand Rapids: Eerdmans, 1986); Michael Perry, *Love and Power: The Role of Religion and Morality in American Politics* (Oxford: Oxford University Press, 1991); A. James Reichley, *Religion in American Public Life* (Washington, D.C.: Brookings Institution, 1985); William Temple, *Christianity and Social Order* (New York: Penguin, 1942); Ronald F. Thiemann, *Religion in Public Life: A Dilemma for Democracy* (Washington, D.C.: Georgetown University Press, 1996). Of these arguments, I have been most influenced by Greenawalt's.

2. Tape of panel discussion on the "Religious Voice in the Public Square" at the 1996 annual meeting of the Association of American Law Schools, held by the Jewish Law and Religion and Law Sections of the Association of American Law Schools (Jan. 3-7, 1996). Produced by the Recorded Resources Corporation (Millersville, Md., 1996).

3. Ibid.

4. Audi and Wolterstorff, *Religion in the Public Square,* 1-2.

5. Audi, "Separation of Church and State," 284, 290. Italics are in the original.

6. Of course, even the term *secular philosopher* is misleading. Kant, Hegel, Rousseau, and even Dewey were all influenced by religion.

7. Ackerman, "Religious Voice in the Public Square."

8. See generally John Rawls, *Political Liberalism* (New York: Columbia University Press, 1993), and Bruce Ackerman, *Social Justice in the Liberal State* (New Haven: Yale University Press, 1980).

9. My argument here echoes Callan's criticism of Rawls that I discussed in chapter 4.

10. Richard S. Von Wagoner, *Mormon Polygamy: A History,* 2nd ed. (Salt Lake City: Signature Books, 1989), 116.

11. *Reynolds v United States,* 98 US 145 (1878).

12. Sarah Barringer Gordon, "The Second American Disestablishment: Blasphemy, Polygamy, and Church-State Relations in the Nineteenth Century," unpublished typescript, University of Pennsylvania, 1997.

13. There is evidence that the New Testament prefers monogamy. See 1 Corinthians 7:2.

14. Philip Johnson, *Reason in the Balance: The Case Against Naturalism in Science, Law and Education* (Downers Grove, Ill.: Intervarsity Press, 1995), 150. Emphasis in the original removed.

15. Deuteronomy 21.

16. About half of all U.S. Christians believe in ESP. Clairvoyance is believed in by 22% percent of Protestants, and 30% of Catholics; 33% of Protestants believe in mental telepathy while 38% of Catholics do. One-quarter of all Christians believe in astrology. Five percent of Protestants believe in reincarnation. See "Paranormal Beliefs," Gallup Poll, September 3-5, 1996. On file with author. Sampling error is ±3%.

17. The efforts of the church to stamp out magic in early modern England is well told in Keith Thomas, *Religion and the Decline of Magic* (New York: Scribner's, 1971).

18. Eamonn Callan, *Creating Citizens: Political Education and Liberal Democracy* (Oxford: Oxford University Press, 1997), 37.

19. John Stuart Mill, *Auguste Comte and Positivism* (1865), reprinted in vol. 10 of *Collected Works,* ed. J. M. Robson (Toronto: University of Toronto Press, 1969), 321-22.

20. This is one of Carter's concerns in *Culture of Disbelief,* 23.

21. Jim Wallis, *The Soul of Politics: Beyond "Religious Right" and "Secular Left"* (New York: Orbis Books, 1994; reprint, New York: Harcourt Brace, 1995).

22. See also Jose Casanova, *Public Religions in the Modern World* (Chicago: University of Chicago Press, 1994), 166.

23. David Popenoe, "American Family Decline, 1960-1990," *Journal of Marriage and the Family* 55 (August 1993).

24. Amy Gutmann and Dennis Thompson, *Democracy and Disagreement: Why Moral Conflict Cannot Be Avoided in Politics and What Should Be Done about It* (Cambridge: Harvard University Press, 1996), 85-91.

25. Ibid., chaps. 8 and 9.

26. "Southern Baptists Declare Wife Should Submit to Husband," *New York Times,* sec. A, p. 1, June 10, 1998.

27. Thomas Hobbes, *Leviathan* (1651), reprint, ed. C. B. Macpherson (Harmondsworth: Penguin, 1968), 331-32, 133.

28. The bill itself contained several values for pi, so it is impossible to say what value for pi the Indiana House preferred. David Singmaster, "The Legal Value of Pi," *Mathematical Intelligencer* 7, no. 2 (April 1987).

29. Carter, *Culture of Disbelief,* 161.

30. Ibid., 229.

31. We generally accord more protection to people than to animals, so while killing animals in a kosher manner may not be the most humane way to kill animals, unless the practice is particularly cruel, we should allow people to continue the practice. The dispute here then revolves on whether killing an animal in a kosher way is especially brutal. I doubt that it is. Few societies that discuss the cruelty of killing animals in a

kosher manner are considering a ban on hunting, surely a crueler practice. But if so-ciety banned hunting, and was convinced that kosher slaughter was also particularly cruel, then perhaps there would be reason to review the matter.

32. My discussion here is indebted to Greenawalt, *Religious Convictions and Political Choice.*

33. See also Greenawalt, *Private Consciences and Public Reasons,* 151-79.

34. Temple, *Christianity and Social Order;* Greenawalt, *Private Consciences and Public Reasons;* Reichley, *Religion in American Public Life.*

35. Reichley, *Religion in American Public Life,* argues that this is what happened to many liberal Protestant denominations in the 1960s, causing many of them to lose members.

7 | *Identity and Discrimination*

1. Quoted from their press release, on file with author. See also the articles in the *New York Times* on March 26, 1996 ("Nebraska Bishop Threatens Excommunication for Dissenters," sec. A, p. 16) and on May 17, 1996 ("Some Catholics in Nebraska Face Excommunication Order," sec. A, p. 23).

2. I ignore the question of whether canon law supports Bruskewitz's decision or not.

3. The reform and reconstructionist movements tend to be less bound to tradition than the other branches of Judaism.

4. I note one case below where a church has been sued for discrimination, though in that particular case I argue the church did wrongly discriminate.

5. The Madison Equal Opportunity Commission later amended its language so that housemates could discriminate. The Supreme Court refused to hear the case, perhaps because the Commission reversed itself on the housemate issue, though the fine still had to be paid. "Lesbian Wins Fight over Housing," *Capital Times,* May 12, 1997, p. 1A; "Equal Opportunity Commission Reverses Roommate Ruling," *Capital Times,* July 21, 1992, p. 3A.

6. "Girl Sues Boy Scouts," *Sacramento Bee,* p. A1, August 25, 1995.

7. "Education Chief Challenges Rule on Campus Mix," *New York Times,* p. 1A, April 13, 1991.

8. For a good explanation of why and when discrimination calls for government action see Andrew Koppelman, *Antidiscrimination Law and Social Equality* (New Haven: Yale University Press, 1996).

9. The policy of Bob Jones University to keep its Black and white students from dating each other caused the IRS to revoke its tax-exempt status. *Bob Jones University v United States* 461 US 574 (1983).

10. Stephen Monsma, *The Mixing of Church and State: Religious Nonprofit Organizations and Public Money* (Grand Rapids, Mich.: Calvin College, 1994), 1.

11. Stuart White makes a similar argument in "Freedom of Association and the Right to Exclude," *Journal of Political Philosophy* 5, no. 4 (December 1997).

12. John Rawls, *A Theory of Justice* (Cambridge: Harvard University Press, 1971), 62, 440. I thank David Miller for pointing out to me the usefulness of Rawls's concept of primary goods here.

13. For an eloquent explanation of this, see Martin Luther King Jr., "Letter from Birmingham City Jail," in *A Testament of Hope: The Essential Writings of Martin Luther King, Jr.,* ed. James M. Washington (New York: HarperCollins, 1991), 292-93.

14. *Roberts v United States Jaycees* 468 US 619 (1984).

15. I would like to add that there is reason to think that the Jaycees might very well have welcomed women on their own, though it would have taken much longer than being forced to by the Court. Women could join the Jaycees before *Roberts v United States Jaycees* as associate members. This led to full membership in some places. In Minneapolis and St. Paul women had full membership in the Jaycees, and in fact women led the chapters in those cities. It was the national Jaycee organization threatening these chapters with sanctions that precipitated the lawsuit.

16. Nancy Rosenblum, *Membership and Morals: The Personal Uses of Pluralism in America* (Princeton: Princeton University Press, 1998), 161.

17. *Board of Directors of Rotary International v Rotary Club of Duarte* 481 US 537 (1987). As in the Jaycees case, it was a local club's acceptance of women that led to the lawsuit by the national organization.

18. Ibid. The Supreme Court cites these reasons given by the Appeals Court, but it passed over them rather quickly.

19. Rosenblum, *Membership and Morals,* 171.

20. Ibid., 93.

21. It is not clear why Rosenblum applies this test to the workplace when she studiously avoids it in other cases.

22. See *Corporation of Presiding Bishop of the Church of Jesus Christ of Latter-day Saints v Amos,* 483 US 327 (1987).

23. David Van Biema, "The Empire of the Mormons," *Time,* August 4, 1997.

24. I have learned a great deal about aid to religious-based organizations from Stephen V. Monsma, *When Sacred and Secular Mix: Religious Nonprofit Organizations and Public Money* (Lanham, Md.: Rowman and Littlefield, 1996), and Carl Esbeck, *The Regulation of Religious Organizations as Recipients of Government Financial Assistance* (Washington, D.C.: Center for Public Justice, 1996).

25. I read about the case in Stephen Monsma, *The Mixing of Church and State: Religious Nonprofit Organizations and Public Money* (Grand Rapids, Mich.: Calvin College, Calvin Center for Christian Scholarship, 1994).

26. See Esbeck, *The Regulation of Religious Organizations as Recipients of Government Financial Assistance,* 32-34 and 62-65. The cases involved are *Wilder v Bernstein, 499*

FSupp 980 (SD NY 1980), *Wilder v Bernstein* 645 FSupp 1292 (SD NY 1986) and *Arneth v. Gross,* 699 FSupp 450 (SD NY 1988).

27. Ibid.

28. It is important that I am talking about adult students here. The private choice of an adult, like where she wants to go to college, should not be regulated by the state. But children are a different and special matter. The state has a keen interest in how children are educated. When they are adults, this interest recedes.

29. Monsma, *When Sacred and Secular Mix.*

30. Susan Moller Okin, *Justice, Gender and the Family* (New York: Basic Books, 1989), 171; Judith Lorber, *Paradoxes of Gender* (New Haven: Yale University Press, 1994), 298.

31. Susan Moller Okin, "Is Multiculturalism Bad for Women?" in *Is Multiculturalism Bad for Women?* ed. Martha C. Nussbaum, Joshua Cohen, and Matthew Howard (Princeton: Princeton University Press, 1999).

32. Ibid. Polygamy is the only complicated case here. Polygamy is a problem in inegalitarian societies, but in societies that have a good measure of gender equality I am not sure on what grounds liberals could object to a practice of people having multiple husbands or multiple wives.

33. I argue that Western states do not have the moral authority to interfere in indigenous communities in "Land, Culture and Justice: A Framework for Group Rights and Recognition," *Journal of Political Philosophy* (forthcoming).

34. Okin, "Is Multiculturalism Bad for Women?"

35. Susan Moller Okin, "Feminism and Multiculturalism: Some Tensions," *Ethics* 108, no. 4 (July 1998): 681–82.

36. Okin, "Is Multiculturalism Bad for Women?"

37. In *Widmar v Vincent* 454 US 263 (1981), the Supreme Court ruled that a public university that opened up its facilities to noncurriculum-related clubs created a public forum that must be open to secular and religious clubs alike. In 1984 Congress passed the Equal Access Act which extended this idea of the public forum to public schools. The Supreme Court upheld the Act in *Westside v Mergens* 496 US 226 (1990). In *Lamb's Chapel v Moriches School District,* 508 US 385 (1993) the Court ruled that if community organizations could use school facilities after hours, then religious organizations must be allowed to use them as well.

38. Greg Ivers, *Redefining the First Freedom: The Supreme Court and the Consolidation of State Power* (New Brunswick, N.J.: Transaction Books, 1993), 39.

8 | Surviving Diversity

1. Charles Taylor, "Atomism," in *Powers, Possessions and Freedom,* ed. Alkis Kontos (Toronto: University of Toronto Press, 1979).

2. Michael W. McConnell, "Accommodation of Religion: An Update and a Re-

sponse to Critics," *George Washington Law Review* 60, no. 3 (March 1992): 694. The court case is *Boerne v Flores* US 95-2074 (1997).

3. Jesse H. Choper, *Securing Religious Liberty: Principles for Judicial Interpretation of the Religion Clauses* (Chicago: University of Chicago Press, 1995), 75. Michael Sandel makes a similar argument that religious convictions should be viewed as a matter of conscience, not choice. Yet right before he makes this argument, he bemoans the Supreme Court decision in 1943 that allowed Jehovah's Witnesses to follow their conscience and be exempt from saluting the flag in public school. If not by compulsory flag salutes, Sandel wonders, how may the state cultivate a common citizenship? Under Sandel's account religious conscience can sometimes be overridden by important state values. Michael Sandel, *Democracy's Discontent: America in Search of a Public Philosophy* (Cambridge: Harvard University Press, 1996), 54.

4. McConnell, "Accommodation of Religion," 700.

5. This school was at issue in *Board of Education of Kiryas Joel v Grumet* 114 US 2490 (1994). I discuss the case in Jeff Spinner-Halev, "Cultural Pluralism and Partial Citizenship," in *Multicultural Questions,* ed. Steven Lukes and Christian Joppke (Oxford: Oxford University Press, 1999).

6. *Smith v Fair Employment and Housing Commission* 12 CA 4th 1143.

7. McConnell, "Accommodation of Religion," 692.

8. *Boerne v Flores* 95-2074 (1997).

9. Many private universities contribute money to the city that they inhabit to help pay for the services they consume. These contributions are voluntary and negotiated between the university and the city, so they are not the same as a tax.

10. The classic argument against taxing churches is Dean M. Kelley, *Why Churches Should Not Pay Taxes* (New York: Harper and Row, 1977). The Supreme Court ruled the tax-exemption of churches constitutional in *Walz v Tax Commission* 397 US 664 (1970).

11. See, too, Bertrand Russell, *Religion and Science* (1935; reprint, Oxford: Oxford University Press, 1961); Bertrand Russell, *Unpopular Essays* (London: Allen and Unwin, 1950).

12. Stanley Hauerwas, *Theological Engagements with the Secular* (Durham, N.C.: Duke University Press, 1994), 105.

13. Stanley Hauerwas, *In Good Company: The Church as Polis* (Notre Dame: University of Notre Dame Press, 1995), 98.

14. For how some Americans have reshaped traditional religions see Jack Miles et al., "God Decentralized," *New York Times,* December 7, 1997.

15. Dean M. Kelley, *Why Conservative Churches Are Growing* (New York: Harper and Row, 1972); Roger Finke and Rodney Stark, *The Churching of America, 1776-1990: Winners and Losers in Our Religious Economy* (New Brunswick, N.J.: Rutgers University Press, 1992).

16. Purity is an important theme in many accounts of religious people. Robert

Eisenberg describes how many Hasidic Jews want to do more than what God prescribes in Robert Eisenberg, *Boychicks in the Hood: Travels in the Hasidic Underground* (San Francisco: Harper, 1995). For a strange but fascinating account of two people's quest for Christian purity in nineteenth-century America, see the story of Elijah and Sarah Pierson in Paul E. Johnson and Sean Wilentz, *The Kingdom of Matthias: A Story of Sex and Salvation in Nineteenth-Century America* (Oxford: Oxford University Press, 1994), chap. 2. For other accounts of why people are attracted to conservative religions, see Nancy Tatom Ammerman, *Bible Believers: Fundamentalists in the Modern World* (New Brunswick, N.J.: Rutgers University Press, 1987); George Marsden, *Fundamentalism and American Culture: The Shaping of Twentieth Century Evangelicalism* (Oxford: Oxford University Press, 1980); Alan Peshkin, *God's Choice: The Total World of a Fundamentalist Christian School* (Chicago: University of Chicago Press, 1986); Susan D. Rose, *Keeping Them Out of the Hands of Satan* (New York: Routledge, 1988); Jermoe R. Mintz, *Hasidic People: A Place in the New World* (Cambridge: Harvard University Press, 1992); Samuel Heilman, *Defenders of the Faith: Inside Ultra-Orthodox Jewry* (New York: Schocken Books, 1992).

17. Kelley, *Why Conservatives Churches are Growing*; Finke and Stark, *The Churching of America.*

18. See Eisenberg, *Boychicks in the Hood,* and Rose, *Keeping Them Out.*

Index

Ackerman, Bruce, 143-45, 154
African Americans, 41, 96, 175
afterlife, 12, 13, 17, 91, 93, 208. *See also*
  Heaven; Hell
Allred, Gloria, 170
Amish, 6, 11, 50, 55, 62, 68, 87, 113, 207, 218
Ammerman, Nancy Tatom, 240n. 16
Arneson, Richard, 232n. 10
Arneth v. Gross, 237-38n. 26
Asian Americans, 43, 50, 175
assimilation, 7, 45
atheists, 11-12
Audi, Robert, 143-45, 154
Australia, 45
autonomy, 5, 22, 172, 217; and children,
  92-93; and Christianity, 14; and citizenship,
  89, 102-3, 105-6; and community, 25, 30,
  46-55, 62-67, 86, 115; conditions of, 32; and
  cultural community, 19, 33-37, 36, 58, 103;
  and culture, 4, 24, 31, 33, 34, 36, 53, 55, 197,
  204; degrees of, 22, 51; and dialogue, 3; and
  group boundaries, 43, 203; and identity
  theorists, 38; liberal, 17, 112, 204; and liberalism, 3, 4-5, 21, 29-30, 48, 86-87, 106, 201,
  203, 205; and manipulation, 32, 69-70;
  minimal, 54; and parents, 110-11; and respect, 134; and restrictions, 56, 57-68, 205;
  and self-denial, 92; and voluntary groups,
  181; and well-being, 52-53

Banks, James, 233n. 26
Bates, Stephen, 233n. 35
Blasius, Mark, 226n. 32
Boerne v. Flores, 239n. 8
boundaries, 44, 153; and community, 47;
  group, 41, 43, 45, 203, 213; and mainstream

society, 50, 204; open, 49; and religious
  liberals, 46
Boy Scouts, 166, 170, 180-82, 210
Brady, Henry, 230n. 15
Brennan, William, 183
Bruskewitz, Fabian, 167-68
Buddhism, 22
Burtt, Shelley, 136, 140

Callan, Eamonn, 69, 99-102, 114, 132, 136, 139
Canada, 36, 45, 73, 197
Carter, Stephen, 95, 161, 234n. 1
Casanova, Jose, 235n. 22
Catholic Church, 55, 171; hierarchical nature
  of, 96; rules of, 167-68, 215-16. *See also*
  discrimination
Catholicism, 9
Catholics, 1, 8, 10, 11, 22, 29, 50, 60, 87, 115,
  175, 186, 188
Choper, Jesse, 239n. 3
Christ, Jesus, 1, 12, 14-15, 16, 91, 129, 147,
  151, 159, 161, 164
Christianity, 16, 208, 214; and morality, 14-16, 98
Christians, 8, 91; conservative, 1; fundamental-
  ist, 1, 2, 25, 62; political views of, 147-48
Christian Science, 162
Church of Jesus Christ of Latter Day Saints,
  55, 66. *See also* Mormons
*Church of Jesus Christ of Latter Day Saints v.
  Amos*, 237n. 22
citizens: and dialogue, 3, 154-55, 157, 163; and
  dignity, 3; equal, 3; and good life, 31; liberal,
  21, 115; and mainstream society, 63; and
  multiple memberships, 49; and mutual respect, 133, 142, 174; partial, 87; reasonable,
  99-106; virtues of, 110; well-being of, 31-32

57-61, 64, 65-66, 69-71, 74-75, 88, 102-3, 167, 197, 205-7

Reichley, A. James, 234n. 1, 236n. 35

religion: and certainty, 17; and civil skills, 96-98; and civil society, 95-96; and classical liberalism, 11-18; as comprehensive view, 145-46; decline of, 27-29; democratization of, 215; and diversity, 6-7, 19-20, 214; and discrimination, 182-85, 198-200, 191-96; as encompassing group, 2, 4; exclusive, 1-3; hierarchical, 7, 8, 46, 194; and immutable beliefs, 16; influence on political views, 146-50, 164-65; infrastructure of, 212; and liberalism, 4-5, 9, 22, 98, 99-106, 214; and liberty, 18; long duration of, 15; as mediating institution, 95-96; and men, 28, 46; and morality, 11, 17, 23, 28, 87, 89-95, 97, 99, 164-65; patriarchal, 7, 27, 194-95, 213, 215; private, 18, 27, 146; public, 27-29, 142, 146; and public square, 142-46, 150; and purity, 240n. 16; and restrictions, 2; and ritual, 8; rules of, 7-8, 18, 46, 94; and science, 160-63; and social services, 185-91; specialness of, 207-14; and tax-exempt status, 211-12; teaching about, 128-35; and truth, 159; and women, 28, 46

religion of humanity, 15-16, 17-18, 217

religions, conservative: and boundaries, 44; and change, 46; and choice, 26, 44; inflexibility of, 212; and liberal democracy, 2-3, 18, 20; as moral community, 97; rules of, 66, 217; success of, 213-14, 218-19

religions, liberal, 10, 18, 201, 218

religious communities, 21-22, 116; and change, 46; and children, 68-69, 107; and choice, 27, 67; and conscience, 27; and liberalism, 202; and liberal values, 197; restrictive life of, 26, 66, 94

religious conservatives, 11, 18, 23; alliances among, 9, 144; and autonomy, 51-52, 54, 68-69, 203; and boundaries, 153; and change, 99; and children, 1-2, 4, 26, 93-94, 97-98, 101-2, 203, 217-18; and choice, 5, 29, 72; and creationism, 161; and custom, 3; defined, 9-10; as different, 5, 25, 27, 29, 55; and education, 50-51, 54, 101, 115, 135-41; and equality, 196; exclusion from public life, 37, 150-56; and family, 94; and identity, 153-54; and individuality, 5; leaders of, 153; and liberalism, 19, 23, 24, 29, 106-8, 118-19, 201-6, 213-14, 219; and liberal state, 205; as

minority, 19; and morality, 89-95; political views of, 147, 149-51, 155; and politics, 213; and restrictions, 5, 25; and temptation, 68; and virtue, 28, 105

religious divisions, 9

religious groups, 36; communal, 74; and difference, 45; joining of, 71-72; and political views, 151

religious humanism, 16, 217

religious liberals, 4, 46, 151; and children, 216-17; and discrimination, 192; survival of, 214-19

religious moderates, 5, 10-11, 218-19; autonomous life of, 23; and children, 68; and civic skills, 103; defined, 9, 194; education, 118; and liberalism, 201, 205-6; rules of, 66

restrictions: and choices, 59-60; and community, 59-67; cultural, 60; external, 58-59, 62, 67, 166-67, 192-93; internal, 49, 58-59, 62, 67-69, 83, 84, 167, 192-93; and meaningful life, 204. See also autonomy

Roberts v. Jaycees, 177-80

Rockefeller, Steven, 223n. 26

Rose, Susan, 224n. 1, 231n. 1, 240nn. 16, 18

Rosenblum, Nancy, 178-79

Rotaries, 178-80, 183

Rotary International v. Rotary Club of Duarte, 237n. 17

Rousseau, Jean Jacques, 104

Russell, Bertrand, 239n. 11

Ryan, Alan, 223n. 30

Salvation Army, 186-87, 190

Sandel, Michael, 27, 239n. 3

Schlozman, Kay Lehman, 230n. 15

schools: accommodating religion in, 135-41, 202; and class, 119-20; common, 3, 9, 114, 118, 120, 139, 210; cooperation between, 123-28; and diversity, 112-15, 126, 139; and equality of opportunity, 119-20; financing of, 118-28; home, 126; illiberal, 119; and inclusion, 126, 128; and mutual respect, 197, 202; parochial, 50; private, 9, 59, 112, 119, 120, 123-28; public, 18, 29, 49, 59, 112-18, 120, 122, 123-35, 199, 213; religious, 19, 105, 113, 115-28; use of facilities, 199-200. See also education

secular reason, 143-44, 146

self-respect, 174

Settle v. Dickson County School Board, 129

Shapiro, Ian, 232n. 10